Harvard, Hollywood, Hitmen, and Holy Men

HARVARD, HOLLYWOOD, HITMEN, and HOLY MEN

A Memoir

Paul W. Williams

UNIVERSITY PRESS OF KENTUCKY

Published by The University Press of Kentucky

Scholarly publisher for the Commonwealth,
serving Bellarmine University, Berea College, Centre
College of Kentucky, Eastern Kentucky University,
The Filson Historical Society, Georgetown College,
Kentucky Historical Society, Kentucky State University,
Morehead State University, Murray State University,
Northern Kentucky University, Spalding University,
Transylvania University, University of Kentucky,
University of Louisville, University of Pikeville,
and Western Kentucky University.
All rights reserved.

Editorial and Sales Offices: The University Press of Kentucky
663 South Limestone Street, Lexington, Kentucky 40508-4008
www.kentuckypress.com

This is a work of creative nonfiction, and events are portrayed to the
best of the author's memory and ability to verify facts. The opinions
and interpretations are, of course, solely those of the author.

Cover art by Sylvain Despretz.

Cataloging-in-Publication data is available from the Library of Congress.

ISBN 978-0-8131-9667-1 (hardcover)
ISBN 978-0-8131-9668-8 (pdf)
ISBN 978-0-8131-9669-5 (epub)

This book is printed on acid-free paper meeting
the requirements of the American National Standard
for Permanence in Paper for Printed Library Materials.

Manufactured in the United States of America

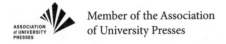

Member of the Association
of University Presses

For Zoe Clarke-Williams and Tomy Perez

Paul Williams—Your "self-indulgence" has been put to good use. While I object ordinarily to the use of autobiography in a thesis, I think that you make the personal and the theoretical hang together very well.

—Erik H. Erikson, 1964

Reminiscence and anecdote, as they tell of one's meetings with the great or the prominent, are an established form of self-enhancement. They make known that one was there. This is not my purpose; my aim is to inform and perhaps, on occasion, to entertain. The risk, nonetheless, exists that critics who are less than tolerant may suggest that I am indulging in name-dropping . . . [but] nothing so disarms a prosecutor as a prior confession of guilt.

—John K. Galbraith, *Name-Dropping*

Paul, of our eight roommates,* you are not the first-smartest in any field, but you are the second-smartest in more than anyone.

—Howard Gardner, later, in 1983, author of *Frames of Mind: The Theory of Multiple Intelligences*

---

* Richard Ferber, chemistry; Howard Gardner, social relations; Eldon Greenberg, history and literature; Jim King, mathematics; Robert Sandy, government; John Veblen, government; Paul Williams, social relations and visual studies; John Young, history.

Contents

Contents

Memories

New experiences are like memes—sticky in the brain and easy to remember. Nevertheless, readers of this mosaic of reminiscences may reasonably be curious to know more about the retrievals of this geezer.

I have journals that I kept in high school and college, notes from psychoanalysis, consciousness-expanding drug experiences, and the year with the Sufis. I have the transcripts from the oral historian Nyra Atyla, with whom I sat for ten two-hour sessions in 1998, when I suspected I would forget details of my history. I also have kept my daily calendars for the last forty years. In 2003, after two years researching Pope John Paul II and the fall of communism in Eastern Europe, Jeff Markey sat me down for long video interviews that became his internet project *Beyond Greed & Ego.*

I started writing this book five years ago, when I was seventy-two. I made a list of all the extraordinary events I could. The early drafts concentrated on these vignettes—they were briefer, like place markers for events I wanted to recall. And I still had a good memory for all my defeats.

Without any conscious intention on my part, the day's work on the draft became the schedule for my mind to germinate its sense memories. I soon enough learned to stop whatever I was doing—resting between crunches or groggy in sleep—and write down notes, until the images stopped appearing. At night, around three in the morning, after two sleep cycles, the markers stimulated deep memory as I continually awoke full of smells, sights, sounds, and feelings. I recovered the interred body of the archive.

Prologue

2021

This morning I sit on the porch and watch the light change out over Rio de Janeiro's perfectly composed Marambaia peninsula. Gray. After an hour, suddenly shards of gold hit a few green vines that hang above me, and my eyes alert toward them, fixated. I'm living life now. Like the period just typed. And this one. What happened before, starts in a couple of pages.

I never wanted to be a writer. No fun. I wanted to be a great character. Since I knew early from abuse that I did not exist, I was fearless in my life and not bored. I became rich and famous and poor and anonymous.

Waldo Salt, one of the best screenwriters of the twentieth century, once said to me while we smoked gonzo weed in the Imperial Gardens, "Write a book about your characters before you start the screenplay, everything, what they put in each of their clothes drawers, what did they do before the action begins? Then all you have to do is pick the location to put them in—that's the work—because they will speak when they are there."

So, has everything I've written for the last five years, draft after draft, polish after polish of this sunset memoir—*An Extraordinary Life That Made No Difference,* after that came *Every Road Is a Path,* before *Harvard and All That . . . ,* and *Calmer in Crisis,* and *Going As Who?*—has it all been simply a preparation?

Are these drafts just research so I can be empty? To simply see what is in front of me, with no past on my mind? Watch the panoramic gray view as shards of gold sunlight start appearing, minute after minute, hour after hour?

I stand in a corner of the porch, in front of a bronze head of a female Buddha, and strike a Tibetan singing bowl with a cloth-covered mallet. The sound expands. I look at the metal face and her eyes open as they usually do when I am calm. They are larger than yesterday and happier. She disappears within a blackness. I watch for a full minute. She reappears, eyes open. I walk away to write as the sound becomes silent.

Is this interesting? I am in bed, waking up in the morning. I want to gargle. I need to sit on a toilet. I feel tired. I think about it.

My rank breath, my tired brain and muscles, my bladder is full. What time is it?

Wanting. Needing. Feeling. Thinking. I want an espresso. I need caffeine. I feel an ache in my lower back. I will ask Vivian to make me a cup of espresso.

I say, "Would you mind making me a *doppio?*"

She says, "We can split it—two *singolos.*"*

---

* *singolo, doppio, triplo*—single, double, triple, in Italian.

Book One

How to Get into Harvard

1

Where I Come From

1946–1952

1946

World War Two is over. We won. Hitler lost. My father is back home from the army. I'm three years old. I don't remember him. Neither does my sister, who is a year older than me.

He is tall and wears a khaki uniform with a khaki hat like an upside-down folded paper boat. He smiles down at me.

My mother says, "That's your daddy."

He says, "Come here." I walk toward him and he picks me up in his arms. He smells wet from the rain outside, and my head is closer to the ceiling than it has ever been in my life.

He smiles and stands straight as he holds me.

I touch a round piece of dark metal with a cross in the middle that is pinned to his jacket.

He says, "That's an Expert medal."

I stare at it.

He says, "I can shoot a rifle better than a 'Sharpshooter,' even better than a 'Marksman.' I'm called an 'Expert.' I was a teacher in the army. I taught soldiers how to shoot."

It is winter. Now he teaches students English at Christopher Columbus High School in the Bronx.

My mother drives from our white neighborhood in the afternoon to pick him up from school; I sit in the back seat of the Chevy—a chrome handle is recessed in the door.

At twenty miles per hour, she makes a left turn onto the snow-covered Pelham Parkway, lined with black-trunked twisted-limbed trees.

The centrifugal force lurches me against the door, and I grab at the handle.

The unlocked door swings open, and I sail into the cold air upside down. I see the snowy road below.

Soon the gliding flight is over—I spear deep into a snowbank, headfirst. My chin hits a cement curb.

I am enclosed by crushed snow—all is white.

She pulls me out by my feet and holds me in her arms; red blood flows from my chin. It does not hurt.

She pushes a handkerchief against the straight split on my chin.

She says, "I almost killed his son. I didn't lock the door."

I am held close.

She says to me, "Don't tell Daddy how this happened. You can't tell him, or he'll kill me. He'll kill me."

He shoots better than a Marksman.

She looks at me, "Okay?"

I say, "Yes."

She says, "Don't tell him. You can't tell Daddy. Or he'll kill me."

I say, "Okay."

I look into her scared eyes.

We understand that my father may murder my mother.

I am a cold four-year-old playing outside in the Great Blizzard of '47. I run up the steps and push open the front door of redbrick row house.

I sit next to the toaster on the high kitchen counter and she rubs my naked frozen feet. My toes warm up.

She says, "Would you like some Droste's cocoa and a roll to dunk?"

I say, "I love you, Mom."

She looks at me.

I say, "I wish Dad would die and we could be alone."

I look at her.

She says, "Murray! Murray! Murray!"

I am astonished. She is hysterical.

She looks toward the hallway that leads to the bedrooms, "Murray!"

I am scared.

I slide off the counter and land on my feet and walk away.

Behind me, I hear my mother repeat the words I had said to her.

I reach the arched entrance to the living room.

A sting explodes on my behind—I am in the air with my ass on fire. I fly slowly, toward our blond wood TV set against the far wall. Below on my left, I notice the rattan couch covered with green jungle floral upholstery float by. Why is there no gravity? I feel pain ringing through my weightless body and watch as I gain upon the eight-inch screen from an elevated scary point of view.

In the nick of time, I crash suddenly on the rug with a thud in a heap, crying helpless tears.

When I lift my dazed head up, I stare horrified at my six-foot, two-hundred-pound father under the archway.

He says, "Don't you ever say that again." And he walks off.

I know I told the truth.

When my bedroom door is closed each night by my mother, she says, "Good night, sweet dreams, I love you."

I say, "Good night, sweet dreams, I love you," to the traitor.

The door opens again. My father says, "Good night, sweet dreams, I love you." The Expert closes the door.

So, if you really love someone, don't say it.

1949

I walk on the sidewalk past the row houses on the left and parked cars at the curb on my right until I reach the empty lot at the corner of Tenbroeck Avenue, our block in the Bronx neighborhood. I watch out for traffic before I cross busy Morris Park Avenue to the candy store. I have my week's allowance in my pocket.

I climb up on one of the six red-vinyl round seats that swivel in the poorly lit narrow mom-and-pop business.

I order a Coca-Cola. The silent mom pumps the dark syrup into the glass.

I touch the nearby transparent plastic cylinder that imprisons the foot-long pretzel sticks that I cannot afford.

She holds the glass under the spritzer fountain and with a long spoon breaks the stream of seltzer into a spray before it hits the syrup.

She keeps an eye on me and the pretzels.

I look behind me at the rack of comic books that my parents forbid me to buy.

She stirs the curvy Coca-Cola glass in front of me.

I hand over my nickel.

She says, "Don't take all day."

Twenty minutes later, I slurp my soda glass dry.

She says, "Time to leave."

Only then do I slide off the tall seat and head for home. I'm from New York City.

1950

In the dark night, I come to. Stars quiver outside the window. I lie on the back seat of the Chevy. My father, my mother, my eight-year-old sister, and my grandmother—who have been cramped with me in this car for a month driving west—are nowhere to be seen. I am six years old. Something is seriously wrong.

I push down the recessed chrome handle and get out. There are many other cars in this gravel parking lot in the middle of a desert. The moon shines in the sky. It is warm. No human beings are in sight.

Thirty feet away, I see a wooden sign.

I walk to it and read the white-painted, whittled letters under a pointing arrow, "To the Top." An opportunity presents itself in the depths of crisis.

Step by step, I climb the steep dirt trail. Every fifty feet I see another sign with another white arrow indicating a 180-degree turn in the uphill narrow path. It gets colder. My life is unraveling. But I follow the signs up relentlessly for an hour.

Suddenly my eyes are up above the vast flat expanse of the mesa top. Surprise.

A hundred yards off, I see a barn fire that dwarfs the forms of an encircling crowd of human beings.

I walk toward the flames.

I hear cries of shock.

I see my mother emerge from the dark as she hurries toward me.

My father follows, just a step behind.

She says, "Oh, my baby!"

She hugs me.

He says, "How did you get up here?"

I say, "I followed the arrows."

He says, "Good boy. If you had made a wrong turn, you would have fallen a thousand feet and died."

So, obey signs to get to the top.

1951

My father takes me on the subway from the Bronx to Manhattan to Broadway for a live play, *South Pacific,* with Mary Martin and Ezio Pinza. The theater is packed with one thousand people. I sit high in the last row of the last balcony—I rest my head against the cement rear wall and touch the ceiling with my outstretched fingers. I am seven years old.

The small beings on the stage far below are a chorus of powerful booming baritone sailors who sing, "It's a waste of time to worry over things that they have not / Be thankful for / The things they've got / There is nothin' you can name / That is anythin' like a dame! / There are no books like a dame . . ."

I feel a sharp pain in my left ribcage. He elbows me again. I look up at my father. His second poke really hurts. He doesn't know his own strength is all I can figure.

He says, "'No books like a dame'? We know better than that. Don't we?" And he gives me another painful jab and smiles.

What? What about Mary Martin? What about my mother?

So, I am supposed to like books more?

1952

I am nine years old on a weekday after my father has left the house for school. My now pregnant mother mysteriously takes me on a subway train that soon elevates high above the streets. I can see Yankee Stadium, the home of the World Champions—the Bronx Bombers. My father often ridicules professional athletes. He says they're ignorant.

I say, "Mom, can we go see the Yankees?"

She says, "We are going to a baseball game now—in Brooklyn."

My first time in a professional ballpark. I play punchball in the gutter almost every day.

I say, "Does Daddy know?"

She says, "No."

I say, "I'm missing school."

She says, "Don't worry. I won't tell him."

I say, "He thinks it's stupid to watch baseball."

She says, "What does he know?"

I get it. I am astonished by her fearlessness.

I say, "Why do we have to go all the way to Brooklyn to see the Bums?"

She says, "Because we're going to see Jackie Robinson play."

I say, "We can see Mickey Mantle here."

She says, "The Yankees are all white. So are the Giants. The Dodgers have Robinson at second base. He's great."

I say, "Better than Mantle?"

She says, "Yes. Robinson's the only Negro in the major leagues."

I say, "All right."

It takes another hour of steel rail bump and screech.

At Ebbets Field on Flatbush Avenue, near where my mother grew up, Jackie Robinson steals a base and gets two hits. Number 42 is quick on the infield and turns a double play, Robinson to Pee Wee Reese to Gil Hodges. We both cheer loudly.

After the win, my bargain-obsessed mother splurges fifty cents ($4.50 today) to buy me a Dodger yearbook that I treasure. The Dodgers have never won a World Series, beaten by the Yankees in the 1941, 1947, and 1949 World Series. That's why the Brooklyn Bum caricature on the white cover holds a hammer in front of a poster that says what all Dodger fans say after each Series, "Wait 'til Next Year."

I say, "Thanks, Mom. What will Daddy say?"

She says, "We know better than that. I'll say you were sick. I took you to the doctor. Okay?"

I say, "Okay."

She says, "Don't let him see the yearbook."

I say, "Okay."

The Dodgers and I secretly wait, for next year.

Gary Cooper is on the screen in the grand Loew's Paradise movie palace on the Bronx's Grand Concourse. He is abandoned by everyone in his town, left to face the bad guy alone, at high noon. Cooper walks down the dirt main street as his fiancée, Grace Kelly, watches from afar. Why doesn't she help him?

The soundtrack's cowboy singer, Tex Ritter, unsettles me as he sings again the movie's opening lyric, "Do not forsake me, oh my darling . . ."

2

Socialization

1953–1955

1953

I have a ten-year-old's crush on blonde, blue-eyed Elaine Babbington, who lives five houses down our block on Tenbroeck.

She is a star pupil like me, tall and thin, and is friendly to me. Her brother, Lowell, is a year older than us and a skilled punchball player—he can smack a line drive half a block with his fist, two manholes beyond the manhole that we call home plate.

In our garage, a carpenter has left two sawhorses that support a sheet of thick plywood. He builds my father's new library in the basement during the week.

The kids on the block play ringolevio—a team tag game—and Elaine runs down the short driveway into the garage under the house. I follow her.

We are on the same team, hiding together.

The light is dim inside. She wears a translucent summer dress. She is beautiful.

I stare at her.

She smiles at me. What a dame.

She says, "Let's play doctor. I'll lie down and you can examine me."

The plywood worktable is bare.

This offer hangs in the air. Fills the garage. Her brother is outside on the block.

I can't move. I am bewildered.

She says, "Come on."

I say nothing, then, "Nah."

Shame on me. Elaine turns away and runs out and up the driveway to the street, never to return.

I did not dare.

Under the wooden deck at Peter Diamond's big two-story, two-family house around the block, we have built a clubhouse of cardboard boxes and army blankets.

The eight club members assemble in the dark fort for the group share of the first issue of *Playboy* that features a full page of Marilyn Monroe, in focus and in color.

She is completely naked. She has red lips and two red nipples and blonde hair. She even arches her back. And smiles.

When I walk home, new synapses multiply in in my brain as I wonder how anyone could be permitted to publish such a photograph of a woman in a magazine. An excitement reverberates around my head.

A photograph.

I bother my parents for months to give me a camera.

My sister and I each open our biggest holiday gift box.

I tear off my wrapping and see "Sportswear" in big letters on the cover.

I say, "Not clothes. No, no, no."

I jump up and hurl the box and its unopened contents into the fireplace. I cry.

My parents jump up from the rattan couch covered with green jungle upholstery and maneuver the box out of the flames.

"Open the box," I hear.

I am bitter. I lift off the cardboard cover. Inside, I see a black Brownie Hawkeye fixed-focus box camera.

Exactly what I want.

I get their joke.

I wipe away the tears to look in the viewfinder.

My father says, "Let's take a walk. Bring your camera."

We head down Tenbroeck to Morris Park Avenue and take a left turn up Seminole Avenue to the construction site of the Albert Einstein College of Medicine. At the cornerstone-laying ceremony this afternoon, Governor

Thomas E. Dewey (who lost the presidential election to Roosevelt in 1944 and again to Truman in 1948) stands ready with a trowel.

My father says, "Get a picture of the governor."

My father told me that a workman must have the right tool to do his work. I now have what I need.

A large crowd separates us from the huge rectangular granite cube.

I push my way forward under the towering adults until I can place my Brownie on top of the near edge of the cornerstone.

A policeman says, "Hey kid. Get outta'dare."

I don't move.

The cop says, "Move."

I don't.

On the far side of the cornerstone, Dewey says, "No, no. It's okay."

I look down into the viewfinder and press the shutter button. I click the handsome man with the black mustache above a toothy smile, four feet away.

I withdraw into the crowd of tall people, back to my father.

I say, "I got it."

He says, "That's my boy."

I learn what it takes. The world I live in is stressful. If I look through the lens of a camera, I can see it from a distance. I am in two places at the same time—here and there. And I have a little magic black box of armor that lets me safely break the rules.

1954

My father's voluptuous twenty-two-year-old sister comes to live with us for several months. My maturing twelve-year-old sister has been rewarded our bedroom upstairs, and my bed is now in the new basement library. Aunt Sydel sleeps there too on a cot across the room.

Most evenings, before a night in Manhattan at the notorious Copacabana nightclub, she rolls up a new pair of nylon stockings onto her long legs. I can't take my eyes off them.

My mother frequently says to my father, "What, she can't wear a pair of nylon stockings more than once?"

Downstairs, Aunt Sydel can hear my angry mother.

And every evening, I watch Sydel undulate into a tight-knit dress—low-cut, and often red.

She looks into the full-length mirror as she shimmies and sings, "Bango bungo bungo, not gonna leave the Congo, no, no, no—Bongo, bongo,

bongo, I don't want to leave the Congo, oh no-no no no-no. Bingo, bangle, bungle, I'm so happy in the jungle, I refuse to go." I imagine a wild Copacabana.

Sometimes she sweetly asks me to zipper up the back of the dress.

Sydel meets and soon marries Teamsters Union president Jimmy Hoffa's tax attorney, my three-hundred-pound Uncle Stanley.

There are people who are so joyful, they sing.

Every morning of my elementary school life, the defeat of the South in the Civil War eighty-nine years ago is confirmed in unison, "one nation, indivisible, with liberty and justice for all."

But on this morning, there is a change. Thirty-two fourth-graders pledge their allegiance to, "one nation, under God, indivisible." I have no idea that the Republican Congress has mandated this Cold War rejoinder to "godless" communism.

I know my parents would not approve. I take a breath when they all say, "under God," and rejoin in time for, "with liberty and justice for all."

From the entrance of revolving, swishing doors to deep within the darkwooded Lüchow's German restaurant in Manhattan, a maroon velvet rope herds the long, stagnant line of long-waiting patrons. The ceiling is thirty feet high, and I see a herd of severed heads of dead deer with open eyes that overlook the big tables with white tablecloths. Fascinating—nothing like the tiny Hebrew National Deli on Lydig Avenue in the Bronx.

My father says, "Where are they? Sydel said six thirty."

My mother says, "What is wrong with your sister?"

Foxy Sydel and massive Stanley appear beaming on the other side of the rope.

He says, "I'll be right back."

I watch him walk to the front of the line and say a few words to a man holding menus. Stanley slides a hand into his pocket and takes out a thick roll of cash and covertly hands a couple of bills to the man.

Stanley walks all the way back to us accompanied by the bribed man who smoothly unhooks the rope in front of us.

He says, "Let me show you to your table."

I am startled and ashamed as our family cuts out, and dumbfounded that my atheist parents do not remain in place for justice for all.

Where have you gone, Jackie Robinson?

1955

The Dodgers lost again in 1952 to the Yankees. And again in 1953. I am given dispensation by my father to watch on the blond tiny TV in the living room, the 1955 World Series—when Robinson dashes from third base to steal home, in Game Six. The white Yankees are caught by surprise. Jackie is safe at the plate. So many people hate him, and he's so great—I want to be Jackie Robinson.

The Brooklyn Dodgers win their lone World Series title in Game Seven.

I had never seen anybody steal home.

In the fifth grade, as the teacher turns to write on the blackboard, I half-rise from my seat and accurately pitch a perfectly timed wet blob past the back of her head.

"Splat." Caught and stuck on the blackboard. My colleagues laugh.

The teacher turns around, surprised, but all my classmates are suddenly calm and quiet.

"Splat." Day after day, numberless times. Perfect throws. No student turns me in.

Throughout the school year, Spitballer is an all-star, and at the start of the sixth grade, he is elected president of Public School 108.

The illegal spitballs become presidential. Each well-chewed wet wad is now composed of an entire three-holed page torn out of my loose-leaf notebook.

It is springtime.

The teacher begins her routine turnaround; I rise and cock my arm.

She swings her chalk toward the blackboard.

I commit to the throw.

But a new thought occurs to her, and she suddenly rotates her head to address the classroom of thirty.

My raised arm is in motion. I am caught red-handed.

The teacher cannot believe her eyes—it is I.

I will not steal home today. The classroom is silent.

She says, "Come with me."

The teacher opens the heavy classroom door. I walk out into the long empty hallway of green tile walls.

She escorts me all the way to the office of Principal Margaret McDade, where my crime is reported.

I sit down in a large blond-wood chair with armrests. Tall, gray-haired McDade turns on a microphone that stands on her desk; she picks up a mallet and strokes a musical phrase on the metal bars of a small pixiphone that alerts all to attention on the school-wide public address system.

She says, "Your president has disgraced himself and all of you who elected him . . ."

I am suspended from elementary school and sent home.

As I walk alone in the midday sun on the sidewalk along Herring Avenue, left onto Lakewood Place, and right onto Tenbroeck, I am surprised that the weight of this disgrace is light on my defiant head. No sweat—a fresh perspective.

My father is angry when he hears about the suspension and public shaming—not at me, at McDade. He takes off from his teaching the next morning to upbraid McDade to her face for her inappropriate punishment.

My dad defends my school record.

Father says, "Tomorrow morning your mother will give both of you an intelligence test. It is most accurate at your ages." I am eleven years old.

My single bed is in a corner of the basement knotty pine library, adjacent to the staircase. Aunt Sydel is long gone. It is late, but on my father's crowded wall-to-wall bookshelves I ferret out the *Administrators' Text for the Stanford-Binet Intelligence Test.*

I read that if a subject draws a face in a profile (like Abraham Lincoln on a penny) instead of drawing a full-face (like Abraham Lincoln on a one-dollar bill), the IQ score will soar.

My sister and I take the test the next morning. Indeed, a face is required.

I draw a profile: a big forehead, one eyebrow, one eyelid with lashes, one triangular profile of an eyeball, the bridge of a nose and one half-moon nostril, half of the upper lip, a crack of a mouth, and the lower lip, angular chin, and a neck.

After bedtime that night, I climb to the top of the stairs and listen at the door.

Father says, "I told you he was smarter than she was."

Mother says, "Don't talk like that. They're both smart."

Father says, "I told you. He's the special one."

I have passed his intelligence test. I stole home.

3

Education

1956–1957

1956

Daniel is my best friend, born in the same year as I. His family's tiny porch adjoins ours. His mother is my mother's best friend. I can hear her screaming at her husband through the adjoining wall, and Danny can hear verbatim from his side, my parents' frequent angry combat.

We grow up together on the block—hurl clods of explosive dirt at the corner construction site where we play war, shout at neighbors who try to quiet us from open front doors when punchball games get raucous. Danny gives a stunningly funny nomination speech for me at the PS 108 Election Assembly that ensures my election (before the spitball scandal).

My father's income jumped when he was appointed chairman of English at Prospect Heights High School in distant Brooklyn. There is a gang murder on the corner, near the candy store. My father informs me that when I finish the sixth grade, our family is moving to Long Island into a big house by a canal and I will have my own bedroom and maybe a boat. With an outboard engine.

I see Daniel on the street by the telephone pole near the fire hydrant. He plays tag with my three-year-old brother, Ted—who idolizes Danny. I know I will not see Danny again after we move. My little brother will be traumatized. It is hard to believe this can happen. I worry about him.

Danny writes in my graduation signature book, "A friend is someone who knows you, but likes you."

He is wry.

The family leaves the Bronx. And I lose my best friend.

I gain my own bedroom. Suddenly, we live in a split-level middle-class house just off the Great South Bay of Long Island.

I say, "Please paint my whole room green."

It is painted green. And my mother adds green sheets, green percale pillowcases, and a green spread on my bed—a green cathedral.

I do not know that green is the color for the Buddhist meditation on the chakra of the heart. I do know that I feel better surrounded by green as the voices of the kids on the block die painfully.

At night, I lie awake on my side with my eyes closed and "feel" the cool percale with my thumb and forefinger and caress my way around the pillowcase edge.

Soon, I fly around the emptiness of outer space and imagine myself dead. This discovery is scary but extraordinarily beautiful—so much space and so many stars and no limit to the blackness; forget staring at the entire Morse Code alphabet that I had carefully written on the ceiling—and the words, ••-• /••- /-•-• /-•- and ••• /•••• /•• /-, ("fuck" and "shit").

I am the king of a celestial space within me. Is it the entire universe?

Father says, "Speak more loudly. Don't speak in a monotone."

He says, "Use your diaphragm to project your voice."

He says, "Stop slurring your words. Articulate."

I obey.

He is hard of hearing. He kneeled next to soldiers for three years to instruct them as they fired their M-1 rifles. But I am told that the problem of my slovenly speech is all mine.

And whenever I utter a mistake in grammar, it is instantly corrected, and I repeat the correction aloud to his satisfaction—there will be no impoverishment of the English language:

I say, "If I was president of the United States . . ."

He says, "If I *were* president of the United States . . ."

I say, "If I *were* president of the United States . . ."

I say, ". . . excuse me being late."

He says, ". . . excuse *my* being late."

I say, ". . . excuse *my* being late."

Family dinner is a time for continuous conversation and, incidentally, eating.

There are no boundaries within which I can create thoughts that will remain private—everything I do each day must be revealed in the evening's eventually perfectly well-spoken conversation, directed and cherished by my father.

I believe this is normal.

1957

In the Bronx, I played stickball in the "gutt-ah" (street).

The ball is a pink rubber "spawl-deen" (made by Spalding) hurled over home plate—a "sue-wah" (sewer cover)—by the pitcher at the next sewer, fifty feet farther not further, of course, farther down the block.

Players call out, "Caw! Caw!" and "Toim owt!" when a car turns into our block and drives through our field of play.

The ball is small and fast. The bat is a broom handle no more than an inch thick. I am a good hitter. I hate the ball. I smack it with all my might.

Now, in the Little League of Massapequa, Long Island, ten- to twelve-year-old boys in color-coordinated team uniforms of shirt, pants, high socks, and rubber cleats play baseball on a grass diamond with dirt base paths bordered by white-powdered foul lines, and padded bases. There is a clay pitcher's mound, an in-ground isosceles pentagon home plate, and many baseball bats—bats more than three times thicker than a broomstick.

It is easy with that fat lumber to punish the hardball with all my anger, long distances. Home runs? A slow runner, I lead the league in triples. I never steal home.

My newfound rich teammates like me, anyway.

I did not see Danny's father, Sidney, that much when we lived in the Bronx. Only when he was shouting angrily at Danny.

"Get in here now."

Danny, from the freedom of our gutter game, "Okay, okay."

"Now."

"I hear you."

"Dinner. Now."

"I'm coming."

Sidney was for many years always busy inside writing his textbook, *Past to Present: A World History.*

He loved to play handball in his free time. I once saw him play at the big cement wall in the school playground. He covered the court like a cat and slammed the black rubber ball with his gloved hand like a shot.

My mother tells me her friend, Danny's mother, is coming to visit us on Long Island.

I say, "Is Danny coming?"

She says, "No. He's in school. Sid had a heart attack on the handball court and died." End of her story.

His, too.

I am startled and still, looking at the image of the handball court in my mind. His death is the first of anyone that I have known in real life. I wonder how Danny feels.

My father tells me that Sidney's textbook is now a huge success, being bought by school systems across the nation.

He says, "Daniel will inherit a lot of money."

I conclude that's good.

It is late at night as the twenty couples of our Family Circle sit in the sunken living room. In the darkness on the stairs from my bedroom, just close enough to hear the conversation and just low enough on the carpeted steps to see some of the illuminated crowd trampling Robert's Rules of Order, I wonder at their enthusiasm and good cheer. They are all in their late thirties or forties.

I look into the black around me in wonder—that one day all of them will be dead and I will still be living.

I close my eyes and the far-off stars of my private infinite space appear, twinkling in serene blackness. Miraculous. My place.

In a brown paper bag, well in the back of my parents' bedroom closet, I discover *Fanny Hill: Memoirs of a Woman of Pleasure*, by John Cleland. And there are many pages of a large naked man with different women in pornographic woodcuts.

I take the volume.

Each night after I read, I hide it behind a small sliding door in the cubby of my bed's headboard. Weeks later, I reach for Fanny, but the cubby is bare.

The next afternoon when I am alone in the house, I search for the book. I find it across the hallway in my sister's room, in the headboard container of her bed. I take it and restore it to my cubby.

A few days later, I find Fanny gone again.

Soon, I again rescue her from across the hallway.

A few days later, Fanny is gone.

Soon, I again rescue her from across the hallway.

After another month of this literary shuttle, my parents go out for the evening, leaving my sister and me home alone.

She is a tall, pretty thirteen-year-old and has breasts. She is in her bedroom.

She says, "Come in here."

I say, "Why?"

She says, "To get your book back."

I walk into her room. She is in her bed under the blanket.

She says, "Lie down here." She lifts a corner of the blanket.

I climb in next to her.

She is naked.

I get in a spoon position.

She reaches down and fondles me. I touch her breast. This is great.

Her hand holds me.

I do not know what to do with my erection.

I get out of the bed.

She throws the blanket aside, naked on her back.

I look at her.

She says, "Stick it in."

I stare at her.

I say to myself, "I can't get her pregnant in the house of my mother and father," though I have never had an orgasm.

I say to her, "You could get pregnant."

She doesn't care that I'm her brother. She wants the physical experience. I just have a penis. That's all she wants.

I walk out of her room, bleak. Scared there is something wrong with me.

Neither of us ever speak again of her experiment gone wrong.

My father requires me to read a book a week in addition to my homework—the entire Landmark Series and the Signature Series, more than a hundred books of historical nonfiction for teens. I travel in time.

I like the Landmark book by Arnold Whitridge about Simón Bolívar, the great South American aristocrat revolutionary—"When tyranny becomes law, rebellion is a right." But I love the one by Katharine Scherman about Toussaint Louverture, the Haitian slave who beat Napoleon and his sick French oppressors—the only successful slave revolution in modern times—"I was born a slave, but nature gave me a soul of a free man."

Freedom comes after rebel violence.

My father says, "Don't fight—that's what stupid people do. Use your brain."

On my back on the grass next to the driveway basketball court, Richie Horowitz sits on top of me and punches me again and again in the face.

I can't move my arms.

I cannot squeeze the slave out of myself.

My family is not religious—no ritual to usher me into the tribal notion of manhood's rank.

I do often recite the Boy Scout Law at troop meetings: "A Scout is trustworthy, loyal, helpful, friendly, courteous, kind, obedient, cheerful, thrifty, brave, clean, and reverent." I assiduously accumulate a moral framework of merit badges on a sash across my chest.

For my thirteenth birthday, my parents give me *My Life and Loves by Frank Harris, Five Volumes in One, Complete and Unexpurgated,* the autobiography of this Irishman who knew all the celebrated writers and political figures of his day. Not only does he report on his daytime activities as a literary critic in turn-of-the-century London, but he also graphically describes the mechanical details of his nightly sexual conquests. The book is banned for sale in the USA.

I read that the best time to seduce a woman is twenty minutes after she finishes a meal because her blood is attracted to the intestines for digestion and so it takes less effort for a seducer to create excitement below. That is why it was the custom to have curtains in the private booths of fancy British dining spots. I am an innocent and I have never eaten in such a place, but I do not forget the data.

Has Frank Harris been presented as my pubescent role model for a career in literature? I don't ask. They don't tell. What am I supposed to do?

The eighth-grade boys are a huddle of flattop crewcuts in the hallway before Homeroom, which starts at 8:15 a.m.

Tom Reuden, who already shaves, holds forth about "jerking off." This is news to me. He makes piston-like gestures and talks of "gray cum."

That evening, after hours of homework in my green room, I get under the green covers of the bed and touch and knead and rub my cock against the green sheets.

Every few minutes it feels more intensely electric. After two hours, I only feel the pinpointed, charged wonderfulness that continually transcends my preadolescent wisdom. No past, no future. Sensations.

And then my first orgasm—a surrender so exhilarating and so slimy and so unexpected. I am in my extraordinary private outer space, vast and black, but now for the first time with an added swoon of love and happiness.

"I knew it. I knew it. There had to be something more to life to make it worth living. This had to be. Why would anybody want to continue to live without this? I know there's no such thing as God, but thank you, god."

This is the opposite of homework.

4

Principles

1957–1961

1957

I have a Porter Chemcraft chemistry set. I sit in my basement laundry room laboratory but do no experiments. I only rearrange endlessly the small chemical bottles in patterns on the narrow metal shelves. I group them by their color, not by their element's atomic number.

The *Porter Science Magazine* arrives in the mail. They sponsor an essay contest each year to attract young people to a career in chemistry, "Why I Want to Be a Scientist."

I write, "I want to go into outer space . . . it would be exciting to be part of that exploration," with no mention of my frequent daily masturbatory expeditions into the extraordinary blackness—my exquisite experiments.

Father vets my essay.

I win the contest—that is, we win the contest. But it appears it is only I that has extraordinary promise as a young mind.

The prize is $1,000 ($9,580 today), a train trip in a "parlor car"—twelve plush swivel chairs in a single line on each side of the carriage—to visit the US Naval Academy at Annapolis and the Porter Chemcraft factory in Hagerstown, Maryland.

My father, sister, and I (for the first time), stay at a hotel—the Lord Baltimore, which was built in the Roaring Twenties. Surrounded at breakfast by polished brass and elegant dark wood, white tablecloths, and plush chairs, we sit with the distinguished, gray-haired Mr. Harold M. Porter himself. I am confused at the outset by my one small glass of orange juice served in an immense crock of crushed ice, and later by a lemon in water that Mr. Porter tells me is a finger bowl.

On the day of our return home, I tell Mr. Porter that I've never flown on an airplane. He discreetly hands my father a fifty-dollar bill as we go down an elevator. It is enough to pay for the three of us to fly to Idlewild Airport (later renamed JFK) on a twin-engine prop Douglas DC-3.

I fly over the clouds. The Empire State Building, the tallest building in the world, looks inconsequential as we descend.

Under the masthead of the *Massapequa Post,* the front-page headline is, "Wins $1,000 Bond." Right below it is a large photo of Porter presenting the prize to me as we stand in front of the Naval Academy statue of the grim Native American old warrior Tecumseh.

I say, "What am I going to do with all this money?"

Father says, "You may invest the money for college."

I say, "It's not mine?"

He says, "No, it's a lot of money."

Flying over clouds will have to suffice.

I say, "What do I say to the kids when they ask me, 'What will you get with a thousand dollars?'"

A new Ford sedan only costs $1,600.

I investigate some stocks and choose to buy one hundred shares on the New York Stock Exchange of the razor company Schick, Inc. He approves.

I return to school. Everybody asks me what I'm going to buy.

I say, "I bought a hunk'a shik."

1958

Our next-door neighbor makes his living buying out-of-date law books from upstate lawyers on driving tours in his Oldsmobile that has a huge trunk and the back seat removed. He buys them for next to nothing and pays fifty cents an hour to six local seventh-grade boys who sit in his garage and sandpaper by hand, the dirty fore-edges of the pages between the covers. It takes them at least twenty minutes to scrape away the decades of embedded dust. That's about seventeen cents a book. He resells the cleaned tan-and-red volumes at a premium to low-rent upstate lawyers who display the fake books on their office shelves to impress clients (they do their research in a law library).

One day, I demonstrate to Mr. Winnette how I can clean a book in twenty seconds. I place a book between my knees and run an electric rotary power sander over the exposed sides—top, side, bottom—one, two, three!

The next day, he fires everybody but me. I earn ten cents a book. In the cold double-garage, steps away from the Great South Bay, I am a solid success.

I read all 440 pages of *The Last Billionaire: Henry Ford* by William C. Richards.

After four long weekends when I am scarce around our house, my mother says, "How much money have you made?"

I say, "About twelve hundred."

She says, "I will talk to Mr. Winnette tomorrow. No more!"

I say, "What? He pays me a dime a book."

She says, "That's too much."

I say, "Why? He's making more than he ever did."

She says, "You're making more than your father—it's not right."

The median yearly income of a family of four in the USA is $5,600.

I say, "It's not right?"

She says, "That's right. It's not right."

I say, "That makes no sense."

She says, "Where is the money?"

I say, "Most of it's in the bank."

She says, "Take it out. We will put the money away, for college."

She lays down her law: don't get too rich. Thus she has spoken—so it shall be.

1959

Okay. There's still baseball. The batting champion of the Massapequa Babe Ruth League will be decided among the top three hitters on this last day of the season. I am fifteen years old and in the running against two opponents on the "Falcons," Jimmy Walsh—his father is the team manager—and Frank Tuffariello—his father is president of the League.

I dress in my cream uniform, "Eagles" in blue across my chest. Black baseball shoes with metal cleats tied are together by the shoelaces and hang from my left hand as I reach with my right for the front door.

I know my current batting stats and calculate how many hits at how many at-bats I must get to win.

"Where do you think you're going?" I hear my father's voice from His Chair in the nearby living room.

I say, "I've got a big game this afternoon."

He says, "The Biology State Regents Exam is tomorrow."

I am taking biology in summer school—so I will have more room in my senior year schedule to take Advanced Placement classes in English and history.

I say, "I know. I'll study later."

"You're not going to play baseball today. You're going to study."

"I can study later."

"Do you know the material perfectly?"

"No."

"Close the door."

"What?"

"You may not leave the house today. You will study for the biology exam."

The stomach of my soul falls out. I do not play baseball that day. There is no leeway.

I study for many hours.

The Eagles simply can't believe that I did not show up.

I get an A on the exam.

Frank Tuffariello gets five hits in seven at-bats for the Falcons and is the Batting Champion. I never play organized baseball again.

Most kids are scared of going to the principal's office—I live in his house.

1960

The school day starts at eight and is over at three. Sports practice lasts at least until five. By the time I walk the mile home and finish the confessional, grammatical, and enunciated family conversation masquerading as dinner, it is seven. Four hours of homework keep me up too late every night to get up at six in the morning without an alarm.

For talking without permission in class, teachers assign detention for forty-five minutes after school. It is the only excuse accepted for being late to sports practice. I play different sports every season—the coaches call me "Nomad." But I love the escape from everyday reality when I am absorbed in physical games.

I wisecrack fearlessly. My oppressed classmates—upper-middle, middle, and lower—are thrilled by my abuse of the authoritarians. I am booked for detention every day with the non-college-bound kids until June, and I am elected junior class president by all.

But I still need an alarm clock to wake up in the morning.

I am told that Mr. Robertson spends the first five minutes in the English class after mine reciting my jokes from the preceding period.

The next day, while thirty-five kids crowd out of the narrow classroom door, I disappear into Robertson's cloak closet in the front of the room. It is black and cramped as I wait four long minutes until the loud alarm bell sounds for the start of the next period.

It takes another two minutes for these students in this next class to take their seats and settle down.

Mr. Robertson says, "You know what he said today?"

I burst out from the closet behind him.

I say, "Did anyone call me?" I tap an imaginary cigar, like Groucho Marx. Howls from the students. And Robertson.

Egregiously late to my next class, that outraged teacher fiercely orders me to appear for a second forty-five-minute detention after the first forty-five— "double detention."

His escalation soon grapevines to all my frustrated teachers and in a few days I have my needed double-detentions booked for the year.

But the teachers who supervise the first crowded detention soon realize that it is I who has given them a second—they rebel at remaining in school another forty-five minutes for a solitary student.

Freedom's just another word for nothing left to lose.

I start to use my alarm clock again.

Paul Goodman's *Growing Up Absurd* explains how delinquency is a reasonable reaction to coping in an absurd American society. Sounds right to me. Class president, I appoint the all-female Junior Prom Planning Committee—half "good kids" and half tough "rocks." The rocks—working-class kids from low-rent North Massapequa—are included for the first time on the committee. The assistant principal tells me it's a bad idea. I insist—he is unable to defend his position against the democratic hero. Fuck him. If I agree with him, we'll both be wrong. Soon the girls, who at the outset had been suspicious of each other, find they like working together and like each other.

Louellen Joe is short but the prettiest girl I have ever seen. She does not take high school seriously and is absent more days than she is present. She dates college guys. To me, her unfathomable lack of attendance is the behavior of a revolutionary.

My crush on Louellen is total, close to lunacy. On days she is not in school, I go to North Massapequa in the afternoon to stare from behind a hedge across the street, at her very small house hoping to catch a glimpse of her. Most of the time, I just see her father's dump truck sitting in front of the house. His name is Lou. Her mother's name is Ellen.

One day in a hallway between periods, Louellen says, "Hello, Paul."

Is this God, again? I am enraptured.

Soon, she tells me I must take her to Greenwich Village in Manhattan to see a singer. I'm all ears.

We arrive at a venue with a two-foot riser in front of the large white-washed store window.

My postponed homework shadows this moment amid a crowd of drop-outs. My father wants his son to go to the pinnacle of the nation's intellectual and moral culture—Harvard College.

I sit next to Louellen. She smiles.

A woman named Joan Baez sings pleasant folk protest songs for a while.

I say, "Let's get out of here." I do not yet have an infinite regard for music.

A skinny kid with long hair, a couple of years older than me, sits just off the left side of the stage.

Louellen touches me with her perfect small hand.

She says, "That's him. I want to hear him. Just wait."

I feel jealous. She is preoccupied by a beatnik singer.

Baez says, "Come on. Don't be shy. Get up here."

The kid stays put.

Baez says, "Please, now. Come up here."

The kid gets on stage, plays his guitar, harmonica, and sings, "I Got a New Girl."

Louellen is happy.

Later, TIME STOPS: she, whom I love, gives me the greatest kisses of my life. She has the long spelunking tongue of a giraffe—it slithers and slides to places hidden and unknown to me until now.

I am happy.

The kid was Bob Dylan.

I love Louellen.

I cannot say the words.

He later wins the Nobel Prize in Literature.

27

Appurtenance. Bellicose. Crepuscular.

Denouement. Eleemosynary. Fatuous.

Genuflect. Heuristic. Interstice.

I have a light-blue box of one thousand vocabulary flashcards that I memorize and use in a sentence before the PSAT—the College Board's Preliminary Scholastic Aptitude Test.

Spelunking. The exploration of caves, especially as a hobby. In a sentence: They spoke of virginal spelunking in the mountains.

At the end of the school year, no one wants to run against me for next year's school president. The college-bound good kids and my detention-buddy rocks are united.

At the last minute, a good guy, John Downey, runs against me.

And he wins. I like the slightly reticent Downey, but the math is all mine. I can't make sense of it.

I go off to work as a waiter in an upstate summer camp. There are two Cuban dishwashers who tell me about the terrorizing of the dirt-poor peasants in their homeland, about maiming of women and brutal murder of men under the government of the recently toppled dictator, Fulgencio Batista.

They are joyous about the triumph of Fidel Castro and his social justice and land reforms, and his universal housing, education, and healthcare for all. I am impressed.

I write many letters to Louellen. Lovesick, I listen to "Maria," from *West Side Story*. All summer long on the radio, the beautiful sounds in a single word, Louellen, Louellen, Louellen, Louellen.

I am quick to mail call every day. But I get no response all summer long. My daily disappointment eventually becomes a joke to all.

During the last week of camp, I am elated to get a small pink billet-doux from her.

I go off to a hilltop far from camp to read. It is oddly written, but I still treasure Louellen's arch expressions of affection. I read the short letter over and over. I read it at least twenty times.

When I return to my cabin, my Cuban friend tells me that the letter is a hoax, perpetrated by the counselors, one of whom on a day off mailed the letter from Massapequa so the envelope would have an unsuspicious postmark.

I grieve.

Then I feel the need for a revolution.

The first day of senior year, the Advanced Placement English teacher assigns an essay, "The Person I Most Admire in History."

I write an appreciation of Fidel's heroic battle against Batista's tyranny.

The next day, over the loudspeakers in all the homerooms, I experience a clear déjà vu: this principal announces that I, a school leader, have disgraced myself and shamed everyone in the school.

I am suspended from high school in fucked-up, conservative Massapequa. I remember the ditty from elementary school, "Whistle while you work, / Margaret is a jerk, / McDade fell down / and broke her crown, / and now we have no work."

Fidel is a Red. A Communist.

Back in school after a few days, John Downey tells me in the hallway that the principal and guidance counselors had met secretly and arranged for him to run. After the voting, they ignored the ballot count, and announced he had won.

Principal power corrupts, absolutely.

1961

I watch outgoing President Eisenhower on TV: "The potential for the disastrous rise of misplaced power exists and will persist. We should take nothing for granted. Only an alert and knowledgeable citizenry can compel the proper meshing of the huge industrial and military machinery of defense with our peaceful methods and goals, so that security and liberty may prosper together."

"Hester Prynne and Her Scarlet Letter."

He sits in His Chair in the living room. He reads my 1,500 words about the fictional adulteress with the "A" over her bosom, ostracized by all, and orders me back up the stairs to my green room to rewrite my essay.

He says, "Remember—in each paragraph: a topic sentence, illustrative examples, rhythmic sentence variety, alliteration, rhetorical questions, climactic order, and a conclusion."

I do as expected upstairs, then return to His Chair; my expert reads it and again orders me up to my room to rewrite with his new notes in my obviously second-rate mind.

Again and again, I walk down the stairs and I believe that imminently I will be free. Eleven times I am wrong. For the last few, I am a demented, angry, disempowered slave in tears. They don't move him.

After the twelfth, I am broken. I surrender to suffering.

In school, I get an A+ from Miss Boetcher.

Six months later, on the Scholastic Aptitude Test Writing Sample, one option for an essay is about an "iconoclastic character from literature"—it takes me fifteen minutes to handwrite from memory.

I even remember my Nathaniel Hawthorne quote, "No man, for any considerable period, can wear one face to himself and another to the multitude, without finally getting bewildered as to which may be the true."

My score is a perfect 800.

I enter the Conference of English Teachers of Nassau County writing contest, "Jobs for the Handicapped, A Community Challenge." The final line in my essay, "It's the ability not the disability that counts." I come in second and win a hundred dollars ($786 today) at a ceremony in a rehabilitation center. A guy plays the piano with a steel hook grabber at the end of one arm. My money is grabbed, hooked for the college fund.

My father often says:

"Get out of the house; put yourself in the way of opportunity."

"All of this could have been avoided."

"Many a slip twixt cup and lip."

"Don't marry for money, but marry where money is."

I hear repeatedly these concise admonitions—rules for a gigolo?

The Kuder Preference Test is a four-hour test that questions your feelings about everything. It discovers your ideally satisfying potential career.

All the twelfth-graders take the test.

I expect a result of "Lawyer" or "Writer" or "Politician," but Kuder recommends only one career for me: "Forest Ranger."

I read *Trees,* by Hermann Hesse. "Whoever has learned how to listen to trees no longer wants to be a tree. He wants to be nothing except what he is. That is home. That is happiness."

Paul does not know what he is. But the image of a small room atop a high tower surrounded by trees seems like a location better than any he knows.

I am drawn to all the short stories that I can find by Frank O'Hara (Harvard College Class of 1950). He never belonged to any class. To the rich he was poor, and to the poor he was poor pretending to be rich.

I read to know how to say what to whom, and when. Class stumbling blocks are often left out of the success story.

In May, I sit in the raised center chair of the city council chamber of Massapequa. Discussing items on the agenda with ten council members, I see that running this city of fifty thousand is child's play. I am hopelessly afraid of my father but fearless of everyone else—and therefore powerful.

These councilmen see as far as their noses. I've learned to think a step ahead.

The *Massapequa Post* publishes a picture of me with a gavel in my hand, "Mayor for a Day."

If I were president . . . of the United States of America. Last year, John F. Kennedy defeated Eisenhower's vice president, Richard M. Nixon, and was elected the first Catholic US president.

I am seventeen years old and receive an envelope from Harvard College—as John Kennedy said, "I have always wanted to go there, as I have felt that it is not just another college."

I am one of the legions of New York public high school boys who applied for admission, who are not athletes and are in need of a scholarship.

I open the letter at the front door.

I read it aloud to my mother. I am to join the Class of 1965, with a scholarship.

My mother holds both my hands and actually jumps up and down with excitement. She screams with joy.

She says, "Oh, god. Daddy will be so happy!"

I got in. I jump with her. I feel relieved that she is happy even though she feels happy because he will be happy.

While my classroom teacher father scored high on a written civil service exam to become a chairman of English, he had once taught a class about birth control, and his Catholic principal blackballed him in the recommendation stage.

My father studied law on his own and sued the board of education, and won, and got his promotion. We moved to Long Island. But the litigation cost him years—he put away his dream to be a district superintendent.

He takes the Long Island Railroad to reach a high school in Brooklyn each day. His best friend, Nat, and his brother-in-law, Lenny, are already high school principals, on their way to super.

My father advises me, Paul William Goldberg, that I shall now change my last name from Goldberg, just before I enter Harvard College.

I am stunned. I am never again to be a Goldberg.

Only I will know that I've lived seventeen years with that name?

I say, "Why didn't you change your name?"

He says, "It never occurred to me when I was young. I should have."

I say, "How can I do this now? Kennedy appointed Arthur Goldberg secretary of labor. You want me to go as someone . . . who I wasn't?"

I will never be able to be the first Jewish president.

He says, "What name shall we change it to?" He waits.

I say, "Hitler committed suicide twenty years ago."

I know I have a middle name, William. I'm used to it.

I say, "Williams."

He says, "OK."

I do not consider that my resulting name, Paul William Williams is too awkwardly alliterative. At least, William Paul Williams could have been a poet—like William Carlos Williams, who wrote in plain American English and just died a few months ago. But I cling to this new name that is almost mine even though it sounds more natural in the voice of da' wabbit Bugs Bunny, "Dat's awl Fowks!—Pawl weeyum weeyums!"

But I never consider opposing my father's will. Looney Tunes.

I am still a minor. He brings his petition to change his son's name to the court. There is a necessary legal notice in the *Massapequa Post.* (I live in the part of town with many Italians and Jews, "Matzah-Pizza" Park).

But what a twist this is. As Peter Pan said, "All children, except one, grow up." Paul Goldberg commits hari-kari. Paul Williams now—if anyone finds out—is a covert, shameful, self-hating name-changing Jew.

Inside my raped surname pretzel-hood, I struggle this summer before I leave for Harvard. In a dream, a beautiful woman murmurs to me, "The less I get to know about you, the more I like you."

At the beach, when kids find out about "Williams," a few say, "How can you do that? Everyone knows who you are."

I say, "After this summer, I'll never see any of you again."

The answer makes me feel alone—it does not feel good, although it is true. I go to Jones Beach less often. I never thought much about being Jewish—now I think about it all the time.

Goldberg is off the radar. He disappeared a virgin. But Paul's body still has a place of black starry infinity in which to take refuge.

I read some books about the college. "You can always tell a Harvard man, but you can't tell him much." That sounds like a good place to start.

In the fall, I shall discover that of the 1,200 Harvard freshman, 400 are Jews.

My father did not know this fact or understand that his renaming of his son was a major wound. A disabled adolescent now goes undercover and tries to live his dream.

Some scars never heal. Here I am, to slay someone else's ghosts: all of his near misses, all of his disappointments, all of his years of want.

5

Harvard College, Class of 1965

1961–1964

1961

I have been assigned two freshman roommates, David Bingham Odell, from Shaker Heights, Ohio, whose grandfather was a two-term governor of New York long before Dewey, and David A. Mersky, from Newton, Massachusetts.

On this first day in Harvard Yard, in the suite on the ground floor of Wigglesworth Hall, the teenage Mersky says, "You're from New York City. You're Jewish."

I say, "I'm from Lawn-gyland."

Mersky says, "I am going to become a very rich rabbi in Newton."

Odell says, "Paul, can you say, 'Long Island'? Two words?"

I unpack my clothes into a wooden bureau.

I say, "These drawz are stuck."

Odell says, "Drawers? There are two syllables in 'drawers.'"

Mersky and Odell out the spy in no time flat.

Is this assignment of roommates a coincidence or the whimsy of a mischievous admissions staffer?

The arch keystone of the entrance to Wigglesworth on Mass Ave. advises in chiseled letters, "Enter to Grow in Wisdom."

Fred Cabot and Harry Parker, the Harvard Crew coaches, ask me to row. From crew-less, clueless Massapequa ("sweet water" in Algonquian), I am six feet three inches tall but weigh 163 pounds—exceptional leverage for a would-be Lightweight. They teach me how.

I am in the first eight-man shell. The best oars—seven of whom have rowed in exclusive prep schools. I sit at starboard number seven oar, in the stern pair—behind Sarge Cheever (Groton), Jack Lowell ("Here's to dear old Boston, The home of the bean and the cod, Where Lowells speak only to Cabots, And Cabots speak only to God"), "T.R.4" (Theodore Roosevelt IV), Galen Brewster (Andover), Bob (FAO) Schwarz, John Young (Andover, who later becomes a roommate), and a guy named Paul Gunderson (later, an Olympian rowing legend).

I like being on the Charles River every day. I like to hear Tim Claflin IV's bark, "Ready? Row!" as he starts to hit the shell with the coxswain's wooden handles as we respond to keep the cadence. I like the small turn of my wrist as I "feather the oar" before the catch and watch the blade enter the water without a splash, and then the slide of the seat as I drive with my legs to power my sweep.

Eight strokes in neural synchrony is serene.

In the boathouse, crewmates detail how they burn more money on a date in Manhattan on a weekend than I have to cover my expenses for the semester. The embers of class rage stir (embers are also known as firebrands).

There is in real life an oligarchy in America. These are the Princes of Maine, the Kings of New England.

And they row, with Williams.

In cavernous Memorial Hall there is an initial dance for all the freshmen. The often plain and brilliant females, called "Cliffies," are integral in the Harvard academic program but live in distant dorms from the males and, though having the same classes with the males, receive their degrees from "Radcliffe College."

I spot a rarity—a winsome Cliffie. I walk to her confidently, with a smile.

I ask her to dance.

She says, "No, I don' wanna' daynce." And walks away.

Her dismissal humiliates me. I polish what I had believed from my father was a Mid-Atlantic accent, as fast as I can. Everybody seems to catch this Gingerbread Man.

Science is not my strong suit, but my plan is to experience firsthand the greatest minds I can find. I want to see and hear how the smartest people think and speak. I work to understand them.

Professor of biology George Wald teaches Natural Sciences 5. With no deus ex machina, Wald spends the year teaching how the four elements C, O, N, and H—(carbon, oxygen, nitrogen, and helium)—by obeying their own rules according to the laws of physics, evolved into the entire biological universe.

After Christmas, I spend days memorizing the sixteen steps of each atom's movement around the chlorine ring in the transformation of fructose sugar into sucrose sugar—how we deliver energy that the body can use. Though a true eye-opener, I know this torture is as far as I will ever submit to biochemistry.

The course ends in May. Wald's final revelation: the head of the male praying mantis emits anti-orgasmic secretions in the initial stages of copulation—which requires the female to bite off his head, to allow the flow of semen to escape.

The biological purpose of male life is insemination, but Wald says, "He who loves and runs away, lives to love another day." Sounds right to me.

(A few years later, Wald would win the Nobel Prize in Physiology when he cut off the head of a rabbit while the bunny was looking at high-contrast black-and-white vertical columns. Wald then pulled out an eyeball, cut it open, and removed the retina, that he put in a photographic fixing solution—and used that as a negative to print a picture of the vertical bars—optography! Your murderer caught in your dying eye is not a clue in solving the case—just the pseudoscience of a mystery writer? Wald's Nobel acceptance speech: "Molecular Basis of Visual Excitation.")

Henry Kissinger is a thirty-eight-year-old academic star of geopolitical thinking. He teaches a graduate seminar in international relations. On the first day, I walk in and ask him if I can audit the course. Kissinger is surprised to see a callow undergraduate. He questions me briefly in a German accent and says yes.

I listen to his genius for four consecutive seminars. I try to understand his realpolitik of the strict objective consideration of power. I listen to how his brain frames his sentences. But I never hear any consideration of compassion. He infuses me with metaphysical gloom. Four times I leave his seminar with a splitting headache. My eyes hurt. I quit.

Most of my time each day is spent at a desk in the stacks of Lamont Library, reading basic works of Western philosophy, United States government, and biology. I am surprised when I find out that I am one of twenty freshman admitted to a creative writing seminar.

In an essay about my first semester, I write about William Ernest Hocking (Class of 1901) and his notions, "If I can reconcile myself to the certainty of death only by forgetting it, I am not happy," and of "life losing its pitch and moment."

I use at one point the longest word in English, "floccinaucinihilipilification"—the action or habit of estimating something as worthless, like my life.

I am personally invited to the office hours of the section man. He says, "How are you? Do you need to talk to a doctor?"

I do not say, "A possum that wants to avoid being eaten pretends to be dead and therefore unpalatable to the predator, or at least, more likely to be spit out whole after being verified as not fit for eating."

I say, "The required reading is a heavier load than my father's, but I do not plan to kill myself."

There is no way for me but forward. Knowledge is knowing a tomato is a fruit. Wisdom is not putting it in a fruit salad.

I read a Government 1 assignment, *The Children of Light and The Children of Darkness,* by Reinhold Niebuhr. I find out that he is a visiting professor, and I make sure to attend the lectures of the greatest American Protestant theologian of the nineteenth and twentieth centuries.

He says, "Nations, as individuals, who are completely innocent in their own esteem are insufferable in their human contacts."

Niebuhr says every political decision is a sin—somebody always benefits and somebody always doesn't.

Live and learn.

I don't quit.

1962

I am hospitalized at University Health Services on Mount Auburn Street with mononucleosis—the shipwreck of my Lightweight Crew career.

Just like Albert Camus' tuberculosis ended his football career at this age.

I read in *The Stranger* how Camus chooses his half-loved, half-deaf mother over communism. I read how Jean-Paul Sartre does not. *Being and Nothingness.*

Camus, in *The Myth of Sisyphus,* has Sisyphus keep rolling his boulder up a hill, never getting to the top. It rolls back down over and over for eternity. But he's happy making the righteous effort until he dies. My man. I read everything published that he has written. "Should I kill myself tonight, or have a cup of coffee?" Hope in caffeine.

No classmates visit. They are busy reading and writing papers.

I feel the distance between the others and me. I have a cheap but solid Argus C-3 35mm camera. I decide to take pictures.

I can be objective when I photograph. Present and apart, out of harm's way. The mythic Argus had a thousand eyes.

There is a six-week competition to join the Photography Board of the newspaper the *Harvard Crimson.* All the other competitors have costly Nikons or Leicas. Argus makes the cut, and I begin to publish photographs.

It takes hours in the darkroom to develop the exposed negatives, enlarge prints, and make photo engravings before the basement printing press deadline of two in the morning.

I often visit the newsroom, adjacent to the darkrooms. Though all *Crimson* members are "editors," as a photog I am often called a "photo-wonk" when I appear. I sometimes venture upstairs to watch the first-rate minds in the Editorial Board meetings.

Once, I am surprised by a short, overweight, hairy Allen Ginsberg, who sits buck naked on the thirty-foot-long conference table. The Beat poet author of *Howl* reveals the power of the open expression of his rage and pain as he sits among the editors, who look at him but don't see him.

He asks the interviewer, "Why don't you take off your clothes?"

This man celebrates everything I try to hide.

I am so far from being naked.

I observe the yet-unknown crowd of undergraduate wordsmiths who hang each afternoon at the *Crimson* building at 14 Plympton Street.

Every day, I review the *Crimson* comment books in which editors scribble critical notes about the day's published pieces, cut out and pasted on separate pages. The books are open on a long, four-foot-high shelf that spans the newsroom. A great way to learn to write.

I particularly like ATW (Andrew T. Weil—later, MD, inventor of the holistic health movement), MMC (Michael M. Crichton—later, author of *Andromeda Strain*, the TV series *ER*, and *Jurassic Park*), HH (Hendrik "Rick" Hertzberg—later, the *New Yorker* political commentator), DEG (Donald E. Graham—later, publisher of the *Washington Post*), WMS (Wallace Shawn—later, actor), and the acknowledged smartest-of-all, JEC (Joel E. Cohen—who later plunks out on an Adams House piano the soundtrack for my documentary *Chanzeaux* and later is the star mathematical biologist of Rockefeller University).

I am now PWW but I imagine PWG whenever I see my initials in the comment book.

I spend a lot of time at the *Crimson* building—but most of it in the darkroom.

I am more comfortable in darkness. When the light goes off, I am absorbed back into my magical black sanctuary where I control the light and produce my own pictures of people I have seen who glow with goodness.

John Winthrop, the first governor of Massachusetts, inspired by Jesus's Sermon on the Mount, authored the undying metaphor, "We shall be as a city upon a hill"—a seventeenth-century forerunner to the concept of American exceptionalism.

My John Winthrop House roommates and I get out of a cab. I have five twenties in my pocket that the other three virgins chipped in on a dare to end my innocence with one of a crowd of a hundred Black sex workers, whom we call "prostitutes," who are known to mass on a corner of Massachusetts Avenue in Boston. There is a long line of taxis parked along the street, as taxis like ours disgorge white undergraduates from all across this city of institutes of higher learning. The roommates quickly disappear into a nearby diner, leaving me in the lonely crowd.

I am tall and can survey the sea of dark faces as the nearest repeat, "You want a date?" I am not attracted to any of them but I see between them and me the figure of a tall woman partially hidden by a column of the building adjacent to the broad sidewalk.

I walk through the crowd ignoring all and stop near her. She is stunning, and shy. I am embarrassed. Maybe she is not so enthusiastic about her job.

I say, "Are you?"

She nods. Maybe I seem more desirable than other customers.

She says, "Get in a taxi over there. I'll tell him where to go. I'll meet you there in another taxi."

Ten minutes later, we enter an old apartment building, and as I follow, she checks each door in the line of bedrooms. All are occupied. We climb the stairs to the second floor. She finds an empty room. On a double bed with a brass headboard, she lies beneath me, naked but for her bra, beautiful.

She says, "No kissing."

We make love. We do it together. I look into her eyes. She is right there. The feeling is overwhelming. And she is orgasmic. A momentary pleasure for her? This initiation is a transcendent milestone for me.

I am still spaced out when I enter the diner and see the roommates lined up on stools next to an overweight plain sex worker.

One says to her, "No thank you. We don't have a hundred dollars."

She says, "Hey, I'll do you all for twenty."

They get up tightly to leave with me. I say, "We have to go now. Sorry."

I write in my journal when we return to our suite in Cambridge, "It feels like a circle of velvet pads, covered in warm honey, pushed from behind by a circle of springs, tightly against me . . ." I am meticulous in my description of the mechanics but don't write anything about that I love her and miss her already.

In the just-published *One Hundred Dollar Misunderstanding*, by Robert Grover, about his crazy love affair with a young Black sex worker, I read what could have been. But I don't even know my first love's name.

I look down at the Charles from our rooms on the top floor of Winthrop.

The phone rings—my best friend in junior high school, Steve, now at RPI in Troy, New York, urges me to drop whatever I am doing and go directly to the address of a dorm at women's Emerson College in Boston to meet Franny. He says, "Make sure you are the first guy she meets. She's a nymphomaniac."

On the porch, shadowed in the bright September afternoon, I ring the bell. She comes out the front door—friendly, trim, a diminutive, dark-eyed, striking-looking descendent from the Fertile Crescent. We kiss. She ascertains quickly that women are allowed in Harvard bedrooms only during several "parietal hours" in the afternoon, and insists we get on my Lambretta and scooter back to Winthrop.

As we speed parallel to the Charles toward Cambridge, I hold the handles with both hands. Franny reaches around and rubs my thigh, and then some. The sun reflects off the water's chop in miraculous sparkling explosions.

As soon as we lock the door, she is naked. She tells me she does not have orgasms so she likes to keep doing it.

She says, "Come without me. I never get tired."

I am skeptical, but she teaches me that recovery time is really only fifteen minutes. I swoon into the transcendent blackness, again and again.

I am happy when we are in my Harvard single bed, which is where we are all of the time.

She visits me throughout the fall, several afternoons a week. Franny is funny and indefatigable; we make a lot of noise. My virgin roommates are in awe.

One day in the spring, Franny disappears.

Gone. From all to nothing. There must be a misunderstanding.

But I can't find out where she is. She is reported no longer at Emerson College, but not a missing person. She is not in Troy, New York, either.

Much later, I discover that the Harvard psychiatrist Graham Blaine had treated Franny briefly and that she had returned home, where she was institutionalized with acute paranoia. I cannot give her a helping hand. A shame.

My teacher is gone.

I audit B. F. Skinner's psychology course in operant conditioning—what happens after a response, not before it, is the key to modifying behavior.

After class, I walk with the great behaviorist across the Yard. I am fascinated by his utopian novel, *Walden Two*.

He seems happy to talk to a naive undergraduate.

We discuss how my parents are at their wits' end—how might they change my nine-year-old brother's troublesome behavior.

I say, "They could give him a quarter after he performs the desired behavior."

He says, "If your subject knows what produces the reward, it is not conditioning; it is a contract. You must wait for the behavior to occur and make sure the reward is unassociated with their deed."

Back at Winthrop, I make a column of my five roommates' names with rows of small empty boxes on a poster board.

I paste the first gold star in the row next to one roommate's name on the "Star Chart" and write the initials "A.B.O." in the second column. And soon another star follows in their row in the third column "A.B.O.T."

Eldon and Bob get many stars for "C.D.B.F.G." in their rows.

The roommates are curious when their stars appear. They see no connection between a star and their behavior—the essence of positive reinforcement.

They compete to get them, without knowing the rules of my game.

They ask what the initials stand for. I do not tell.

After a few weeks, they become rebellious and want to know.

I say, "Cool it. It's my chart. None of your business."

After another week, they threaten to destroy the Star Chart. They demand to know.

One says, "A-B-O?"

I say, "A-B-O—Admits-Beating-Off. It's good to be honest and open. A-B-O-T?—Twice."

(Philip Roth's *Portnoy's Complaint* is seven years in the future.)

Eldon and Bob say, "C-D-B-F-G?"

I say, "Cleans-Dishes-Before-Football-Game." I have thereby avoided having to help clean up the suite in preparation for our weekend dates—as the roommates busily emitted behavior that yielded the stars.

You can fool all the people some of the time, but they tear up my Star Chart into small pieces.

I do all the dishes by myself before the next game.

I exit the Crimson Building and walk downhill on Plympton Street toward Winthrop House. President John F Kennedy informed the nation on TV last night that the US has imposed a naval embargo on Cuba, and that a Soviet cargo ship with missiles on board is heading toward Havana to add to the nuclear capability already in place. Kennedy says the US will not let the ship reach its destination and will use military force if necessary to remove the nuclear missiles in Cuba.

This afternoon, an unthinkable war suddenly seems quite possible.

I imagine a mushroom cloud at the horizon beyond Lowell House. Dread.

The next day, the Soviet premier, Nikita Khrushchev, halts the ship short of the blockade.

But the Russian nuclear missiles remain in place ninety miles away.

An American reconnaissance plane is shot down over Cuba on Saturday.

Defense Secretary Robert McNamara (Business School, Class of 1939) later says, "I thought it would be the last Saturday I would ever see."

Two days later, Khrushchev agrees to remove the missiles in Cuba, and Kennedy secretly agrees to remove American missiles from Turkey.

World War III is called off. The Cuban Missile Crisis is over.

I am not dead.

In the Winthrop private dining room, John Kenneth Galbraith asks his six economics tutees, "Do you mind if I bring a noneconomist to our lunch next Wednesday?"

It is a rhetorical question: he is the Paul M. Warburg Professor of Economics, the US ambassador to India, and a presidential adviser to Kennedy. An unabashed liberal Keynesian, he is the most-read economist of the twentieth century. He is six feet, nine inches tall and has a wry, confident way about him.

I wonder if next week's guest will shed light on Galbraith's thesis that people focus on wealth and ignore problems in society. He is after all a disciple of the grandfather of my roommate, John Veblen—Thorstein Veblen, the seminal American economist who wrote *The Theory of the Leisure Class*.

I have read all JKG's books, including *The Affluent Society* and *American Capitalism: The Concept of Countervailing Power*. He warned that an economy in which artificial need for a product is created by the industry producing the product is immoral. I love the history of economic theory: Thomas Malthus, David Ricardo, Adam Smith, Karl Marx, Joseph Schumpeter, John Maynard Keynes. I do not know how anyone can understand their actual condition in life without understanding how worldly economic systems work. Economics is the Holy Grail.

At the next lunch, all the wannabe knights around the economics roundtable are stunned mute. My jaw hangs limp when I behold the noneconomist. TIME STOPS.

I have never been in the presence of such an Earthling. Every transfixing part of her is otherworldly gorgeous.

Galbraith says, "I would like to introduce you to our guest, Miss Angie Dickinson. She is not an economist but does sincerely appreciate your letting her join our discussion."

She smiles with the light of a star (as she did in director Howard Hawks's *Rio Bravo*).

Finally, clear as a bell, I hear my own thought, "Whatever field this woman is in, I am going there."

The sirens have no need of an irresistible call for me. I have seen their light.

Galbraith, I find out, is bearding for JFK and escorting Dickinson to the White House.

1963

Winthrop is known as "The Jock House" and is famous for its prior resident, John F. Kennedy (Class of 1940). Robert F. Kennedy (Class of 1947) and Ted Kennedy (Class of 1956) were also in Winthrop—Teddy left his original class when suspended for several years for cheating on exams. The house is also known for the hockey team's cross-dining hall aerial mashed potato fights. Along with Elliot House next door, Winthrop is a preppie bastion and a fecund source for the State Department and CIA.

Our suite of eight nerds are House anomalies. We eat lunch most days with government policy wonk and assistant senior tutor Barney Frank (Class of 1962)—later, the first US congressman to come out voluntarily as a homosexual and the coauthor of the Dodd-Frank Wall Street Reform and Consumer Protection Act.

I prefer the company of the senior tutor, historian Standish Meacham— intelligent, open-minded, witty, and in my experience, always kind. I enjoy his seminar "History of Western Europe to 1715" more than any other. He likes my contributions of what was going on in the worlds of art and music contemporaneously with the various European political movements. And during all the sections, we laugh together quickly and often. His first published book, *Henry Thornton of Clapham*, was a biography of the nineteenth-century English abolitionist.

Straight A's for a semester put a scholar in "Group 1," the top 3 percent of the class, and their parents receive a letter of praise from the dean, John Munro. The student is rewarded with a Detur Prize—any published work you may choose. Standish is master of ceremonies of the presentation in the Winthrop dining hall.

One chooses *The Complete Works of Freud;* another picks the entire *Oxford English Dictionary* of twenty-six volumes. A heavy-duty dolly carries these expensive prizes on and off the low stage. I am the last scholar summoned

(*W*, after all). Standish and the audience have a chuckle when he hands my choice to me between his thumb and pinky—*Henry Thornton*.

I start to wear tortoiseshell eyeglasses, like he does. A Christian from Yale.

At the first session of my junior year honors tutorial in economics, Ec98, the professor writes a simple calculus on the blackboard and says, "This is our starting point in econometrics."

I do not understand the starting point.

Econometrics is the use of mathematical methods (especially statistics) in describing economic systems.

A lively question-and-answer exchange follows between professor and students.

I cannot do the math.

I am stunned. Ignorant.

I get up from my seat after fifteen minutes and exit.

I cannot be an economist. I never thought this science dismal. But now it is astonishingly incomprehensible.

I have two additional suitemates this year, John Young of the Lightweights and his sophomore roommate, Howard Gardner.

Howie meets me on Mount Auburn Street. We walk to Winthrop for lunch. I tell him (later, a MacArthur "genius," and the world-renowned educationist author of *Frames of Mind: The Theory of Multiple Intelligences*) about my traumatic morning.

He says, "Switch into the psychology of perception—you'll get to the head of the field in no time. Right now, you're way ahead of everyone else in visual matters."

I say, "I can write papers for the academic psychologists objectifying the relevance of their work in fine art. I can write papers for the fine arts professors about the relevance of their work in the psychology of perception. They'll love to realize that their work has any relevance in the outside world. I'll enlarge their context."

He says, "Paul, of our eight roommates, you are not the first-smartest in any field, but you are the second-smartest in more than anyone."

William James wrote, "The more experiments, the better. Life is an experiment."

1964

Howie and I are admitted to the select tutorial of the German American psychologist and psychoanalyst Erik H. Erikson, author of *Childhood and Society* and *Young Man Luther*. Erikson shifted the focus of the study of man from childhood to the entire life cycle. This is the great man who originated the concept of the "Identity Crisis." Right up my alley. I feed off his dialogue.

The seminar never starts until he arranges around a notepad on the desk before him, three pens and two pencils and a tin of ten Schimmelpenninck cigarillos, in a perfect composition. Erik H. Erikson started his career as an art teacher in Anna Freud's school for children in Vienna. And she was his shrink.

The greatest psychoanalytic thinker of the second half of the twentieth century, I learn, changed his last name from Homburger to Erikson. That's what the *H* stands for. That's how the confused young Erikson became fascinated by the question of identity formation.

I am not alone.

I meet with him to discuss my paper, "A Study in Identity and Ideology," which builds on Robert Park's concept of the "marginal man."

I say, "I feel super-marginal as 'Williams'—not a bona fide member of the Christian world or of the Jewish world. I'm an outsider even to the outsiders."

Finally, I say, "Why did you change your name from Homburger to Erikson?"

Blue-eyed, Nordic-featured, white-maned Erikson says, "My father's name was Homburger, but I was brought up by my stepfather, and I identified with him as my father, and so I took his name."

It sounds simple.

What he did not tell me is that he changed his name, as I did, only days before he began his life at Harvard (as a teacher at the Medical School).

Nor did he tell me that he was ignorant until adulthood about the fact that he was born to a divorced Jewish mother as the result of an extramarital affair. She only later married Dr. Theodor Homberger. Erik never saw his birth father.

Erikson's book *Gandhi's Truth* is a Pulitzer Prize and National Book Award winner.

To me, he says, "You are like many Blacks, defining yourself by what you are not. You have developed a negative identity. You must find out what you are for, and be positive about your identity."

That sounds right to me.

And I am too scared of being found out.

Decades later, I wonder if his birth father were a Nazi.

I'm sure he did, too.

On November 22, I walk on the path between Widener Library and the Houghton Rare Books Library on my way to Emerson Hall for Erikson's seminar. It is early on the cold afternoon.

I hear a nearby undergraduate say, "Kennedy is dead. He was shot."

Then it is quiet in the Yard.

I see Memorial Church, far in front of me. I see Emerson Hall, to my right. Suspended animation.

No thought. The most powerful educated man in the Western world has been shut up.

He was fed up with the Joint Chiefs of Staff and the CIA—after the humiliating Bay of Pigs defeat by Fidel Castro and Che Guevara. Jack's younger brother, the attorney general, Bobby, is in the midst of prosecuting the Mafia bosses—after they delivered critical Chicago votes to elect JFK.

"Don't ever say that again." I hear my father's voice.

I go into my private blackness. No one is safe.

The rest is silence.

Three days later, all the roommates drive down to DC for the funeral. It is cold, and I duck in and out of a public bathroom to warm up.

When the horse-drawn caisson with Kennedy's body aboard passes us by, I see a jet-black horse with a riderless saddle above two empty boots facing backward tied in the stirrups. The horse is skittish, shoed hoofs rapidly clicking on the street, moving side to side as its long lead pulls it behind the coffin.

It rains on the cloudy day of the first lecture in Music 1. My black-felt wide-brimmed hat is soaked as I take a seat in the balcony of the hall.

I notice a pretty, wet Radcliffe student who sits nearby. The Cliffie smiles at me.

Susan Carey (Class of 1964) is exceptionally bright and curious. We soon audit a graduate psychology course together, "Need Achievement in Greek Society," taught by Richard Alpert and Timothy Leary. We attend the lectures faithfully.

After each, we hurry toward the lectern to chat one of them into inviting us to join in on some of their rumored LSD experiments. Every time, there is an impenetrable gaggle of young male graduate students between us and the psychedelic pioneers.

Alpert and Leary prove with their analysis of ancient Greek literature that the frequency of heroic individual "need achievement themes" predicts the rise and fall of the power of the Greek economy, with a lag time of twenty years—one generation.

All that heroic nonfiction in my youth—I understand how deeply programmed a horse I am, racing for my father.

1964

Our real goal is to get mind-blowing LSD, that is, to get our consciousness expanded. And we fail.

But Sue is so bright and beautiful, I imagine us together for a long time. One night, after some of my photographs appear in the newspaper, we make out in the shadows outside her Radcliffe hall.

She says, "I don't like most of the *Crimson* Jews . . ."

Thunder strikes Sisyphus, a Jew only to oppose anti-Semites. Even a micro-aggression. Lockjaw sets in—caught in a need for moral redemption, absolution from my past sin, but I say nothing. I'm so brave and so chickenshit—it's over. I'm not the one she's looking for.

Andy Weil starts to investigate the Alpert and Leary scene for the *Crimson*. He discovers that they are using the drug to seduce male students. ATW meets confidentially with Harvard president Nathan Pusey (Class of 1928), who then meets with the professors, who then agree to leave Harvard with the public explanation that their procedures were in violation of university research policy and they "failed to keep classroom appointments." There is no public mention of sex.

Andy later creates the field of holistic medicine; Sue is the Henry A. Morss, Jr. and Elisabeth W. Morss Professor of Psychology at Harvard; Alpert becomes Baba Ram Dass; Leary writes *Turn On, Tune In, Drop Out.* Paul remains a spy.

The most wondrous class I attend at Harvard: the final lecture of Professor G. Wallace Woodward in Music 1. His course has been rigorous, from the ancient monody of Gregorian chant to modern post-Stravinsky atonal music, but his lectures are a weekly awakening, noted at full tilt.

On this day, only a single chair and a record player atop a small table occupy the stage of Paine Concert Hall. No lectern.

Woodward says, "Put down your pens, shut your notebooks."

A welcome relief.

He says, "Close your eyes, and just listen."

Woodward sits down on the chair and listens silently with his two hundred students as they escape time for forty-five minutes.

They do nothing but take the sound adventure of Beethoven's Sixth Symphony, the *Pastoral*. No intervening computations are required: just the natural resonances among brain, body, and place are sufficient.

The movements: "Awakening of cheerful feelings on arrival in the countryside," "Scene by the brook," "Merry gathering of country folk," "Thunder. Storm," "Shepherd's song. Cheerful and thankful feelings after the storm."

Clearly, this is the radiating anthem of a forest ranger, balancing his soul.

"When we are stricken and cannot bear our lives any longer, then a tree has something to say to us: Be still! Be still! Look at me! Life is not easy, life is not difficult. Those are childish thoughts. Let God speak within you, and your thoughts will grow silent," wrote Hermann Hesse.

Clearly, I need to listen to trees.

A sexploitation film opens in Boston, *Heavenly Bodies,* the first commercial success of campy director Russ Meyer. It tells the story of a delivery man who goes to the dentist and, after the nitrous oxide wears off, discovers that each large-breasted woman who crosses his path appears naked. The responses of the ticket-taker, candy counter matron, and usher to the sly film are the subject of an early *Crimson* review for the Editorial Board.

It gets good reactions for PWW in the editorial comment books from ATW, HH, DEG, and others.

I am welcomed onto the Board as a reviewer of the arts. My pieces are pasted in the comment books, and I read the criticism carefully.

When Federico Fellini's incomparable *8 ½* opens a few days later, Don Graham writes a brilliant, explanatory review.

I am not that smart. I jump over lower hurdles. I cheated on the intelligence test.

I ask administrators at Radcliffe if I can meet with the most beautiful women in each residential house for a *Crimson* photo-essay.

Upset at the ease with which these exclusive dinners are arranged, I feel the unfair power of beauty. If I were a female, I wouldn't pick me.

I dine one night after another with tables of attractive Cliffies, for a week.

I select my subjects and shoot for ten days in Cambridge locations.

At breakfast on the day that "Bright & Beautiful" appears, undergrads without *Crimson* subscriptions wait to borrow copies of the newspaper in the Winthrop dining hall.

My Argus may be mightier than my pen! Why transmute all of life into a literary experience? William James, the father of American psychology, wrote in his *Letters,* "It would be an awful universe if everything could be converted into words, words, words."

In the public lobby of the Time-Life Building in Manhattan, I ask the guard behind a desk to direct me to someone who can look at my pictures.

On the twentieth floor, I show them to the editor of the "Miscellany" page, Ann Guerin. She chooses a photograph every week as the last page of *Life* magazine. In her late forties, she is sweet behind her horn-rimmed glasses.

She says, "These are good individual photographs. But if you want to work for us, you should do a picture story. Take a subject and cover it completely."

I return to Harvard and spend two months on the Charles River, shooting my old crewmates, who are heavily favored to represent the United States in the Tokyo Olympics next summer.

Soon, the *Life* editor looks at my pile of new contact sheets.

She says, "Take them to George Bloodgood at *Sports Illustrated,* up two floors."

Bloodgood is a lithe, redheaded forty-year-old, with bright eyes. After a look at the sheets, he takes all my negatives and says their lab will make hundreds of eleven-by-fourteen-inch prints for their designers to use to prepare a major picture story for a *SI* summer issue.

This is the best of all possible worlds. I am on my way.

Back in Cambridge, I study fine arts and imagine a trip to see the great art in Europe's museums. I need to see how the great artists saw. But I need financing to get to Europe.

I research anthropologists who might want me to photograph their field work. I discover that Laurence Wylie, C. Douglas Dillon Professor of the Civilization of France, is writing a book with his students about the provincial French village of Chanzeaux. An unusually open, red-haired, freckled, friendly, and generous man, Larry is an ardent photographer and appreciates my work. He proposes to finance a summer trip so I can take pictures for the book.

C. Douglas Dillon is the US secretary of the treasury, and Wylie gets Dillon to add to my stipend—enough to shoot a documentary film.

My summer vacation plan is to expose all the film in two weeks in Chanzeaux and then to wander the great cities of Europe, to see the art in the National Gallery and Tate in London, the Rijksmuseum in Amsterdam, the Louvre in Paris, the Uffizi in Florence, the Vatican, and the Borghese Gallery in Rome, and all of Venice. I can sleep free many nights by shuttling between cities on a Eurail Pass.

I will live as a poor man, with enough money.

Eldon in Sorel hiking boots and I in thin rubber-soled sneakers follow the trail composed of broken shards of granite to the top of Britain's highest mountain, in the Western Highlands of Scotland. He waits every fifty yards, sipping water, while I struggle over the sharp rocks to rejoin him. When I do, Eldie marches up another fifty yards. The ascent takes three hours.

We are a thousand feet high, below a perfect hemisphere of baby blue. We are above an unbroken panorama of gray stratocumulus clouds that stretch to the horizon—endless time appears as an endless moment. Absorbed, perfectly still. I resonate and harmonize. My small self expands to the limits of sight of the external. The blue sky above is the constant observer, the serendipitous cloud cover below just passing weather. I am so small and have never felt so big, exhausted on this summit rock of Ben Nevis.

For thirty minutes I just breathe and perceive that my detachment has utility. It is a transparent moment: I escape from human misuse.

After our quiet time on top of the world, I stand up and discover my feet are raw with pain.

I say, "I can't walk."

Following Eldon's suggestion, I slide on my ass straight down the bumpy slopes of Ben Nevis for almost two hours.

From the sublime to the ridiculous.

In London, Eldon drives me to St. Pancras Station in his new two-seater MG sports car that he will have shipped back to Cambridge for senior year. I get on the Night Ferry train to Paris with my copy of *Europe on Five Dollars a Day,* by Arthur Frommer.

I arrive at Paris Gare du Nord eleven hours later in the early dawn. I walk gingerly to the produce market, Les Halles, and breakfast on richly flavored *soupe aux oignons.* Then, at Le Louvre, nearby, feast on the luminous invisible glazes of the Mona Lisa. When I look into her serene eyes, she looks at me with a cool smile. But when I look directly at her smile, I see it has more color—and it has transformed into a smirk.

It is a sunny July day as I rest upon a bank of the Seine with an *International Herald Tribune,* ready to leave for Maine-et-Loire to begin the Chanzeaux project. I read on the front page that three civil rights workers, Chaney, Goodman, and Schwerner, have gone missing in Mississippi as they attempted to register Black Americans to vote. The South is in turmoil.

Another headline catches my eye: "Vesper Boat Club of Philadelphia Upsets Harvard in Olympic Trials." Our eights will not be at the 1964 Tokyo Olympics. Fuck. *Vanitas vanitatum!* Vanity of Vanities. Sayonara, *Sports Illustrated.*

The motto of Harvard is *Veritas*—Truth.

In the weeks that follow, every farmer in Chanzeaux is gracious with their stash of homemade wine in the cellar. I photograph from morning to evening every day, pleasantly drunk. *In vino veritas.*

Afterward, I crisscross Europe, visiting the great art museums, improving my vision. Highpoint: Cézanne's compositions.

6

Coincidence

1964–1965

1964

Surfeited with Rembrandts, I visit the seven-hundred-year-old puppet theater in the Royal Palace in Amsterdam that is a scaled-down, child-size hall. I am the only visitor.

I sit in solitude on a miniature bench in the dormant space, but I feel the excitement of a young audience at a performance. It is palpable and constant. I even hear the distinct high voices of children.

I am transfixed in the utter emptiness for three hours until a guard appears and informs me that it is closing time.

In the farthest reaches of the last balcony, I see young man and woman about my age. They use improvised hand signals to tell me to wait for them after I exit the theater.

They emerge from a small hidden door into the grand baroque hall of the Palace and walk to me.

I say, "How did you know about this place?"

She says, "We live here. I am Marie-Claire."

He says, "Hans."

I say, "Oh, I'm Paul. How long were you two up there?"

She says, "An hour or so. We were watching you."

I say, "Did you hear any sounds of children?"

Marie-Claire's smile is beguiling.

I say, "I heard kids."

Hans smiles.

She says, "Come with us to dinner, Paul. It is a special day—graduation day for all the students of Amsterdam. We will go to the Toro Negro. It is a wonderful restaurant."

We walk to it, in the center of town, one floor up from the cobblestone street.

It is elegant. It is crowded. Hans and Marie-Claire order. I know I can't afford this meal. We eat dinner.

Marie-Claire says, "Hans, get the coats and wait downstairs." He gets up from the table and heads to the cloak room.

She says, "Just wait, now. When I say so, get up, and once you are out of this room, start running and don't stop."

She has a Dutch accent and that bewitching smile.

I am nervous. They live in the Royal Palace. She watches the movement of the waiters.

She says, "Now."

We get up and walk out of the dining room into the corridor. She runs to the staircase. I follow. We are outside in a moment, running with her brother and the coats.

Eventually we reach the celebratory spot in a small park. I join them as they run in circles around the Maypole and they sing the graduation song.

They invite me to stay overnight at a four-story house, near the Palace.

She says, "It's our hideaway."

I join them and drink wine and we are merry. She says, "You know, maybe the curators have a recording of children to provide atmosphere in the theater."

I say, "And you're just telling me now?"

She laughs.

I say, "I'm sticking with a miracle. I have to get up early. Where do I sleep?"

She says, "You must never leave a party when you are having fun."

I say, "I'm going on a bus tour of your socialist schools and hospitals. I live in a greedy capitalist culture—I want to see how it works here."

She says, "I can show you some more miracles . . ." She makes fun of me but I am adamant.

I like her. And she likes me, a peasant. Alas, one in a big hurry. In the future, I believe, I will never be able to afford another trip to Europe.

Hans walks me up two flights to a bedroom with a mattress on the floor. I thank him and fall asleep.

The next morning I wake up, say goodbye to my smiling new friends, and hustle out to be on time for the tour.

I get on the Pullman. People smile at me. I feel attractive.

At the first restroom stop, I head for the men's room door, acknowledging the many smiles of nearby women who openly maintain their admiration as the *bon vivant* returns their smiles.

After I wash my hands, I look up into the mirror and stare at a bold floral design carefully applied with charcoal that covers my entire face.

How miraculous is that?

I love this Marie-Claire.

I can't afford romance.

I have a schedule. No time for parties.

In Manhattan when I return, Bloodgood confirms that *Sports Illustrated* will run only one or two crew photos. He surrenders to me the hundreds of stunning eleven-by-fourteen black-and-white prints of my negatives made by the *Life* photographic laboratory. He consoles me with a promise to hire me for a hundred dollars a day during the academic year to stand with the main athletic events at my back while I photograph the spectators—the "background color." I shall shoot only reactions and dump my exposed rolls at the conclusion of the races into a burlap sack that is helicoptered away.

At Harvard, John and Faith Hubley give a course in animation. They pioneered a new minimal graphic style in *The Hole* and won the Oscar in 1962 for Best Animated Short. Two hundred undergraduates apply for the twenty places.

At my interview with the Hubleys, I volunteer to photograph each day's student drawings, one by one, on a state-of-the-art Oxberry animation stand. I know no Harvard student wants this artless boring job. I am accepted on the spot without any questions. Earlier in his career, John Hubley created the myopic cartoon character in *Mr. Magoo*. He knows one when he sees one.

Late each evening, I collect the repetitive drawings from the nineteen student artistes to shoot on the Oxberry. It takes me an hour do the task.

Then I hide in the basement of Le Corbusier's eminent Carpenter Center until the building is locked up, in the men's room.

Then I go back to the Oxberry and work until after daybreak on *Crew*—zooming and panning the king-size *Life* prints onto the movie camera's 35mm film.

During the day, I edit the documentary footage of the French village.

Since Winthrop primarily houses jocks, the House has never used their yearly Ford Foundation arts grants. Standish liberates the accumulated

Ford funds for me to shoot my first dramatic short, *Don't Walk,* starring elegant Libby Buxton (Radcliffe '65) and ill-of-face David Odell, who reveals early on why my freshman roommate got the part—he smiles in a big close-up to reveal a freshly punched-out front tooth. Serious student cineastes dismiss the film as shallow and stupid, but I am happy with it—every scene was concocted to require a different cinematographic experiment: how to shoot from different angles and distances the same action so it appears smooth shot to shot, how to choreograph long mise-en-scène sequences, how to transition from tripod to hand-held traveling shots. The actors run, jump, skip, and get in and out of and ride in various types of vehicles.

I am a workaholic opportunist, like Henry Adams (Class of 1858): "By twisting life to follow accidental and devious paths, one might perhaps find some use for accidental and devious knowledge."

"Ten thousand men of Harvard / want victory today," is the famous first line of Harvard's football fight song. I watch the marching band at halftime sing the second verse in Latin. Winthrop buddy and classicist George Cushing says, "The band now is actually singing Latin nonsense."

Few Harvard men in the crowd have any idea, including me.

George says, "The first line they sing, 'illegitimum non carborundum,' roughly means, "Don't let the bastards grind you down."

George, Eldon, the Johns—Veblen and Young, Bob Sandy, and I sit for the law school admissions test. None of us want to leave safe Harvard to go to war in Vietnam.

A spunky redhead sits for her interview in the small office in the basement of the Carpenter Center. She is vibrant and confident.

I sit with the professor of Harvard's first course in photography, Len Gittleman. Though I am still an undergraduate, he has hired me to teach one of the three, eight-student sections.

One hundred fifty students have applied. Most of them are rich kids who can afford to take such an impractical Harvard course. They ride big motorcycles and wear expensive leather boots.

Elizabeth, the self-assured redhead, impresses Gittleman with her notion that photography can improve her vision as a painter.

I say, "Yes, but of course you believe that photography is a second-rate art?"

She is flustered. She looks at me. I like her and smile happily.

She smiles back and then regally and skillfully improvises the truth of her plan.

I ask Len to put her in my section.

He does.

I like this girl. She has a quick wit and wide perspective. She's got a good eye for composition and an eager sexiness. For the first time in three years, since loving the African American sex worker on Mass Ave., I do not use a condom. I am at once privately humiliated and relieved to learn that the primary sexual organ of the female Caucasian is not a racial deficiency. This invalid biological assumption was only a slander caused by latex insulation and a colonial male oppressor's stupidity.

For three months Liz and I are lovers at every opportunity—we spend a lot of adventurous time in the darkrooms. We laugh a lot.

I am happy. She says she loves my blue eyes.

I say, "I like Henry Miller's vocabulary—the 'Cosmodemonic Telegraphic Company'!"

She says, "Henry Miller? He's so bourgeois. You should read Virginia Woolf's *Orlando*—'it is clothes that wear us and not we them.'" I read it.

Josef Albers, the great color theorist and painter, lectures a hundred students in the Carpenter Center. We listen from the back of the hall. How the color red changes its tone when adjacent to yellow, or green, or blue? She takes my hand and leads me to an alcove behind a circular concrete support, six feet in diameter. We make dangerous love.

She is well-read and highbrow.

One afternoon, Howie leads me into my room in our Winthrop suite. He sits down on my bed.

"Do you know who you're dating?"

I say, "Yes. Liz. Sure."

He says, "Do you know about her family?"

I say, "No, I don't. Why?"

He says, "Her grandfather founded Sears Roebuck—they are one of the richest families in the world."

I say, "Oh."

He says, "Sit down."

He informs me that Liz's grandfather, Julius Rosenwald, created the Sears fortune (the *Sears-Roebuck Catalog* was the Amazon.com of the first half of the twentieth century, with the first mass mail order distribution system, and the largest chain of retail stores—Sears taught America how to shop). The Rosenwalds sold Sears at its height, and now they own Wall Street investment banks, mainframe computer industry, Western Union, and the Empire State Building. Liz's dad is a founder of the principal Jewish charity in the USA, the United Jewish Appeal.

That night I prevail on Winthrop friend Rodge Cohen to lend me his car. On the way over to pick her up, I remember Albert Einstein's line, "Coincidence is God's way of remaining anonymous." I sit in the front seat with Elizabeth. She sits close to me.

"How come you didn't tell me that you were so rich?"

"Do you love me any less because I'm rich?"

"No."

"Is it okay with you?"

"Yeah."

"Do you like it that I'm rich?"

"Yeah. It's good. Sure."

"Okay, then, it's fine with me if you like it, because it's one of the things about me."

Rather than objectively ask for a loan, I say, "I changed my name to Williams just before I left home for Harvard. I took it from my middle name, William. My last name had been Goldberg."

She says, "I would not have gone out with you if your name was Goldberg. I'm glad you changed your name."

I hear my father's voice, "*If* requires the subjunctive: '*Were* Goldberg. *Were!*'"

And then my own, "What the fuck? Even the Princess of the Jews won't go out with a Goldberg?"

Later, I read in a poem by W. B. Yeats: "How in the name of Heaven can he escape / That defiling and disfigured shape / The mirror of malicious eyes / Casts upon his eyes until at last / He thinks that shape must be his shape?"

Elizabeth is my unindicted co-conspirator.

During Christmas vacation, I meet Liz's family in Manhattan.

Her father, Bill, is almost my height and looks a bit like me. Ah-hah.

His shirt collar is many sizes too big; his shoes, too.

I say, "I hate tight clothes." He smiles. He does not need to look up at me.

Her mother, Mary, is a gracious, gray-haired German-accented fiddler, whom Bill rescued from a club in Nazi Berlin. She brought along her two brothers—one accompanied Isadora Duncan in his youth and the other had been Anna Pavlova's principal musician. Now the taller one conducts the Houston Symphony and the other is a concert cellist.

On the walls of the duplex apartment at Seventy-Ninth Street and Park Avenue are paintings by Degas, Braque, Bonnard, Seurat, and Pierre-Auguste Renoir, among others. I spend too much time looking at them.

There are many Irish maids in uniforms—some cook, some serve, more perform household chores.

Black-suited Caucasian chauffeurs hang out in the kitchen, available twenty-four hours a day.

Brunch is served in the main floor dining room. Guests include the febrile pianist Byron Janis; his gorgeous, thin wife, Maria Cooper (*High Noon* Gary's daughter); big Sol Hurok, the legendary impresario; Mary's brothers—the squat cellist Edmund Kurtz and the tall conductor Efrem Kurtz; Efrem's pretty blonde wife—the first female concert flautist, Elaine Shaffer; and me—a veteran of Music 1, whose childhood's musical highpoint was, "Come mister tally man, tally me banana."

When it is my turn, I talk about how people perceive causation.

I hold up in front of my face one steady fist. Then I bump it from the side emphatically with the other fist. After two seconds of hesitation, I move the first fist as if it had been propelled by the hit of the second fist.

I say, "Did the second fist cause the first fist to move?" The guests agree, no.

I continually repeat the bumping but hesitate shorter and shorter periods of time between the bump of the second fist into the first, until finally it looks as if the second fist "causes" the first fist to move.

They all smile. I am satisfied that everyone seems to have learned how this gestalt phenomenon works.

When coffee is served, Bill has a kettle of steeping tea and three teacups of hot water placed in front of him at the head of the table. He removes the tea infuser and dips it momentarily in the first cup. Then he pours a drop from that cup into the second cup. Then he pours a drop from the second cup into the third cup. He takes a sip.

I look at him quizzically, sitting on his right.

He says, "I like very mild tea."

Andy is the chief driver, bodyguard, and factotum. Liz introduces me to the overweight, short but powerful, nice guy from Brooklyn.

Liz leaves us alone; we have a quick rapport.

I say, "What's with these guys, huh?"

Andy says, "They're a little crazy, but they're really okay."

In the living room, Mary plays "my fiddle," a Stradivarius, with Byron on the Steinway piano, brother Edmund on his Hausmann cello, and Elaine on her sterling silver handmade flute. I join them and can follow the melodic strains of the vibrant quartets.

Liz walks me to the door when I leave the apartment.

She says, "They like you. And Andy is the guy they really trust, and he said you're a good person."

Andy told me earlier in the day, "Put a rubber band around your driver's license with a folded hundred-dollar bill. When you get stopped, give the cop the license. If they ever say anything about a bribe, say, 'Oops, it's my secret emergency money.' But you'll almost always get it back without the hundred, and you're on your way."

I need a hundred-dollar bill.

1965

Howie advises me to take the pioneer course, Social Relations 120—"The Life Cycle of the Group."

He says, "You really can have fun if you sit opposite the professor at one end of the long conference table and make it your goal to attract all the other students to your end before the term finishes. Try to isolate the professor."

He knows the history of my Star Chart.

Dexter Dunphy is the teacher, a slight fellow. Most of the other professors of the Soc Rel Department sit invisibly behind a huge one-way mirror where they make observational notes for their seminal work on the life cycle of groups.

On the last day of the course, Dunphy is alone at his end. I have turned the table. The dozen students flank me at my end.

Dunphy offers objective observations about the group's desire "for camaraderie in the face of the impending death of the group."

I say, "We have been the guinea pigs for them," and point to the glass rectangle that defines the wall. "Why do they get to look at us and stay anonymous? It is time to claim our equality."

I say, "We are not piglets. Stand up. Don't be frightened. Get out of your chairs. We will look at them. Follow me!"

I jump out of my chair, open the conference room door, and heroically run down the hallway with the dozen behind me.

We circle the hallway and I open the door to the large darkened observation room.

We all walk inside. We stand still and look at our academic adversaries and their graduate students in their comfortable seats. They look back, nonplussed.

The consciousness of humankind is one. No one says anything. Not a word.

After a minute, we walk out.

We stole home too, Jackie Robinson.

It's a matter of Principal.

Two blond wooden eighteen-inch-tall artist's manikins—one with two clay breasts that I have added—stand on a black piece of plywood. I ask student subjects to create various scenes between this yellow woman and yellow man that express contrasting emotions and qualities: Aggressive/ Unaggressive, Female Initiating/Male Initiating, Loving/Unloving—twelve pairings in all.

It is an intense eight weeks of eighteen-hour days. Elizabeth stays with me on the all-nighters in a deep basement room in Winthrop, as I absorb the scenes and make detailed charts. I find the family resemblances of emotional significance that emerge: for example, Arm's Length—beyond? at? within? Arm Positions—one or both—extended? creating an enclosure? against the body? Relative Head Levels? And so on. I take photographs of each of the subject's creations. I am present but distant. Later, comparing the 1,200 pictures, I sort the data and trust my insights to understand what is being communicated.

A summa cum laude, "with highest honors," is bestowed on this senior thesis, "The Expressive Meaning of Body Positions in the Male-Female Encounter." I am told that the reason is that I "created completely new knowledge." This is not nothing.

I must prepare during the two weeks that I have available before the exalted summa oral examination—the pathway to Harvard professorial academic success.

But I find it impossible to focus my eyes on even a sliver of the background literature. I am exhausted from around-the-clock effort. B. F. Skinner taught me that, after it pushes the reward bar to exhaustion, a rat will not touch the bar again until after a recovery period.

My father surprises me with a handout of cash so I can go socialize with the affluent roommates in Nassau on spring vacation. My sister is livid when she hears about that money since she had to clean bathrooms as part of her financial scholarship package at Bennington College. I agree with her—it's not fair. But I am his surrogate. She's an underfunded girl, a victim of his sexist resentment. It's 1965.

We fellows eat the soup made from the daily catch of the not-yet-endangered sea turtles and stay drunk. If the oral examiners just ask me about my thesis, I'll probably be a Harvard professor one day!

I may have hawk eyes but I am a rat.

On the top floor of William James Hall, three academics sit in front of me in small one-piece student desks. I sit in the office's plush leather desk chair that has been placed to face them, five feet away. A half century ago, when William James was the first psychologist at Harvard, he had written, "The greatest weapon against stress is our ability to choose one thought over another."

Professor John P. Spiegel is an expert on violent combat stress, and is the 103rd president of the American Psychiatric Association.

He says, "Your thesis is excellent. There's no need to talk further about that. So, we will spend the next two hours discussing the background literature."

Hearing those words, I jerk back in the desk chair. It tilts and topples over. I am on the rug.

I get up. I right the chair and sit back down.

My thesis supervisor, Pavel Machotka, says, "Are you all right?"

I say, "Yes."

Professor Dexter Dunphy says, "You can go on?"

I nod, stressed.

Spiegel asks, "What do you think about 'bird whistle'?"

Birds? Whistles? Years ago, I read *King Solomon's Ring* in the introductory Soc Rel 10 and now remember Konrad Lorenz walking with ducklings who thought he was their mother. And then I remember Lorenz's crows—the jackdaws. It's not the sounds they make that communicates to their young, it is the position of their beaks!

I begin to improvise—I flap my imaginary wings and imitate adult jackdaws.

I open wide my jackdaw beak: "CAW! CAW!"

And close it shut: "CHYAK-CHYAK!"

I say to the professors, "Look at how open my mouth is? See my open beak? CAW, CAW!"

I say, "Or—how it continually closes? CHYAK!-CHYAK!-CHYAK!"

I say, "This visual signal of the bird's beak—not the whistle of the audio, is the imprinted cue for my hungry infants."

I look down at the imaginary little jackdaws below me, and say, "If I am coming to the nest, I CAW! CAW! with my beak wide open."

As I turn my head and take off from the jackdaw nest, pumping my wings for emphasis, I say, "If I am leaving to hunt, I CHYAK!-CHYAK! with my beak closing after each CHYAK."

The three examiners laugh louder and longer than I consider appropriate, more than merely appreciative chortles for my hyperexpressive and brilliant bird-whistle dramatization.

But then they guffaw and must rise out of their tiny seats.

They are doubled over and break up in near-schizophrenic cachinnating hee-haws.

I wait. Nervous laughter can be contagious.

They have trouble recomposing themselves.

I wait.

The three finally subside. They lower themselves and slide into their pupil seats.

Spiegel says, "Professor Ray Birdwhistell is an anthropologist who founded 'Kinesics'—that's *your* field—as a field of inquiry and research."

I shift in my seat and recalculate their recent jocularity. I say, "Oh."

He says, "Please wait outside."

The Department is too embarrassed to flunk their one and only summa thesis writer who created new knowledge. I receive a "low pass" and will only graduate magna cum laude, with high honors.

Williams, the Harvard professor of expression, has committed suicide.

I find out that Dexter Dunphy, on whom I turned the tables during the "Life Cycle of the Group," advised his associates that "Williams has problems with authority." If he only knew.

Last month, my senior supervisor, Robert Gardner, the documentarian of *Dead Birds* and the head of film and photography education at Harvard, introduced me to charming Leni Riefenstahl—Hitler's prized Aryan director of the most innovative propaganda film ever made, *Triumph of the Will*. Now, Bob stands in the large vestibule outside the Carpenter Center darkrooms and introduces me to the seventy-year-old second son of the French impressionist Pierre-Auguste Renoir.

Jean Renoir made two of the greatest films of all time, *Grand Illusion* and *Rules of the Game*. François Truffaut wrote, "He never made mistakes, because he always found solutions based on simplicity—human solutions."

The perfect director has just given a speech in the adjacent auditorium. I tell Renoir about two short films that I am finishing, *Crew* and *Chanzeaux*. He has made forty films.

He says, "A man only has at most three original stories to tell before he starts repeating himself, so try to keep a sense of balance and live your life. Enjoy life."

That sounds wise. Three? I did not mention *Don't Walk*. But all three are just short films. Do they count? The only thing I know for sure is that I am here and that this life is full of wonders. Renoir's words hit home.

When I open my mailbox that evening, I find a letter of admission to Harvard Law School—the dream of my father—and my Get Out of War Free card.

The very next day in the very same spot, Elizabeth says, "I don't want to be married to a lawyer. Boring."

My destiny teeters.

I say, "Are you serious?"

She says, "No, I'm Roebuck—who's minding the store?"

Serious-Roebuck. Must be a Rosenwald family joke.

I recently read that Truffaut married Madeleine Morgenstern, daughter of Ignace Morgenstern, the head of France's largest film distribution company, who financed Truffaut's first films.

I decide in an instant. No digestion, all impulse. I'll stick with Liz, love, and fortune. I will try to become a director, unshackled from the need for lunch money—but with a Boy Scout's courteous resolve to find my own financing for my movies. I don't have a faint heart. No more school. I'm done.

I say, "I'll give the movies a few years—see what happens." My life is living me.

In a flash, Williams the Harvard Lawyer has committed suicide.

I'm living a dream, as usual.

But whose?

7

Onward, Backward

1965–1967

1965

The demented Vietnam War expands. Without Harvard Law, I need another avenue to avoid going to the criminal carnage.

Standish Meacham suggests, and then quickly arranges for me, admission to Cambridge University's Trinity Hall to read fine arts. I am amazed by his generous and snazzy solution so late in my last days at Harvard. Elizabeth's father calls the Anglo-French financier Sir "Jimmy" Goldsmith, and Liz is admitted immediately to the preeminent Slade School of Fine Art in London, in Bloomsbury.

Mr. and Mrs. Goldberg make the two hundred-mile drive from Manhattan up to Cambridge for the ceremony and the admission of the Class of 1965 into "the fellowship of educated men and women" (responsible for the production of trustworthy knowledge). Even Socrates champions those attributes possessed at the end of a basic education over innate knowledge. My parents beam at my election to Phi Beta Kappa, Alpha of Massachusetts at Harvard College, the most prestigious and oldest academic honor society in the USA.

My parents are Democrats, and I am happy for them as they listen to their hero, Commencement speaker Adlai E. Stevenson—who ran and twice lost the race for president to Eisenhower. They are in jolly spirits as they meet all my roommates and their proud parents. They are greeted as "Mr. Williams" and "Mrs. Williams," but of course my parents happily correct them—and reveal my Goldberg shame. Everyone but me smiles in the photograph of the roommates on this graduation day.

Crimson president Steve Cotton asks me to be the photographer for the *Southern Courier*. It will be a summer weekly by *Crimson* editors that fills the gap of accurate reporting of the civil rights protests erupting in Mississippi. I like the idea of a righteous adventure in the Deep South, but I recommend John Young, and he is excited to take my place—and takes excellent photos during the summer in the *Courier*'s "hot car" that crisscrosses Mississippi, Alabama, and Georgia.

I remain in Cambridge, Massachusetts, all summer to finish *Crew, Chanzeaux,* and *Don't Walk*. I manage to get to Cambridge, England, a day before the mid-September deadline.

Each cold morning at my Trinity Hall digs, a manservant, Harry, brings me a small bottle of milk and lights the gas heater before I get out of bed. But I take a train down to London on Thursday afternoons and don't come back up until Monday night. In London, I live with Liz in a four-story townhouse that she rents on Herbert Crescent, behind Harrods. We have a cook. I have some bespoke suits made. I am a rich man with no money.

My grandmother dies in New York. She is eighty-six. I miss the funeral.

Two weeks later, I wake up in the middle of the night and sit upright in the dark upstairs bedroom. A pulsing, protoplasmic alabaster bust of Grandma Ruth, wearing nothing but a black slip, appears five feet in front of my eyes.

Startled, I breathe in time with her breath for a minute.

This must be a hallucination. I test it. I hold my head with both hands and keep my eyes steady as I turn from side to side—and the image too moves side to side. I look up and down, and the image moves up and down.

I conclude that my brain—not the retina—supplies the image for me to see.

I wake up Liz, "Do you see anything?"

I point.

She says, "No. I don't see anything."

I see the blood pumping in my grandmother's carotid artery.

I turn on the bedside lamp.

The room brightens; my grandmother dissolves slowly as the world comes back. I leave the light on for thirty minutes before I go to sleep.

It is uncanny.

After soft-boiled eggs, toast, and tea, Elizabeth taxis to the Slade each day in WC1 to paint, and I take a short walk to the Harrods food court to bring back a half quart of heavy double cream and a ripe pineapple.

I return to the townhouse and draw a warm bath.

All day in the tub with my food on a chair within arm's reach, I read all the novels of Hemingway and most of Fitzgerald. I read until she returns to me, pickled by their whispers. *The Beautiful and Damned.* Many weeks of immersion in their exciting, exemplary lives.

I do not want to be nothing but a cranky old man. *For Whom the Bells Toll.* How will I negotiate the shadowy passages, unrevealed in this world, and derive as much astonishment as I can while being alive? Simply explore. Each adventure must be a new beginning for me, kiss the last one goodbye—a life of beginnings and celebrations.

Habit is my enemy. As Oxford's Gilbert Ryle observed, not the flexible habits that intelligently hone skills but the repetitive and stupefied habitual responses that are activated by familiar cultural cues. A Monday through Friday sort of dying, as Studs Terkel put it.

People will only say time after time as they did on the TV series of my childhood *The Lone Ranger*—played by Clayton Moore, who spoke in perfect English even in the Old West—"Who was that masked man?"

At a Thanksgiving party in Cadogan Square, the privileged Harvard roommates rendezvous safe from the draft—enrolled at the London School of Economics (Howie), Oxford (John Veblen), the Institut d'études politiques de Paris (Eldon), and the University of Madrid (Richard Ferber). John Young is absent, now in Chicago at law school, and Jim King is at Berkeley Graduate School.

Ed Pressman is at the party, too. Enrolled at the London School of Economics, he actually spends his days in the halls of Columbia Pictures in London hoping to learn something about being a producer. A short, balding fellow who looks like Napoleon at a distance, Ed has a mother who wants to buy him a seat on the board of directors of any big movie studio, but he wants to make the movies.

He says, "I hear that you made some films."

I say, "Today I spent all the money I had for the spring semester to rent a 35mm camera for this weekend and to buy a thousand-foot roll of Eastman color film. My cast is from the Cambridge Footlights players. I wrote the script, *Girl,* and I'm going to shoot just one take of each shot so I can cut together enough shots to make a big-budget-looking ten-minute short. But I still need money to develop the roll and money for postproduction."

He says, "I tried to produce a movie with my friends from Fieldston School, but the director, the writer, the cameraman, and the editor just argued with each other and they never shot a frame."

I say, "You'll have no one to talk to but me. I do all the jobs. I'm shooting tomorrow morning in Cambridge."

He takes the train up the next day and watches me shoot the modest sex scene between attractive Footlighters Susan Kingsford and David Collins.

New York is about money. Washington is about power. Hollywood is about sex.

Ed insists at a dinner the following Tuesday at the Connaught Hotel that we sign a contract.

He says, "We can call it Williams Pressman Enterprises."

Instinctively, my impulse is to be less visible.

I say, "Ah, it can be Pressman Williams, if you want."

He says, "Okay, that's good."

I say, "You'll seem more important."

Ed looks older than thirty. He has the name of the family's Pressman Toy Company. He graduated from Stanford. He will appear to be an older, responsible producer, even though we are both twenty-three years old—a quiet Mutt to my overamped Jeff.

He says he will finance the completion as soon as I sign.

Liz advises me not to sign anything without a lawyer. She does not trust Ed. She does not volunteer a loan. I am afraid to ask.

When we meet the next day, Ed says I can consult a lawyer when we get back to the USA and he will make any changes I want.

I am undercapitalized, insecure, and trustful. I sign. I need a father figure, even if he's not a six-foot two-hundred-pounder.

I like Ed. He's bright and thoughtful. But just "having no one to talk to but me" turns out not to be so simple. A couple of times, Ed's jaw spasms shut from tension, and I speed him to hospital to get it injected with muscle relaxer so he can talk again. It is clear to me that Ed also has some unresolved childhood traumas. We take care of each other.

Ed arranges a meeting with the Beatles producer, George Martin, to get the rights to their recording of *Girl*. We meet in his office on Wardour Street. The Beatles are too expensive, but Martin gives us a new group of his, the Saint Louis Union, to record the song cheaply. The music costs Ed more than I spent on filming. "Produced by Edward Rambach Pressman" takes two lines on-screen to include his mother's maiden name to fit in his single card credit.

Girl wins the CINE Golden Eagle Award for Best Dramatic Short Film of the year.

Unbeknownst to me, Ed falls into unrequited love with Elizabeth.

Two multimillionaires under my wing, taking care of their hearts, and I'm still broke. I may not understand greed, but I do understand the rich egoist's fear of being hit up for money. The thing that is on my mind—survival.

I am not bored.

1966

One night in London, I see the German comedy version of Thomas Mann's *Confessions of Felix Krull*. Horst Buchholz stammers his way through a crazed appeal to his draft board to get him into a war so that he can torture the enemy to death. As Krull planned, the board dismisses him as unfit for military service.

I soon find myself in the King's College bathroom of my supervisor in fine arts, Michael Jaffe. He had recently bought a cheap painting at an estate sale and then sold the Rubens for a small fortune. Ample, dark-haired Jaffe is naked, bathing in the tub, preparing for a night out.

He says, "Your idea of going to the locations of Cézanne's landscapes to shoot his point of view on film, and then to dissolve into the actual paintings to show how he altered objective reality in his compositions, is an exceptional one, but beyond our resources. Also, the history department is arguing that it should be their project."

I say, "I don't think I have time to do the project before the end of the term. Perhaps it's better if I just leave in June."

In Trinity Hall, I write a passionate letter to my draft board. I ask for immediate induction so I can fulfill my desire to murder the yellow Vietcong commies. They write back and advise me to finish the term at Cambridge and then to come to see them.

Hi-yo, Silver, away!

Lee Marvin, Jim Brown, Donald Sutherland, John Cassavetes, Telly Savalas, and the rest of the all-star cast of *The Dirty Dozen*, shooting at Shepperton Studios during the week, play softball on Sundays in Hyde Park, near our Knightsbridge townhouse.

I brought my old Babe Ruth League mitt to the United Kingdom—God knows why—and of course a softball is huge compared to a baseball, let alone the bat many times the diameter of a broomstick. I go every Sunday and wait on the sidelines while the self-confident actors, who I think make more money than professional baseball players, choose up the teams. One Sunday, they are one short and Harvey Orkin, the London head of Creative Management Agency and the game's organizer, invites me to play in the outfield.

Charles Bronson is the bare-chested pitcher when I get up to bat on the nippy morning. Needless to say, I smack the grapefruit-size ball into Carriage Drive for a home run. Six sewers, easy. Bronson is pissed. None of the others befriend me, either. I have a glove and can hit. That's all they're interested in, kind of like my horny sister when I was twelve.

Orkin tells me to come and bring my glove the next Sunday. I become a regular.

I'm an unknown in the big leagues.

In June, Liz books a first-class cabin, and I, to keep up appearances for her family, book a room of my own in steerage on the *Queen Mary*.

I never see my cabin. We actually eat at the captain's table; I am surprised by the dull conversation.

During the five-day ocean crossing from Southampton to New York, I write a screenplay treatment, *The Man Who Killed Men*. The leading man lives on Park Avenue, but every time he looks out a window he finds himself in the midst of a war—in Vietnam, in World War II, in the Old West, in the Crusades. It makes it difficult for the character to live the high-society life of Manhattan.

Personal feelings can make passionate art.

And I'm on the *Queen Mary*, not the *Titanic*.

The night before the duty call to the Selective Service, I read Dalton Trumbo's novel *Johnny Got His Gun*. Johnny has had his four limbs and face blown off in the war but still has his mind and communicates by wrinkling his forehead in Morse Code.

After the four-hour physical, we three hundred inductees are in our underpants in a single line with backs against the cold tiled wall—remarkably similar to the tiles in the hallways of PS 108 that I remember passing on the way to my elementary school suspension.

An officer says, "Anyone who wants to see a shrink, take three steps forward."

A short, morbidly obese young man shuffles out. A tall, anorexic Black man with a ponytail that reaches his ankles, and I, also step forward.

The officer says, "Stand at the door behind me. You will be admitted one at a time."

I am the last soldier boy in the line of three at the psychiatrist's door. We wait, watched by the 297 draftees that duty is calling.

Twenty-five minutes later, across the desk of the German-accented doctor, I am careful to speak disjointedly and slowly. I do not want to give him any extra information or time to delve deeply. I continuously stutter and stammer as Horst Buchholz did, and add a repetitious spastic flinch throughout the interrogation. It takes me a full minute to utter even a short sentence, but I make sure to say that when I imagine myself in the army, the pictures in my brain break apart (a sure sign of potential psychosis) and that I dread the doorless toilet stalls (a shamed child?).

Soon enough, I am in front of an overweight sergeant at a small desk. There are two doors open behind him: through one, I see several of my Massapequa High School classmates lined up to take the oath to serve in the bloodiest years of the Vietnam War; and through the second door—I see a bright open exit to Brooklyn.

The sergeant says, "You son of a bitch."

He raises his arm and stamps my psychological "2-S Deferment" card.

War does not determine who is right, only who is left.

I step outside—no more school, no need to work, ready to make movies.

I stand in sunlight.

David Picker runs United Artists. He is the smartest executive in the business, and everyone knows it. The Pickers and Pressmans are society friends. Ed arranges for me to meet him.

I wait outside David Picker's office in the cramped anteroom. He has three secretaries who line up and prioritize the continuously incoming calls.

I hear the secretary say, "No, Mr. Picker will not pick up unless you have your party on the line."

The door opens and I walk toward his desk. Before I can reach the chair to sit down in front of him, the large, fit man in his mid-thirties says, "I like the treatment. We'll buy it."

I say, "I want to direct it."

He says, "How old are you?"

I say, "Twenty-three."

He says, "Don't be silly. This is a big-budget story."

I say, "You can have it for free, if I direct it."

He says, "Come back in a week. Talk to people. We want to buy *The Man Who Killed Men*."

I enter the office a week later. David has Chris Mankiewicz, the United Artists' house intellectual and head of development, next to him at one end of the desk. I sit in the only empty chair.

Mankiewicz says, "It is a very good treatment."

I say, "You can have it for free, if I can direct it."

Picker says, "Are you serious?"

I say, "Yes."

He says, "You won't just sell us the story?"

I say, "No."

If I sell it to them, what will Ed do? How will I feel, Mom, if I make more money than a principal?

Picker says, "Well, then, go home and write a low-budget movie, and then maybe we can do it." I am an old hand at going upstairs to write again.

I say, "Okay," and leave.

My goal is to direct, and I'm in a suicidal hurry. Why? I don't have any reason except that it passes muster as a career, and I find writing is no fun.

I rent a studio apartment on Fifty-Fifth Street and start the process of writing a low-budget screenplay, one index card at a time. I base *Out of It* on my high school experiences—football, Louellen, prom—a drama about transcending the belief in the norms of suburban high school.

I survive on winnings from a weekly poker night with Ed's brother-in-law and his colleagues in the rag trade.

Seven months later, I am again in front of David and Chris Mankiewicz. David says, "We'd like to buy the screenplay."

Mankiewicz says, "It's fresh. Nothing like it. It's a nice movie." Herman Mankiewicz, Chris's uncle, wrote the screenplay of Orson Welles's *Citizen Kane.*

I say, "Thank you. I want to direct it."

David says, "You're still too young. We'll buy it."

I say, "Only if I direct."

David says, "You're too young. I can never get it past our board of directors."

I say, "I'm going to direct it." I walk out of United Artists.

1967

Ed says he will go and try to sell it to the other major studios or, if that fails, he will get independent money.

I say, "How long will that take?"

He says, "It could take a year."

I play poker once a week to make ends meet. Another person named Paul Williams founds the first national US rock magazine, *Crawdaddy*—a year before *Rolling Stone.* Ironic. In the meantime, I'm not bluffing.

I read in *Variety* that a new organization, the American Film Institute, is being formed in Washington, DC, by the son of the great director George Stevens (*A Place in the Sun* and *Giant*)—George Jr.

I jump on a train in Penn Station with the show business newspaper under my arm. In DC, I walk to the address of the "AFI." There is no identification of such an organization in the building, but I wander up and find a few large, completely empty rooms, one with and a folding table, a black desk dial telephone, and a chair. I walk in.

I say, "Hello? Hello?"

I sit down on the folding chair and stare at the black dial.

George Stevens Jr., in his mid-thirties, tall, blond, handsome in a well-pressed white shirt with rolled-up sleeves, walks in from an adjacent almost empty room.

He says, "Who are you?"

I say, "I saw the article in *Variety* today, that you're going to help young filmmakers."

He says, "Well, we're really not ready yet, as you can see."

I say, "Too bad. I could use you. Let me know when you're in business."

He laughs.

Do not believe what you read in the newspaper.

Stanley Kauffmann, author and also the movie critic for the *New Republic,* sees *Chanzeaux* and puts it on his local New York television show. He praises the film as "authentic and sensitive to the culture in which it was shot," and compares it favorably on the air to George Roy Hill's "flawed blockbuster, *Hawaii.*"

Ed suggests that I should learn something about acting before I direct my first drama. The next night I go to HB studios in Greenwich Village. After his introductory class, I meet Herbert Berghof. He saw the Kauffmann TV show and *Chanzeaux* the night before.

He walks me down the hall and introduces me to his wife, the legendary acting master Uta Hagen. They take me under their wing and I start to learn.

I watch Robert Duvall do a riveting scene at the studio, relaxed and focused, alone in a one-room log cabin set just doing bits of activity. It lasts twenty minutes. He says not a word.

This is new fun. I am where I need to be.

And three times a week, at Elizabeth's urging, I take a subway to Brooklyn for my psychoanalysis with Boris Heller, MD. His office is not far from the defunct Prospect Heights High School where my father had been chairman before he became a principal.

I had a recurring dream all through high school that ceased when I was admitted to Harvard.

Now I say to the psychiatrist, "I am alone in the cavernous ground-floor cafeteria of PS 108. It is quiet, empty. Then an angry bull suddenly charges into the room at me. I barely escape through a side exit into a stairwell. I run up and onto the first floor. Rest. I hear the bull violently climbing up the steps. I run to an exit at the opposite end of the long hallway and race up to the second floor. I rest for some moments but soon hear thunderous banging up the metal stairs. I run to the opposite end of the second-floor hallway to the exit into that stairwell and race to the top floor. When I finally hear the bull crashing in that door, I run into a classroom and stand still. I hear the bull snorting and sniffing at the door and hide in the teacher's cloak closet. The bull crashes into the classroom and bangs around until a sharp horn pries open the closet door. His ferocious head is only feet away when he thrusts to mortally gore me—but I wake up."

I say, "How would you like a domineering father like that?"

He says, "Did you ever consider that it is your mother?"

Week after week in the Brooklyn office I remember, further and further back before I knew what remembering was.

After doing something so inexcusable, I run.

She chases me.

I run.

She holds a five-foot broomstick bobbing over her head, ready to strike.

She says, "You lousy kid!"

I run from the living room, into the foyer.

She runs through the arched entrance into the living room.

I exit the living room on the run into the foyer and circle through the dining alcove where a glass of milk and giant pack of Oreos are abandoned on the table.

She screams and does not slow down as she transits the foyer and reaches the dining alcove.

She's in the kitchen as I run out.

I round the bend through the arch into the living room again.

She's almost out of the kitchen.

I run.

She runs.

Around and around we circle the apartment. I am faster and keep ahead of her. I stay beyond the reach of a whack.

She tires.

I slow down.

She stops in the living room.
I stand in the foyer, ready to bolt.
She laughs out loud, "You lousy kid."
I watch her.
She puts down the broomstick.
Am I safe at home?

Before that, my father tells me he has "professional privilege" and can get the PS 108 principal to admit me early—so I can start my education sooner. I am surrounded by kids a year older than me—in high school, it's impossible to make the varsity baseball team.

A boy beats on a small snare drum and marches around the large kindergarten. I sit on a small chair in the back.

All the girls and boys sing, "Soldier boy, soldier boy / Where are you going / Waving so proudly the red white and blue. / I'm going to my country / Where duty is calling. / If you'll be a soldier boy, you may come, too."

The drummer boy then picks somebody to follow him. They sing another chorus, and the second chosen picks a third to extend the line. Each time a soldier is added, another chorus is sung.

One by one, the older children leave their seats and join the elongating snaking parade behind the drummer.

I listen to the ditty twenty-nine times. I am the last chosen, the end of the line.

Before that, when I am four years old, I stand in front of the many square windows. The panes of glass are six inches high and wide, and set with putty into the metal frame of the large casement window of the living room.

The checkerboard metal frame looms over me. Like prison bars.

I punch out the lowest window. Then the one next to it.

My mother rushes in and ministers to my bleeding hand.

My father arrives.

He says, "Why did you do that?"

I say, "I don't know."

The next day, I stand in front of a three-foot-square glass panel below the screen on the front door.

I punch out the glass panel.

My hand does not bleed. I hit it just right.

I feel better when I break windows.

Before that, my father gives me an allowance every Saturday. A nickel (a half dollar today). He or my mother drive me to Woolworth's Five-and-Dime Store. I have exactly one hour before they come back from their grocery shopping to meander the aisles that brim with possibilities for the rich.

Then, with only a few minutes left in my hour, always, I run back to where I know I can get the best value for my nickel—a 3x5 pad with fifty multicolored pages. I run to the cash register.

There are darkest No. 1 pencils in the tool drawer at home, for free, that my father brings home from school.

A pad and pencil is my jackpot.

Before that: I fly out of the Chevy into the sky and land in the snowbank.

She says, "Don't tell him. You can't tell Daddy. Or he'll kill me."

I say, "Okay."

I understand that my father may murder my mother.

Before that: I fly across the living room propelled by a wallop from my father, after I told her that I love her and she betrayed me.

The recurring dream?

Tyrannical Murray may propel me to achieve, but this shape-shifted bull destroys my achievement so I have nowhere to go but her embrace.

The good father loves me as his star surrogate but the good mother can only love me as her dependent infant.

Put that in your pipe and smoke it.

Oh yeah, Doctor Boris also mentioned that I jerk off so much to make sure my pen is working.

Book Two

How to Get into Hollywood

8

It's Not Just You, Murray!

1967–1968

1967

I apply to NYU to be in their inaugural graduate class in film. I am one of the two admitted—the other is Martin Scorsese, who has just made a short film, *It's Not Just You, Murray!* What a coincidence. Marty implores me to enroll with him and extols the virtues of Haig Manoogian, who will teach us.

We start to hang out. His knowledge of movies is encyclopedic. He seems to know nothing about the acting process but knows from old movies every performance of every emotional quality he might need to request of his players.

He says, "Do it like Lauren Bacall in the doorway when she turns back to Bogart in *To Have and Have Not*." (She said, "You know how to whistle, don't you? You just put your lips together and blow.")

He is a dark young man, and a very friendly, very short, very fast talker. All of his focus is on movies. A unique monumental monomaniac.

Soon, Ed announces he cannot get any studio to do *Out of It*.

But he says he will get his mother to put up some money for a low-budget production. His mother is a capitalist. She runs the toy company.

We will make the movie.

I tell Marty I will not be enrolling at NYU. Unlike him, I don't know much about American movies. I don't like violence. I don't like lowest-common-denominator aesthetics. The Scandinavians make hot movies like *I Am Curious Yellow* and censor violent ones. America censors humane carnal love.

I know a lot about photography and something about human behavior. Not that much about drama.

Quiet hubris will have to suffice.

I find a young production manager and camera operator, John Avildsen, to generate the budget. He is a friendly, knowledgeable hipster, an early LSD explorer. John has a friend, Moe Odegaard, who can light.

John says, "I will do the preproduction organization and budget and schedule, if I can have the credit as director of photography. And I'll operate the camera."

I say, "If it's okay with Moe, it's okay with me."

Ed says we should use Barry Gordon, the kid from *A Thousand Clowns,* who starred with Jason Robards.

I say, "He has none of the tough or sexy qualities of the lead character."

Ed says, "We must have a name."

I say, "It's just a completely different character."

Ed says, "He's a name." Ed signs a contract with the short, soft-featured actor to play "Paul." When the film opens, Molly Haskell refers to him as a "super-Semite squirt."

The next day, I meet Jon Voight at a William Morris Agency casting session with agent Marty Davidson. Jon is tall and charismatic, quick-witted, charming. I love him. Jon will make the main character as full as I wrote it— he's a wonderful actor.

But Ed refuses to switch to Voight. Ed already signed and committed money for Barry Gordon—the "name." I can't get Ed to see. He will not budge. Just as well, I excuse myself: with the justification that the damaged child within me needs one hand tied behind his back. I blame myself, not my abuser.

I promise Jon I will write a film for him to star in after this one—and he says he will play the bad guy, Russ, a supporting role in *Out of It.*

Ed is my producer, I am the worker. Ed may be chronically shy, but he is an immovable boulder, beyond Sisyphus, dictating the path. In fact, since early childhood, this need for and inability to stand up to a strong-willed, powerful collaborator is a continual, tragic flaw. It's this disability, not the ability that counts.

My otherwise fearless confidence and charm, presented to the rest of the world, hides my deep shame in an exceptional defense and otherwise exceptional offense.

In Manhattan, I get onto the set of *Up the Down Staircase* and watch director Robert Mulligan at work. The set is tense. Mulligan demands complete quiet and quick obedience. He is an autocrat, all day long. His focus is complete.

My first big surprise is how the subtle and delicate actress Sandy Dennis belches. Louder than a cow. All day long. Her focus is complete.

My second, that Mulligan covers this simple school classroom scene from every imaginable angle—close-up, medium, and wide shot, on every character—for three days. And then he spends two more days with dolly shots of small actor movements and tracking shots of longer ones. Mulligan was a top editor and this little piggy makes sure he has a thousand bricks to build his house.

I imagine how I will have to shoot the scene on my low budget: one long mise-en-scène and then some coverage. One day.

There will be few alternative ways to cut the scenes.

Mulligan might as well be Fred Astaire (née Fredrick Austerlitz) because I will be Ginger Rogers (née Virginia Katherine McMath) dancing backward in high heels.

Julie Christie takes off her shoes and strides down a man street in *Billy Liar*. It is electrifying. She commands attention doing nothing.

In 1965, she is Lara in *Doctor Zhivago* and wins the Best Actress Oscar for *Darling*. She is the most soulful actress in the Western world. Two years later, it is decades before the internet exists and a Western Union telegram is expensive. Telegrams are used only for singular terse communications, usually the notification of a relative's death.

Now, I write a twenty-page telegram to dazzling Julie that asks her to let me come to John F. Kennedy Airport next time she visits this country so I can get a five-second shot for my "dream of the future" sequence in my first feature film.

She responds—a sweet note and the promise to send some outtakes from the documentary film she is shooting with Peter Whitehead, *Tonite Let's All Make Love in London*.

Dream girls do exist. I knew that.

John Avildsen operates the movie camera (a decade later, he directs *Rocky* and later *The Karate Kid*).

The first day of shooting, John says to the production manager, "Alvin, there's no fucking eyepiece. See my eye?"

John must press his eye firmly onto the metal reflex camera eyepiece to prevent light from leaking in. His eye is red raw.

I say, "Alvin, get it."

For three days, John fumes and his eye is crimson. Finally, obese Alvin brings a spongy oval designed to slip around the eyepiece of the Arriflex camera.

John says, "There's no fucking chalk. We need chalk to make marks. For the actors to hit their spots."

Alvin says, "I'll get you chalk."

We all eat cheese sandwiches for lunch and work twelve-hour days.

The next week, Alvin delivers a box of chalk.

As top man below-the-line, John complains, "No more cheese sandwiches for the crew."

After two days, hamburgers appear at lunchtime.

After two weeks, John says, "Alvin, no more hamburgers!"

The third week, hot pizzas arrive on set.

Avildsen soon says, "No more fucking pizzas, Alvin!"

By the end of the fifth week, we eat steak sandwiches. The crew is joyous.

I ask producer Ed why he has not fired our production manager Alvin for doing such a poor job.

Ed says, "Alvin says, 'I give them cheap stuff to complain about. Eye-piece guard, chalk, hamburgers. Imagine if they wanted more film stock or better lenses! This is a low-budget shoot.'"

I play the cards that are dealt. I know how to suffer.

1968

The film is shot and edited. Carl Lerner, an older, expert editor (*12 Angry Men, The Swimmer*) is a mentor friend of my young editor, Eddie Orshan. Lerner comes into the editing room once a week and amazes me as he takes out a few frames of the head and the tail of shots within dialogue scenes to make the speeches flow and overlap. I can't believe the difference it makes.

The ending is better than I had written—Jon brilliantly improvised dialogue in the men's room where the bully humiliates himself and capitulates in front of a pistol held by nerdy Barry. It turns out not to be a prescient Columbine High School massacre only when Barry flicks his fake pistol to light his cigarette.

My sister has a friend from Bennington College, Lynn Goldberg, whose husband, Michael Small, is a composer for commercials and is eager to do movies. I like him immediately and he turns out to be a bit of a musical master. His enchanting score pulls the movie together (he later scores my next two movies and sixty others, including *Klute, Stepford Wives, The China Syndrome,* and my *Miss Right*).

I am too nervous to watch the projection of the movie in the evening with David Picker at the UA screening room. Ed goes alone and returns to my apartment after midnight.

Ed says, "Picker got in at eight and we watched the English-dubbed version of *Elvira Madigan* and then *Out of It*. When it was over, he got up and said, 'We'll buy it! What do you want to do next?'"

I am relieved and exhausted.

I watch as Ed proudly repays his mother at her desk at Pressman Toy Company with a Pressman Williams Enterprises check for $132,000 (a million today).

Ed tells me there is no profit, no money for me. No big deal.

I made a movie. United Artists (UA) will distribute it. I feel legitimate, enough to get married. Liz and I have been together for three years. A June wedding is the plan. She insists that I sign a prenuptial agreement worth $300,000 ($2,200,000 today). I'll sign anything.

Keep moving forward, Kemosabe.

The dangerous anticapitalist, antipoverty Martin Luther King Jr. is shot dead on April 4, in Memphis. The cruel day is right after his televised speech, "Free at last, Free at last, Great God a-mighty, We are free at last."

I photographed King close up for the *Crimson* when he visited Harvard. I cannot help but link the assassination to John F. Kennedy's. The reactionary Right simply kills the decent charismatic leaders of the Left.

The country erupts in a hundred riots from coast to coast—the greatest wave of social unrest since the Civil War.

Right on. Right on Time.

Robert F. Kennedy is the presidential candidate calling for peace in Vietnam. JFK's younger brother is shot on June 5 in Hollywood, just after winning the California Democratic Primary. Bobby dies the next day.

My generation has lost all three of its compassionate leaders by coincidence at the hands of solitary magical marksmen murderers.

We are traumatized, if we know it or not.

We repress the memory and the fear. But it weighs for decades like a hidden nightmare.

The course of history will veer to the right for half a century. The Republicans morph into reactionaries under Ronald Reagan, and the Democrats become centrist Republicans, under Bill Clinton. The progressive income tax that reduces the incentives for the very rich to pillage their companies or rip off their workers withers away.

Within a year, an American walks on the moon for the first time and distracts everyone on the planet.

There is no Left left.

The lower classes are left behind. Abandoned to an economy that shall only enrich a few and wage endless war while it destroys the climate.

9

Big Time

1968

On June 22, there is a drunken stag party with the gang of old Harvard roommates in a suite at the Americana Hotel in Manhattan. I am frightened by the looming next day's milestone. I expound to the group on the gutsiness of this life decision as I stagger and fall on a chrome and glass coffee table, and split my scalp open.

The next morning, Ed drives on the Westside Highway as I sit in the passenger seat when suddenly the front hood slams open obscuring the road ahead. We are not hit by any cars before he manages to stop. He had neglected to fasten the hood after an oil check. Another Mister Magoo.

At the Anchorage, the Rosenwalds' Connecticut estate on Long Island Sound, a doctor is waiting to stitch up my head before the ceremony in the garden of the manor.

As we take our vows, Elizabeth looks radiant and happy. I am too thoughtful. This is who I am? I have a bandage over my brain, but I want to spend my days and nights walking through this crazy world with her.

Below the hill upon which we are married, on the acres of lawn—beyond the tennis courts, three-hole golf course, the dock and saltwater swimming pool—a two-pole white circus tent has been erected. Hundreds of reception guests arrive in shuttle vehicles.

The great and the near great of Manhattan society are there. And my relatives from Brooklyn and the Bronx. And the roommates and a few *Out of It* personnel. Chamber music performers in white tie and tailcoats begin to fill the air with polite sounds.

It is impossible to see the interior canvas walls of the huge tent because they are completely covered with recently living white flowers.

Ed is my best man and makes a long, emotionally generous toast, concluding, "and may they be out of it, together."

The preeminent families of Lehman, Astor, Sarnoff, et al., and the families of public school educators Goldberg, Gelber, Schwartz, et al., all foxtrot.

After twenty minutes of classical pieces, the crowd is astounded when the musicians pull off their breakaway tails. This is the New York Rock and Roll Ensemble—loud, baroque rockers. They play a "Whiter Shade of Pale" for Liz and me. Then a tsunami of raucous rock 'n' roll.

There is confusion in the tent.

But then John Avildsen's wife, Melissa (née Marie Olga Maturevich), an ex–Las Vegas showgirl in a minidress and bare long legs, lets her pelvis swing. Most of the elders have never seen such dancing in real life. It makes them happy. Elizabeth and I are driven to the Plaza Hotel in Manhattan. We are happy.

I took four years of Spanish in high school. I did not get to Spain and the Museo del Prado when I first went to Europe. Elizabeth and I have been living together for years so the honeymoon is more of a vacation. Ed is my best friend and has started to dabble in oil painting and wants to come on the trip to Madrid, Seville, and Toledo. Liz agrees.

The next day, we meet Ed and fly to Spain. I remember Calderon's *La vida es sueño,* which I read in the original Spanish. Tell me about it.

Upon their return, Mr. and Mrs. Williams sit with four couples and a young Israeli army commander at a round table on the floor of the immense banquet hall of the Americana hotel. Up on the stage, my father-in-law, Bill, stands at the lectern. Nelson Rockefeller, the governor of New York, sits to his left. The Israeli general Moshe Dayan, with a black patch over one eye, on his right. On either side of the distinguished guests sit the richest of the Jews of New York. In front of them on a lower riser sit the next dozen richest.

At our table on the floor, the young Israeli battle-hardened warrior propositions two of the wives. He ignores their husbands.

On the stage, Bill says, "On behalf of my family and I, I pledge one million dollars." (That would be seven million today.) He continues, "And in honor of our guest, General Dayan, I pledge an additional two million dollars to the Six-Day War Fund." (Another fourteen.)

Applause fills the hall.

Then the elevated others announce their gifts: a million here, a million there. All are loudly applauded.

At our table, the Commander Benjamin Netanyahu announces aloud the number of his hotel room for the benefit of the women. Real scholarship calls for my contemplating and theorizing in the persona of the philosopher:

I say to Liz, "He's a pig."

At the lectern, Bill says, "We will not announce Governor Rockefeller's gift, but I can tell you, it is quite substantial."

Applause. It seems an awkward exception to me, but he is after all not Jewish.

The owner of Korvettes Department Store now stands up to make the first pledge from the tables on the floor.

He says, "On behalf of my wife, Myra, and me, we pledge $75,000."

There is no applause. The room is silent.

After several moments, Bill says, "Let's hear it for the little givers!"

Polite applause follows.

I say to Liz, "When they call our name, I'm going to pledge two BILLION dollars."

She says, "They won't call us. We're part of the family gift."

I am a strange fellow, even to myself—an odd fellow is in the family.

I have been happy—without working on a movie.

I hire my freshman roommate, Odell, who had been writing computer manuals in Boston, to come to New York to write for me—*Blown and Blasted* is about a factory that supplies penis-shaped explosive sausages for Vietnam until it blows itself up. The other one is about an aspiring actress who joins a sex commune, *Come Together*. She ends her Hollywood career as a sex worker. But Ed insists he will not do either of them. I can make no serious headway with him.

Ed walks into Micucci's custom tailor shop above Fifth Avenue and hands me a slim novel, *The Revolutionary,* by someone named Hans Koningsberger. Ed says, "I think you will like it."

I read the intelligent, timeless radical drama, but I want to do outrageous and funny, radical stories. I want to do Odell's scripts. Ed is insistent that I get back to work and dismisses David as "too far out." I am an overworked vassal since the earliest stages of life. I empower Ed, saddled now with a new overlord.

I start looking for this guy Hans. I like my suspicion that I may spend some time with a hippie radical writer in a walkup on the Lower East Side. A real cohort.

But Hans Koningsberger, it turns out, has written ten well-received books since 1958, contributed to the *New Yorker,* the *Atlantic,* the *New York Times,* and was a hero in the Dutch underground during World War II.

A few days later in Switzerland, on their stone veranda high on the side of an Alp, I eat quiche and sip wine with the tall, handsome, graying Hans and his friendly, younger, blonde third wife, Katie Scanlon. He invites me to go with him to a location in nearby Austria to see John Huston direct *A Walk with Love and Death,* based on Hans's novel, that stars Huston's daughter, Angelica, and General Moshe Dayan's son, Asaf.

John Huston sits absorbed in the *London Times* in a director's chair with two custom-designed pouches that hang from each arm with pockets for the *New York Review of Books,* the *Daily Racing Form,* a shooting script, pads and pens, and other items. I sit nearby with Hans in the high mountain valley of grasses and wildflowers.

Beyond Huston's chair, a company of three hundred prepare the location for the setup of a hundred yards of dolly track and a line of a dozen huge arc lights. They practice the camera move to smoothly follow Asaf on horseback. He chases one of the medieval peasant foes whom he smites to death with a harmless rubber mace and chain. Then he gallops across the fields to his damsel and jumps off his horse near Huston—whose eyes remain on his reading material. Asaf gathers Angelica in his arms, murmurs romantic dialogue.

The assistant director has the battalion of Hundred Years' War combatants, the platoons of grips and electricians, and the squad of camera people rehearse the elaborate shot again and again. After two hours, the assistant director (AD) is satisfied and slowly approaches the preoccupied director.

The AD says, "Mister Huston?"

He says, "Yes?"

The AD says, "Sir, would you like to take a look now?"

Huston says, "Well, yes, yes, let's take a look."

The complicated sequence is run again as Huston watches, for the first time.

He says, "Yes, good. Very good." He gets out of his chair and walks the twenty feet to the spot where Asaf cradles Angelica in his arms.

Huston says, "Try it like this." He kneels down and replaces Asaf, cradles his daughter in a slightly different position, and says the brief dialogue.

Asaf rehearses the slight adjustment with Angelica.

Huston says, "Let's shoot it."

After two takes, the director is satisfied and he is not tired.

At the lunch break, I see no cheese sandwiches, only Viennese *Apfelstrudel,* Wiener schnitzel, sausages, and *Käsespätzle.*

You are what you eat.

My father-in-law says, "There's a movie studio up for sale. American International Pictures. I can buy it for you. What do you think?"

I say, "I don't think I want a job of sitting at a desk, talking on the phone, and looking at pieces of paper with numbers on them. I don't want to spend my life calculating."

I am too small at this point to imagine that I could just hire some smarty pants executive to do the paperwork, and I could re-create this low-budget studio into an artistic haven for Marty, Jon, Ed, and an unknown new wave of young filmmakers.

I have been working too hard my whole life and find no time to do nothing, which is what I'd really like but am too scared to do. I am an overachiever who realizes the extra effort he needs in order to turn in something first-rate. I'm looking for a way to get out, but I keep falling up—I am too big to fail.

Later, William Rosenwald, the son of the titan of American industry, Julius—the inventor of the industrial production line which the anti-Semitic Henry Ford copied—says, "Would you like to run our whole operation?"

I say, "How long will it take to be in charge, to run the show?"

He says, "You'll have to go to business school, then about ten years until you're in charge."

I say, "I don't think I can wait that long."

I don't imagine a long life. Thirty is old. Another decade of work feels unthinkable. The load is not too heavy; I am too weak.

Eventually, Bill says, "You could run our enterprises and still make a movie during the summer."

I say, "I can't make a movie in three months."

He says, "When I was at MIT, I dreamed of designing bridges. But when I graduated, I figured I could always hire someone to build a bridge. My older brother, Lessing, was in charge of increasing the family fortune. I was given the job of giving away the money. My shrink told me that I had to go out and make my own fortune to feel good about myself."

He did so with a mainframe computer company and a secret investment banking operation—no one knew when or what he bought and sold. *Fortune Magazine* observed, "Nobody knows the size of the Rosenwald fortune."

Bill says, "In the end, I figured wrong. I wish I had designed those bridges."

He is a kind man.

I still have my Music 1 list—the great Western sacred and classical music of the last two thousand years.

I assemble a list of the best-reviewed LP recordings.

One afternoon, I go to Sam Goody's record store and buy most of them. The piles of vinyl records stand like solid piers of a bridge on the checkout counter.

Five years ago, in this same store, I was intensely present when I shoplifted an LP of Gregorian chants.

Now, I encounter the cashier and pay with a credit card.

I say, "I can't carry them."

The cashier says, "We'll deliver. No charge."

Live your life. Don't repeat yourself.

10

The Prophet
1968

Waldo Salt, the screenwriter of *Midnight Cowboy*, has an elder daughter, Jennifer, who is in love with Jon Voight. She insists to everyone who will listen that Jon should play Joe Buck in *Cowboy*.

The director, John Schlesinger, finally grants a screen test. Jon does not portray the character—he completely inhabits him. Jon shows me how he practiced for months how Joe smoothly taps his foot out of rhythm to the music—when I try to do it, I can't. United Artists agrees to take a chance with him instead of Michael Sarrazin, the star of *They Shoot Horses, Don't They?* Dustin Hoffman is already Ratso Rizzo.

I will gladly wait for Jon before we do our next movie together.

David Picker says to me, "We are not going to release *Out of It* until after *Midnight Cowboy* is released."

I say, "No, no, no, no . . ."

He says, "You have no stars now. Maybe Jon will be a star."

I say, "That is going to be more than two years from now. No one has made a movie about high school in the USA today. We have the first one. The audience is there now. Believe me, it is ripe. It will rot."

He says, "It's in black-and-white and has no stars. It can do well if Jon becomes a star."

I say, "This is the critical cultural moment for this film. You can't put in on the shelf. It will be old hat by the time you release it. The movie will die."

Out of It is shelved by Picker, who says, "You can bring it to the film festival in Berlin."

I could have been a prophet but I see that one day I will be a martyr.

Liz and her best friend, "Weezie" Duncan from Louisville, and my fifteen-year-old brother, Ted, and I take off to Paris and Amsterdam for ten days. In the sky over Europe, I imagine in the hundreds of towns below, individuals absorbed in their wants and feelings. I feel so distant.

At the Lasserre Restaurant in Paris, a sliding roof opens to the night sky, as we sit for dinner.

An elegant waiter speaks English with a French accent to Ted, "And for monsieur?"

Ted says, "I'll have a hamburger with ketchup and some french fries. And a glass of milk. Can you do that?"

He says, "Ah, but that will be easy."

Dinner is served.

Ted says, "I would like the milk to be colder."

The waiter promptly picks up the glass. Three minutes later, a cold glass of milk is presented.

Ted says, "How did they do that?"

I say, "Put it in a bucket of ice and twirled it?"

He laughs.

Elizabeth is downtown painting at the New York Studio School, which she anonymously helps fund. I am in my study, writing.

I hear the ring of the doorbell of our fifth-floor apartment at 210 Central Park South.

I walk from my study, past the living room, and open the door.

Julie Christie stands there.

She smiles.

I am stunned. Evidently so was the doorman, who did not announce her arrival.

She says, "Hello there. I'm Julie."

I stand still and look down at her. Her eyes are clear but vulnerable. She is soulful and gorgeous—beyond Angie Dickinson. Did my heart love till now?

I say, "Why don't we go downstairs and have a drink?"

We spend a couple of hours in conversation in a dark hotel bar near Columbus Circle. She has a heavenly speaking voice filled with overtones, devoid of any pretension. We like each other and have an easy rapport.

Richard Lester's *Petulia,* with George C. Scott and Julie, has opened. The divine beauty is alone in town to do publicity.

She is also charming and friendly. But I am short of the selfish Dionysian strength to force the moment to a crisis.

What odd timing.

I am married.

Another meeting with David Picker at UA: he likes the idea that Jon—creating a riveting Joe Buck in the daily rushes of *Midnight Cowboy*—wants to play the lead in *The Revolutionary.* But David doesn't like the commercial possibilities. I argue for the morality and timeliness of the project.

Picker says, "I'll think about it."

That weekend, the head of the American Broadcasting Company (ABC), Leonard Goldenson, and his family visit the Rosenwalds at the Anchorage.

Goldenson asks me in front of my father-in-law, "You know what's a good movie?"

I think of Fellini and Truffaut movies but do not come up with my answer before he speaks.

He says, "A good movie is a movie that makes money."

I think he's a jerk and walk away, a spoiled prince, high and low.

I fly to Chicago to join the protests at the Democratic Convention. Each night one large page is composed underground by graduate members of the *Harvard Crimson* with the guidance of ex–sports editor Joe Russin and the stewardship of radical *Ramparts* magazine's executive editor, tipsy Warren Hinckle.

Before daybreak, hundreds of *The Wallposter* appear on building walls around Chicago to inform the thousands of protestors of the next day's plans—the same method used by the French revolutionists of the eighteenth century.

The police of Chicago riot. Abbie Hoffman, Tom Hayden, and fifteen thousand protestors in Grant Park are tear-gassed and clubbed on live national TV, as I snap away and avoid arrest and billy clubs.

Chicago mayor Richard J. Daley says, "The police are not here to create disorder, they're here to preserve disorder." Months later, Abbie Hoffman's conviction for crossing state lines with the intent to incite a riot is overturned.

By the evening we know that our antiwar candidate, George McGovern—who was meant to pick up the torch of assassinated RFK—is a distant also-ran to the new nominee, Hubert Humphrey.

The massed police surround us and simply push everyone in a crush against the huge plate-glass windows of the facade of the Hilton Hotel. Finally, the glass gives way and shatters down on protestors. I keep taking pictures.

The next morning, I fly to New York and take a cab from JFK to Moder-nage Labs to have rush prints made. Then I go to meet with Picker again.

I show him the photos and urge him to make *The Revolutionary.*

He says, "I make one or two movies every year that I know won't make money. This is one of them. But you've got to shoot it in London—it'll cost a lot less. And everybody flies Air India—we have locked funds from distributing *The Sound of Music* in India."

Hi, Mom? Thanks, Ed?

11

Icons and Demons

1968–1969

1968

I visit the set of an abandoned loft in *Midnight Cowboy* to see how John Schlesinger directs.

I watch Joe Buck realize that Ratso Rizzo is dying, and walk across the set to a cot where he lies down and snuggles into his pillow to listen to a tiny radio at his ear.

Schlesinger tracks with Ratso and Joe, then follows Joe to the bed. Joe lies down. But the dolly track cannot get near enough to get the extreme close-up of Joe's private fear that Schlesinger wants.

He calls for a break, stymied. He mutters about his friend, director Richard Lester, knowing everything about the camera, while Schlesinger berates his own lack of abilities. He lauds Lester's stylish *Petulia,* which recently opened.

The set becomes tense.

He says, "Does anybody have an idea how I can get this shot?"

After moments of silence, the sound man walks up to him and quietly says, "Put on a zoom lens. When the camera reaches the end of the track, push all the way in with the zoom to Jon's face."

Schlesinger says, "Yes. Yes. That's what we will do!" Everyone can hear his enthusiasm and the sound of laughter is heard.

He has a good way of looking at things—the dramatic moment always dictates Schlesinger's camera placement. The film wins him the 1969 Oscar for Best Director.

This is a good way to direct.

I'm invited to meet Brian De Palma on the opening night of his new film, *Greetings*. He's only three years older than I am; he could be a buddy. The cast and crew are in high spirits in a small Manhattan hotel suite when producer Chuck Hirsch runs in with the hot-off-the-press *New York Times*. Without a preparatory scan, the excited Hirsch reads aloud the review that seems to never end, but it does: "Next time De Palma might try for something that matters instead of the tired, tawdry and tattered."

Within minutes, everyone leaves and only De Palma, his mother, and I are in the room. This is my first encounter with Brian and I am bewildered by the exeunt of his ignoble friends and associates.

I say, "Don't worry, as Mike Nichols said, 'Critics are like eunuchs at a bang gang.'"

I say, "at a bang gang . . . I mean, bang gang . . ."

Brian stares at me.

I say, "Eunuchs at a . . . Gang . . . Bang."

We are upset. I am more upset than Brian. We become friends. That's about it.

1969

Jon and I work for months in my study to dramatize Hans's narrative screenplay of *The Revolutionary*. We improvise each scene many times with a tape recorder in the afternoons. I continually rewrite at night. The Communist Hans does not object to our rewriting the dialogue, as long as we agree that the screenplay credit is not communal—that he shall receive sole credit.

One day, Jon says that Waldo, who recently won the Oscar for Best Screenplay Adaptation for *Midnight Cowboy*, offered to doctor our script.

Blacklisted in 1951 for refusing to testify for Joe McCarthy's Un-American Activities Committee, Waldo said, "I wish we had done something to deserve being blacklisted. I wish we'd had that much influence on film or on politics at that time. I think the world might have been different. But we didn't."

Instead of now taking advantage of Waldo's incredible generosity, my *Scarlet Letter* essay rewrite trauma makes it impossible for me to accept his priceless offer.

Waldo later writes *Serpico* (and is nominated for an Oscar) and *Coming Home* (he wins it).

I am disabled.

On most Park Avenue Sundays, I harangue the luncheon table about the thuggish stupidity and murderous criminality of the Vietnam War.

As a favor to me, "the office" anonymously contributes via the tax-exempt American Friends Committee in Boston, the largest share of the funding to establish antiwar GI coffeehouses around all the army's basic training forts in the nation. The activities in the coffeehouses help build resistance inside the army.

It is crucial for outsiders to protest, but their voices have limits. Change happens only when the war of ideas is won among the powerful. Eventually, I convince Bill, who then starts to convince His Crowd downtown. Wall Street starts a slow turn against the war. Richard Lester's comedy *How I Won the War* just came out, starring John Lennon, not me.

The nation's young men are betrayed by their own government. Fifty-eight thousand American soldiers die—more than two million North and South Vietnamese. Secretary of Defense Robert McNamara, who brought his brilliant Harvard Business School systems analysis to its prosecution, later sobs in tears regretting his direction of the insane war.

Jon commits to play the lead in *The Revolutionary* for actors' union minimum, and Bob Duvall commits to play one of the two key supporting roles—a traditional Communist. Duvall says, "I've got to find the right hat. Then the character will come to me."

I sit outside with Al Pacino at a Central Park restaurant to discuss his supporting role.

I describe a smart Yippie—Abbie Hoffman.

I say, "Mark Twain said that 'against the assault of laughter nothing can stand.'"

Pacino loves Abbie, knows all his comedic moves, and acts them out for me. He holds up an imaginary jacket with his right arm to shield his wild conspiratorial Abbie, who ducks and spurts out comic radical insights in mock confidence, "Avoid all needle drugs, the only dope worth shooting is Richard Nixon."

He can do Abbie's voice perfectly. Al is excited about doing the role.

Voight, Duvall, and Pacino.

Two weeks before we start to shoot, Pacino wins the Tony for the Broadway play *Does a Tiger Wear a Necktie?*

I get a telephone call from his agent, Stevie Phillips.

She says, "You better find someone else. We don't want Al playing second fiddle to Jon Voight."

"I need a way to go," is what we said in the Bronx.

Jon suggests we cast Seymour Cassel, who can be funny, and I do so quickly.

Tommy Lee Jones (Class of 1969), whose Dunster House roommate is Al Gore, flies to Manhattan to see me.

He says, "I've got to get a SAG [Screen Actors Guild] card. No one will hire me. I can't do anything in this business without one. Can you give me a day with dialogue?"

I say, "It's low-budget and we're shooting in London. SAG minimum. You'll have to pay for your flight and expenses."

He says, "No problem. Thank you so much."

In *The Revolutionary,* he plays a guard at the army camp who questions Jon before he goes AWOL to warn the Black revolutionaries of a planned military clampdown.

After his scene, Tommy gets his SAG card and subsequent employment and four Academy Award nominations. His roommate, Al, learns about deadly CO_2 emissions from his Harvard professor Roger Revelle, that the air will kill us all if action is not taken promptly.

Ten years later, Representative Al warns the US Congress, and twenty years later tragically gives up the presidency that he had actually won at the ballot box to his opponent, the climate-yahoo Yalie George W. Bush. Al wins a booby prize six years after that—an Academy Award for documenting this *Inconvenient Truth.* PS—W's climate change denial mimicked the advice he got from his White House buddy MMC (Michael M. Crichton, AB Class of '65, MD '69).

I am staying alone at the Dorchester Hotel during a short preproduction visit to London. I have been meeting with potential department heads for *The Revolutionary.* One evening I walk toward Mayfair along the narrow back streets beyond the hotel.

I see my mother standing under a red light in a doorway. I am shocked. But then I decide this a gift from the Freud God. Since that day when she warmed my toes when I was four, it has been impossible to love her because my father is such a great big man. Now, I will fuck my mother.

I walk to her and she agrees to go upstairs. I never before heard my mother speak with a Polish accent. In the room, I am resolved to pursue this Oedipal opportunity into my unconscious. How amazing will this be? I pay her.

We start to undress.

I see tattooed on her left forearm, a row of six numbers.

This is not my mother. And I am a monster.

I say, "Never mind. I am going to leave now. Please keep the money."

She says, "Don't be nervous. This is your first time?"

I say, "No. No. But, but I must go."

She says, "You are a nice man. Don't worry. I will show you what to do."

I say, "Thank you, thank you, but no."

I leave, trembling.

Elizabeth and I are asked to go to Morocco to check out a family concern. I take out a week from the film prep. In Rabat, I eat couscous with my fingers and get lost in my first casbah.

I do not know that the Israeli Mossad's Misgeret Division covertly provides full-time security for the liberal king of Morocco against the threats of assassination by other right-wing Arab heads of state.

King Hassan II has allowed secret emigration of Jews from Morocco to Israel. Bill Rosenwald, head of the United Jewish Appeal, has philanthropic American Jews pay the king more than $50 million ($350 million today) for "indemnities" to move the dark-skinned Jews who flee the Atlas Mountains.

Liz and I drive down to Casablanca. We are there to see how the operation works. We are told to refer to the emigrants as "Texans" going to "Texas."

I want to see Rick's Cafe, where Humphrey Bogart listened to Dooley Wilson sing "As Time Goes By." It doesn't exist.

We walk in the narrow back streets of Casablanca near the port, from where the Texans are shipped at night. In the small bedrooms of the apartment buildings we see sheets and pillow cases made from American Aid burlap sacks. The sight moves me to tears. I can't even say why.

We are with four liaison people at lunch at a nearby restaurant above the surf. The waiter appears. I wait for my turn.

I say, "I'll have the lobster. Do you have a small one?"

Our hosts stare at me. I smile. They do not.

Elizabeth says, "Lobster—not kosher."

I say, "Why ya'awl, sons of Texas, that's our cov-ah!"

The story of *The Revolutionary* is set "Sometime in the Twentieth Century." I tell the production designer, Disley Jones, "I want no recognizable products. No labels. No advertisements for real products. Design a unique cigarette pack. No cars, just trucks and trains. This film should seem timeless and placeless to someone living east of the Soviet Union in 1969."

Disley makes a thorough design effort and skillful selection of London locations that are generic. He gets it. Revolution is a state of mind. Hell is a state of mind—in which people are trapped.

When Jon arrives, I tell him to rent a basement flat with minimal utilities. He should start living the life of his character.

He says, "Really? You mean it?"

I say, "Yes."

He finds accommodations in a dingy basement flat in Brixton. After three days, he and Jennifer move into posh digs.

Near their hotel in Hyde Park, Jon and Jennifer agree to play a game of touch football against diminutive Ed and lanky me.

During warm-ups, Jon runs for a pass. Ed rifles the pigskin so fast that Jon can't get his hands up in time and is struck in the middle of his forehead.

He collapses onto the grass.

Jennifer runs to his still body.

Ed is observant.

I say, "You killed our star. He's working for nothing."

The Midnight Cowboy lies on the turf, splayed on his back.

I say, "Jesus, Ed."

Jennifer is in tears.

We are being annihilated.

I see a small movement.

Jon regains consciousness. He is alive, not dead.

Jon says, "It's a node on my forehead. I'm okay. Don't worry."

I say, "Ed, where did you learn to throw a football like that?"

Ed says, "I played quarterback on the Fieldston varsity."

There's a lot I don't know about Ed.

12

The Canary Tweets

1970

1969

A silk shirt, double-vented suit, Lobb high-top shoes, and a velvet bowtie from Turnbull & Asser—I am dressed. I sit on the edge of the bed in the Dorchester Hotel and wait for Michael Braun to arrive for dinner.

Michael wrote *Love Me Do!,* which was only published in paperback. *Rolling Stone* said it was "The first and best Beatles book." And John Lennon said, "He wrote how we were, which was bastards." He is the Beatles' "Paperback Writer."

Dressed with nowhere to go, I walk into the bathroom and stare with total concentration at the reflection of my own eyes.

Dear Reader: If you prefer, as many of my friends do, to skip detailed reports of nonordinary realms of consciousness via mind-altered states or psychoactive drug journeys, I have indicated those exit points as: [SPARE ME], and reentrances as: [RESUME]. No harm, no foul. (Unless you are interested in Book Four, "How to Get Into Heaven"; then, do read.)

[SPARE ME]

After thirty-seconds, the two-dimensional plane of the looking glass dissolves into an unreflective three-dimensional black space, and two gruesome slimy giant bizarre insects arise and claw in my direction with their menacing mandibles. I am fascinated but detached and look for a full minute.

I look away. I no longer see the bizarre images.

I walk back to the bed and sit. "Beware the Jabberwock, my son! The jaws that bite, the claws that catch!"

I rest a couple of minutes at the Tumtum tree and walk back into the bathroom. I look intently into my eyes. Within seconds, up come the oily insects with their slimy clawing multijointed protuberances. After ten more slithy seconds, I look away and see only the shower. This is not a hallucination that travels with my gaze like my dead grandmother. I walk out.

I sit for a few minutes and decide I must go back one more time to verify the phantasmagoric visions that I can see only in the mirror. Shortly, I again focus on the reflection of my eyes. After three seconds, up come the silent wild things—only now with eyes aflame and fuming angry aggressiveness.

I turn away quickly and sit on the bed until Michael arrives. I watched this all with a strange detachment, not terrorized. But I have no idea how to bridge this chasm. I've never done drugs. I have seen something I don't know what. Does looking in the mirror allow my brain to enter another dimension?

[RESUME]

I do not mention anything about fraternizing with demons from the darkest depths to my Paperback Writer amigo ("If you really like it you can have the rights. / It could make a million for you overnight"), nor to anyone else. Even scientists can only examine and verify the observable universe. I have known of no path to knowledge other than critical reason. Certainly not revelation.

I am overwhelmed in silence. Just an ignorant witness.

Years later I read about insect residents of a low bardo, the place between death and rebirth, in *The Tibetan Book of the Dead*. The Buddhists say these creatures impel the spiritually unprepared into choosing a lowly reincarnation. Motherfucker.

Ed is staying at the Connaught Hotel. He has flown in from New York to visit. I meet him in the too-dark dining room.

He says, "They all offer me lousy deals. I can't find anyone to give us a good deal on a movie."

I say, "But they'll put up the money?"

He says, "Yeah, but we get the short end."

I say, "Ed, you're rich. And I don't need money. Forget about the extra nickel—make the movies. We are young; nobody else our age is making movies. Just make bad deals now, but make the movies. Get us established."

Ed says, "The heads of the studios keep postponing my meetings. One is still postponing after eight months."

I say, "We're just the low men on the totem pole. Keep making appointments and don't worry about postponements. Be happy they're willing to schedule. That's a big deal. When it comes that they have a slow day, you're sitting with the head of the studio."

Ed says, "It takes too long."

I say, "Keep track of our movie ideas and on the day that a meeting actually happens, just pick the best one."

He carries the black-and-white speckled composition notebook with movie ideas under his arm, almost everywhere for the rest of his life. It becomes his trademark.

At an Ed Pressman retrospective at the Museum of Modern Art twenty-five years later, Ed makes a speech. Among his remarks, he says, "Paul taught me how to be a producer, and he's here tonight." I take a bow, broke.

This is my first real crew. Union workers. They all call me "Guv."

I am twenty-five years old, and the young production assistants are older than me and resent it. I cannot get a proper morning coffee—too much sugar, too little sugar, too much milk, too little.

Finally, my elderly Bentley driver, George Hart, reliably brings me coffee. I like George. He is my friend on the set. A gentle man.

One day after shooting, George invites me into his row house for tea on the way home.

I sit in a large, high-backed wing chair in their living room. His wife prepares the tea.

As I sit, a bird chirps in my ear. I look around—no bird. I sit and the bird resumes its tweet. I look around again—this time more deliberately, up and to my right. Emptiness. I pay attention in my life—alertness is my guide.

George says, "Is there anything wrong?"

His wife enters with the tea tray.

I say, "No, there's nothing wrong, but there's a bird that keeps tweeting right in my ear. Don't you hear it? Like a canary?"

George and his wife look at each other.

She starts to cry.

George says, "Three years ago, our canary, Bungie, died. We had him for twelve years. He lived in a cage right behind your chair."

What is going on? The canary tweets. I hear it. I am committed to truth. It can't be, but it is—some connection beyond my prior notion of reality.

I hear Bungie somehow from another dimension.

The ancient mystics believed nothing exists until the observer and the observed overcome the illusion of separation.

I simply pigeonhole Bungie and throw myself into rehearsals. Jon and Jennifer are naturals together—plenty of everyday "prior-life experience." And, once Bob Duvall finds a little black cap for his character to wear, he fully inhabits the role. There is no other place on the planet with the joy and creativity of working with actors in rehearsal.

During the weeks exploring the characters before shooting, trust deepens between the cast and me. I suggest that after we get the good take—"print it"—we can do an extra couple of takes where the actors can make bolder choices, choices that they would never make if they did not know we agreed that they already had a good one. It is fun. When we shoot, this freedom to be dangerous provides a surprising number of moments that we find we can use in the final cut.

But the shoot is difficult and exhausting. I have no assistant director on the set. I have to keep the crew moving as well as guide the actors' performances. This on-set production job is an absurd addition to my job description.

Ed never visits the set. At dinner, I say, "It's not right, Ed. I am doing too many jobs."

Nothing changes.

After two weeks, my righteous director of photography, Brian Probyn—who had lit *Poor Cow* with Carol White and *Downhill Racer* with Robert Redford—goes to the production manager, embarrassed by the absence of the assistant director. All the crew has known that the AD has been spending his days at a pub since the shoot began. The production manager, John Pellat, was hired by Ed—and the AD was hired by Pellat, to try to help his alcoholic buddy get back in the business.

I feel abandoned by Ed. But I carry on.

When I come home at night enervated, Elizabeth complains that she feels left out of the event, like an outsider.

One night, we go out to dinner in Knightsbridge, and the director John Boorman and his wife and two kids are at the adjoining table having fun. Boorman is in town directing *Leo the Last* with Marcello Mastroianni.

I ask him, "How do you do it? You look like you don't have a care in the world. Weren't you on the set today?"

He says, "When we wrap, the day is over. Five o'clock, I'm done."

I don't know how to take care of Elizabeth while we shoot.

I can't switch off my concern over the next day's scenes. I am overloaded. She doesn't want to hear all about it.

Seymour Cassel was nominated for an Oscar in last year's *Faces,* directed by John Cassavetes.

Late in the shoot, he arrives in town.

I walk into an elevator with Seymour and he immediately steps behind a pretty woman who studies the floor selection buttons. He rests his head on top of hers. He speaks his pickup lines with a spot-on Donald Duck imitation.

He is a randy, funny man.

But the next day on location in Brixton, he repeatedly makes an incomprehensible mess of the long, key climactic radical speech of the movie. He is not an intellectual and can't play Abbie. This is an utter disaster.

I say, "Seymour, just say, 'You want to talk dialectic? I'll talk dialectic!' And then do the lines in your Donald Duck voice."

The nonsense sounds work in the scene but lack dramatic impact. *The Revolutionary* climax will be significantly thinner than I had imagined.

No Pacino, matters.

At Twickenham Studios, I work with editor Henry Richardson. While he does the mechanical 35mm film edits, I wander around the small movie park.

Sometimes I have lunch in the commissary with Richard Lester, director of *Petulia,* the movie that had Schlesinger doubt his own abilities on the set of *Midnight Cowboy.*

He says, "To be successful, a film must appear while the zeitgeist is right for that sensibility. When that invisible cultural moment changes, and it changes every six months, a wonderful film can easily flop." Like *Out of It?*

One day, director Lindsay Anderson, leading light of the "British New Wave," telephones and invites me to meet him at the Royal Court Theatre where he is rehearsing David Storey's play *The Changing Room.*

Lindsay is a kind, intelligent fellow, and a great director (*if....* introduced Malcolm McDowell; *This Sporting Life,* Richard Harris). I watch him work. I like him.

He is attentive to me and volunteers to look at *Out of It,* still being held from release by UA.

I set up a screening at Twickenham for him. He gives me a signed edition of the comic *Doonesbury,* by Gary Trudeau. After he sees the film, Lindsay suggests two cuts—a long talky scene at the end of the first act, so to speak, and another at the end of the second.

He says, "Those two scenes explain too much. Leave the audience in mystery; let them be eager to discover what will happen. Don't tell them what you're going to do."

When I cut out those two scenes, I watch the film fly forward as it never did before. I look at the drama with new curiosity. On the live-and-learn program, I am helped by a master.

I call New York and tell David Picker that I will pay to make the hot splice cuts by hand to every one of the 115 prints they have in storage.

My knowledge is far less great than my ego.

In December 1969, *Out of It* opens, three years after it was shot. All the reviews in New York are good, though as Ed says years later, "By then, it looked like a period piece. Yet it had been one of the first of the coming-of-age pictures, like *The Graduate.*"

Just as Richard Lester had warned.

Preeminent British critic David Robinson writes: "It is fairly rare that a first film excites the confidence to predict that its director has a very good chance of becoming a major talent." Although Molly Haskell in the *Village Voice* says that "Williams makes films under his breath."

Out of It has no significant box office.

Nevertheless, Ed tells me that I am well regarded and that the next film I make will be critical.

I implore him to option *Being There* by Jerzy Kosinski, but Ed vetoes my plan. He says it's too expensive. I get him to read *A Clockwork Orange* by Anthony Burgess, but he says it will not work.

Eventually, I persuade him to option *Player Piano* and *The Sirens of Titan* by Kurt Vonnegut.

Ed tries to find a studio interested in Vonnegut while I write a screenplay of *Player Piano.*

Kurt and I drink at the St. Regis bar and commiserate. He tells war stories as he gets drunker, about the firebombing of Dresden that killed more people than the atom bombs dropped on Japan.

There are a half dozen different realities that run from start to finish in *Slaughterhouse-Five*. The kids' voices in the Dutch puppet theater, the slimy insects in the Dorchester Hotel mirror, and Bungie the singing dead canary have made me entertain the existence of unseen universes.

In his novel, Vonnegut cut in and out from the six realities—the chosen scene becomes the next scene in the narrative.

I say, "We stack six small rectangles along the left side of a normal big movie screen. Each little rectangle contains a continuous two-hour movie without sound. When we hear a tone, one of the small rectangles goes dark and its image fills the large full screen with a full soundtrack. When the scene is finished, it returns to its small spot and becomes a silent movie again. The next scene enlarges from one of the other small rectangles and continues the drama."

Kurt is enthusiastic.

But no studio in Hollywood wants to finance the film.

I am too discouraged to write anymore. I feel like an imposter.

I am in London again on *The Revolutionary* postproduction when Kurt's *Slaughterhouse-Five* becomes a best seller.

At two in the morning, my phone rings.

The Universal Pictures executive responsible for the huge hit *Airport*, Jennings Lang, says, "Kid, I hear you've been trying to sell Vonnegut to everybody. I'm going to offer this to John Schlesinger and George Roy Hill, and if they won't direct it, I'm going to hire you. Come and see me when you get back to New York."

George Roy Hill jumps at the assignment and creates the movie *Slaughterhouse-Five* as a conventional narrative.

And so it goes, as Kurt would say.

Jon and I go to dinner at Parke's Restaurant on Beauchamp Place in London. We walk down the steps to the basement dining room.

In the far corner table, I spot John Lennon, Paul McCartney, George Harrison, and Ringo Starr. The Beatles.

I say, "Jon, I'll get you a napkin and a waiter's coat. You can go over and take their order."

He says, "Are you kidding?"

I say, "You're famous all over the world now—*Cowboy* is huge. You don't understand."

I get a jacket from a complicit waiter and hang a napkin over Jon's forearm.

He says, "No. You're crazy."

I say, "I guarantee you that they'll be happy to see you." And I give him a strong push toward their large corner table.

John Lennon greets him. Then the other Beatles recognize him.

Ringo says, "Hello, there. You're that cowboy. Yeah."

Jon realizes he's famous.

Things can change in a moment.

On TV that day, Neil Armstrong steps off the ladder of the lunar module onto the moon, "That's one small step for man, one giant leap for mankind."

1970

After *The Revolutionary* sound mix is completed, I return to New York and follow up with my invitation from Jennings. *Airport* opens to huge box office and eventually wins nine Academy Awards. It spawns the tent pole "disaster movie" genre. Lang is the supervising studio executive.

I invite Ed to come along with me. Never leave your friends behind.

We both walk into Lang's huge office at the Universal Pictures office in midtown.

Jennings promptly offers to bring Pressman Williams to the studio. I will direct the movies, and Ed will be the producer, financed completely by Universal.

I have broken through into the major filmmaking arena.

Finally.

Ed says to Jennings, "But who is going to write the checks?"

I look at Ed, bewildered. What has this got to do with our becoming an established studio production company? He ignores me.

Jennings ignores Ed, and continues to paint a bright picture of us as film-makers at Universal.

Ed says, "But who is going to write the checks?" Is he afraid of being pushed to the side by Jennings, who would be signing the checks?

Jennings takes off a shoe and smacks it on the desk. He says, "[Sidney] Sheinberg [the president of Universal] is doing the same thing for Steven Spielberg. He's setting him up!"

Ed says, "But who is going to write the checks?"

Jennings says, "What are you talking about? You don't know what you're talking about, kid—who writes the checks? What's wrong with you? Get out of here. Get out!"

Jennings is a huge six-footer and rises from his desk with his shoe raised over his head. He gets out from behind the desk and heads toward Ed to smack him, but the quick quarterback runs out of the office with me right behind him. My trust trumps his treachery.

I am loyal. That's what I tell myself. Something is wrong with me.

I cannot admit that Ed has sabotaged this breakthrough moment. Is he afraid I'll leave him behind, independent of him?

After all, Jennings did not invite him.

At the Berlin International Film Festival in July, George Stevens, legendary director of Hollywood classics, is head of the jury. *Out of It* is nominated for a Golden Berlin Bear and two other awards.

Stevens says, "You made a wonderful movie. I'm going to give it some kind of prize for best first film."

The film will have a historical milestone.

Brian De Palma hangs out with Elizabeth and me. He has *Dionysus in 69* in competition.

I am excited.

And so are the thousands of student radicals in the streets of Germany in 1970. They riot two days before the prizes are announced. On July 5, the festival closes down. The competition is canceled.

No Bear.

I visit with the young Germans when they occupy some buildings. They seem like extras to me. The protestors speak and dress like clichéd American TV characters.

While I am at the occupation, Brian tries to seduce Elizabeth. They are both cynics, but she wants nothing to do with him.

Brian says, "You ruined her for the film business."

That's his whole story.

In my apartment that overlooks the treetops of Central Park, I sit on a blue-velvet-covered, king-size mattress copied from John Lennon's Apple office on

Saville Row (I had helped a friend install John's unique transparent plexiglass desk).

I am high. It is late at night. On advice of my shrink, I try not to provoke antiweed Elizabeth, who is asleep in the bedroom.

I listen with headphones to the new Beatles song "Revolution."

John sings, pooh-poohing wanting a revolution, cynically singing, "We all want to change the world."

Treason! The Betrayal of the Musicians. The world will be lost.

Suddenly, three powerful white lights skim over the treetops from the north of the park. They head directly toward me. I see that the alien invasion from outer space has certainly begun.

When the blinding lights are a quarter mile away, they suddenly stop and descend straight down, below the treetops. All is black again. I feel as if the rug has been pulled from beneath me.

I do not wake Elizabeth when I climb into bed and hug her.

No way I'm going to face the aliens stoned.

The next morning, the *New York Times* reveals that President Richard Nixon arrived in Manhattan by helicopter last night.

An alien.

Jack Valenti (Harvard Business School, Class of 1948) and I are buckled into our seats in a small private plane, bouncing in some turbulence. Valenti was Lyndon Johnson's press secretary and now is president of the Motion Picture Association of America. He's sociable and loquacious, a tightly built, handsome little Texan in his mid-forties. Our destination is Dartmouth College for a preview screening and discussion of *The Revolutionary*. David Picker is an alumnus of Dartmouth.

Valenti says, "What's the point of the film?"

I say, "If you're not willing to die to advance your revolution, you're just a bullshit college kid trying to avoid the army. I don't think they want to hear that."

Valenti laughs.

I say, "But the most important thing in a political film is to allow the audience to make their own ethical choice."

He says, "I take no sides in my mind. I accept what is out there and try to work to achieve the goals that I am given by the organization."

I say, "You're kidding me. You could represent any political party?"

He says, "Yes, if that is the job."

I say, "That's hard to believe."

The little plane hits an air pocket with a big bump.

He says, "I flew a lot of bombing missions over Germany. Never knew if I'd live through a run. I became dispassionate. I became objective."

He is wiser than I know. He flew fifty-one missions in a B-25 medium bomber—the survival rate was 40 percent.

The Revolutionary ends as Jon holds a bomb, ready to blow up the reactionary judge who just condemned a radical in his court. We do not know if Jon throws it or not. The audience makes its own choice.

I make a brief appearance in the movie, reminding Jon's character of the German philosopher Johann Fichte: "A public intellectual's duty is to inspire the right sorts of feelings in their fellow citizens rather than transmit systems of knowledge or ethics."

The young Ivy Leaguers hoot angrily at this lady-and-the-tiger ending of the movie. In the two long years since we began *The Revolutionary,* radical ideas have emerged as mainstream ideology on campuses. They don't need to be educated. And they feel righteous. In this case, self-righteous.

Yet are these Dartmouth students ready to die for what they believe in?

Early the next year, Project VOLAR, for "Volunteer Army," is implemented.

Henceforth, poor kids will be the soldiers of the USA.

The US Congress responds to its constituency and takes care of the upset rich kids. Wealth of the few is growing and incomes of the many are not—but thank you for your service.

Each year, the Julius Rosenwald grandchildren spend most of their working hours evaluating to whom to gift nine-tenths of their yearly income—and thus maintain their classification by the IRS as "Philanthropists." Philanthropists are not required to pay any federal income tax and are able to sometimes secure benefits from their contributions. Of course, one-tenth of their yearly income is a quite a fortune. More than anyone needs.

I suggest to Elizabeth that we allot two weeks a year, max, to this chore.

I say, "We should manage the money and not let the money manage us."

We are twenty-five years old. She agrees.

We develop a procedure of tossing, from the couch, various requests into piles on top of large index cards demarcating areas of the rug as "$10,000"

($64,000 today), "$25,000," "$50,000," "$100,000," and "$250,000." Then the batches are picked up by a messenger from the office.

I tossed Harvard on the $25,000 pile. Money speaks loudly—Robert Gardner asks me to be on the Visiting Committee for the Arts. I pass.

Weeks after the New York opening of *Out of It, The Revolutionary* opens to good reviews from all the media and, like my first feature, to paltry box office. Six years of effort revealed in a month.

I have lunch with critic Penelope Gilliatt, who writes a particularly detailed and evocative review of *The Revolutionary* in the *New Yorker*.

Gilliatt alternates six-month stretches in the magazine with Pauline Kael, also a critic. Penelope is an Oscar nominee for her screenplay of Schlesinger's *Sunday Bloody Sunday*.

Ed does not like my idea to publish the entire Gilliatt review in a half page of the *New York Times*.

I say, "Everyone in the business will be impressed by how deeply United Artists believes in the film—why else would UA invest in such an unprecedented and expensive marketing ploy for a small film?"

Ed will not do it. This is the only time Elizabeth agrees that we use her money for my movie business. The ad is bought.

It works. Everyone is impressed. Pressman Williams is a solidified entity in the biz.

Ed is of course a blithe beneficiary of the albeit contradictory fight against the destructive grip of capitalism from within.

Also, I feel less invisible.

December. Twenty-one-year-old charismatic Panther Illinois chairman Fred Hampton is assassinated in his sleep in his apartment in the middle of the night by eight Chicago policemen—eventually, the courts rule justifiable homicide.

It is murder. The good guys are the bad guys.

Book Three

How to Get out of Hollywood

13

Revolution

1970

I go to the Morosco Theatre on Broadway to see David Storey's *Home,* directed by Lindsay Anderson. It is the same theater in which I saw my first play, *South Pacific,* when I was seven. I wear a light-blue work shirt with no tie under my Micucci sport jacket.

When Sir Ralph Richardson makes his entrance onstage, he is a parody of the grand Englishman. Just wacko. I laugh aloud. No one else in the New York audience does.

As he continues his fatuous dialogue, I laugh louder. Around me, the bourgeoisie turn with dirty looks and some say, "Shhhushh!"

And then Sir John Gielgud enters with an odd flourish. He sits with Sir Ralph at a small table downstage. A demented Gielgud prattles on. I laugh more, still alone.

Along with Sir Laurence Olivier, Richardson and Gielgud are the trinity of actors who dominate the British stage for much of the century. In this play, they are clearly playing parodies of themselves.

But after a while, the hostile stares of the nearby theatergoers become too intense and I get out of my seat, leave my row, and exit the building.

As soon as I get home, I call Lindsay in London, even though it is three in the morning.

I say, "Lindsay, I just had the worst experience I've ever had at the theater at *Home*!"

He says, "What happened?"

I say, "I was the only one laughing."

He says, "Oh, my."

I say, "They hounded me out of the theater."

He says, "Yes, of course. They paid good money for those tickets to see Gielgud and Richardson, and they want to see what they paid for—serious British theater."

Home is set in an insane asylum. The audience missed it.

On a Sunday morning, I enter 895 Park holding aloft the *New York Times* with a three-line headline stretched across all six columns on the front page—that's as big as the *Times* ever gets. It proclaims the antitrust victory of The People of the United States over the defendants Western Union and Western Union International.

After an eleven-year legal battle, the US Supreme Court finds that control of all communication between North America and Europe via satellites and also via cables is a monopoly, and therefore orders Western Union to divest one of these methods of transmission.

I say, "They got you now, Bill!" I smile kindly at my father-in-law, who owns both companies.

He smiles and says, "Come with me, Paul."

He leads me into a small vestibule office between the dining room and living room, closes a slatted wooden door, picks up the phone, dials, waits, and says, "Sid? Yeah, did you see the *Times* this morning? Ah-huh. Well, suppose you take the satellites and I'll take your steel mills?"

He listens and says, "Fine. I'll send some of my people down there Tuesday morning and you send some of your people up here. Okay. That's fine." He hangs up and smiles at me.

TIME STOPS.

There is something amiss with our democracy. It is a mesmerizing theatrical presentation that shields greedy capitalism. I am beyond amazed. I knew money is power but not on this scale of theft. The Supreme Court is impotent.

I am speechless.

The raw power of the mandarins takes place behind an opaque screen of propaganda—simply hidden from and even inconceivable to hoi polloi. The public trust is betrayed by a tiny handful of hoarding, unreachable oligarchs.

I am radicalized for life. No more, a conscious citizen accepting the inequities of the present. Hope is a dangerous barrier to courageous action. It is time now for the revolutionary to liberate the future.

"FBI Brands Black Panthers 'Most Dangerous of Extremists,'" reads the *New York Times* headline a week later.

"FBI director J. Edgar Hoover says in his fiscal 1969 annual report that the increased activity of 'violence-prone black extremists groups' had put more investigative responsibilities on the FBI."

"'Of these,' Hoover said, 'the Black Panther party, without question, represents the greatest threat to the internal security of the country.'" Sounds to me like J. Edgar is on the wrong side.

As any concentrator in the Department of Social Relations knows, Émile Durkheim, Karl Marx, and Max Weber were the architects of modern social science. In *Elementary Forms of Religious Life,* Durkheim wrote that when a clan gathers together they form a sacred group and often excitedly create a totem of a shared morality. I decide to make a documentary. It will star Eldridge Cleaver, author of the celebrated prison memoir *Soul on Ice.* The film will raise political consciousness and aid the legal defense of imprisoned Black Panther Party cofounder Bobby Seale, and New Haven Panther leader Ericka Huggins.

A few days later, we film the demonstration of twelve thousand people in New Haven in support of the prisoners. I sit in the back of a convertible and direct John Avildsen, who operates the camera. Julie Christie is incognito in the passenger seat. Her boyfriend, Warren Beatty, who played Clyde in *Bonnie and Clyde,* is six years older than me and wears sunglasses and drives slowly in the crowds. Power to the people.

Elbert "Big Man" Howard, a huge man with a prodigious Afro and one of the six original Panthers, introduces me to the New Haven Panther captain, short, wiry Don Cox. He brings us upstairs to a small narrow room in a two-story house in the neighborhood. There are green 16mm film rewinds on a cheap table adjacent to an old empty editing bin.

Big Man says, "You can work here with Newsreel. They work with us."

The Newsreel crowd of white radical filmmakers made an antiwar film of protestors storming the Pentagon.

I say, "I don't want to work with other filmmakers."

He says, "They're okay."

I say, "They don't really understand."

Big Man says, "They'll do what we tell them, or we'll cut their hands off." I believe him.

I say, "I want to make the film that says what you want it to say, not some angry white guys. I'll pay for it and I want no credit."

Don Cox says, "Okay. No Newsreel people."

I say, "I just want the honor to serve and learn."

Big Man says, "Right on."

The next day, Big Man says, "Eldridge says you gotta go see him."

I say, "He's in Algeria."

He says, "Yeah."

National Guardsmen open fire on protestors and kill four students at Kent State University. Madness is in the air. The next day Liz, Michael Braun, and I arrive at JFK for the flight to Algiers.

Waiting for us at the sidewalk are Black Panthers Don Cox and Big Man. So are Kathleen Cleaver, smart as a whip, and observant Angela Davis. They are all dressed as conservative businesspeople, with their Afros now shaved.

At Orly, the Paris police escort me off the plane and hold me alone in a locked room until our flight to Marseilles is ready. I do not see any of my traveling companions. At the Marseilles airport, police again put me in temporary isolation. I realize this trip is no secret (years later I learn that the FBI's COINTELPRO, or counterintelligence program, had infiltrated the Panthers).

In a field outside Algiers, before anybody else shows up, Liz and I discover we did not bring an empty take-up reel for the tape recorder—unprofessional. I take a full 1,200-foot tape reel and place a pencil through the core and Liz runs to the other side of the field and back several times until I have an empty reel spinning on the pencil. We quickly gather the recording tape into a ball, which we duct-tape tightly and throw into the woods.

Just as we finish, Eldridge drives up. He wears a safari jacket and khaki pants and wears his glasses. He has a small goatee on his chin. I encourage him to speak with honesty. The 16mm camera is on a tripod, and soon we begin exposing film.

But Eldridge has no authentic presence in front of the camera. The fugitive minister of information and head of the International Section of the Panthers—in Algiers only because Fidel banished him from Havana when El Comandante discovered his mistress in bed with this man—speaks in a dull monotone like an emotionally cutoff professor. After a half-dozen attempts to get him to relax, I stop shooting. The camera does not love him.

Diminutive North Koreans in black suits visit Eldridge each morning in his second-floor apartment in a two-story house outside of town. North Koreans? We must wait for them to leave in their black limos before we go in for our early-afternoon meetings.

Eldridge informs us that the Panthers plan a kamikaze attack on New York City—the "Flash of Lightning"—for June 19, in four weeks. There is no time to raise money for Bobby Seale.

Cleaver is confused by Michael's repeated suggestion that Eldridge go back to college and get his degree, and taken aback by Elizabeth's sharp question, "How do we know if you get power, you will rule any better than Nixon?"

My mind explodes with these illuminations that my friends lack revolutionary spirit.

Elizabeth's question, however, stymies Cleaver for some time.

He says, "You're right. You don't know. It's a matter of trust."

And each evening, Liz, Michael, and I are escorted past the six black German shepherds on the staircase while Eldridge makes telephone calls to Panther cofounder Huey P. Newton in the States.

On the way back to our hotel in town, we drive around the plaza where so many French soldiers were killed by the revolutionary Algerians, re-created by Gillo Pontecorvo in his *Battle of Algiers*. The plaza is empty of life and movement, eerily silent.

Don Cox says, "This is what it will be like. Nobody will be on the streets of Manhattan except cops and Panthers." Movies aren't scary. Life is scary.

We agree that the impending surprise attack makes the documentary irrelevant.

Eldridge says, "Your job in New York is to identify and locate power stations. And figure out possible locations for field hospitals."

I say, "Just in Manhattan?"

He says, "Yes. How much money do you have left?"

I roll my eyes up, as if adding numbers. I need a number that makes sense but does not reveal our deep pockets.

I say, "Seventeen thousand."

He says, "Chump change. David Hilliard is giving a speech at the Americana Hotel in a couple of weeks. Meet him in the men's room and give him the cash. They'll need it."

The "historical cause" of the rift between Elizabeth and me (that is, like the shooting of Archduke Franz Ferdinand in Sarajevo "causing" World War I) is this seventeen thousand dollars destined for the Panther's chief of staff.

Back in Algiers from that afternoon with Eldridge, Liz stops me as we walk in a narrow alley.

Liz says, "I will not give the Panthers anything."

I say, "What do you mean?"

She says, "I'm not going to do it."

I say, "It's a cheap way to get out gracefully."

She says, "I don't care."

I say, "I think we may be in real danger."

She says, "I don't think so."

I say, "I'll use my own money."

Have I been sharing my bed with the wrong woman?

Eldridge lectures us on the postulate of North Korean leader Kim Il Sung: that anything is justified "if it advances the revolution a half step." I see that if the plotters discover Liz is an heiress (they think she's my sound person), we will at least be kidnapped for ransom.

On my back in the grass on the *croisette* of Algiers, across the street from our hotel, I hear each breath move inside my body. Below the dome sky, the high palm fronds wave in rhythm in the light wind. I feel the lovely long trunk bend and sway, and I feel each blade of grass touching my skin—all is present. I love that tree. I love the blue sky.

I realize that my fear of death at the hands of my new comrades is no greater nor different from my fear of using the wrong utensil to eat my lobster at Sunday-morning brunch with my legendary in-laws.

Fear is only an emotion. "Motions," Shakespeare called them.

They change. I watch the clouds drifting eastward.

These bones shall live.

Cleaver escorts us to the airport. My lie to Eldridge about how much money we had left bothers me. And my certainty that I will not do the site research he delegated to me.

We hug at the departure gate. I see behind him the small terminal hall and feel like a traitor.

I leave the exposed film in an airport locker at a stopover in Paris for the Parisian Panthers to retrieve. I don't want it found by the feds at JFK.

In the Americana Hotel auditorium in Manhattan, I see only Black faces.

Then I see a white one. It is Rodge Cohen—who had lent me his car our senior year the night Liz admitted to me that she was so rich.

I make my way down the rows and sit next to him, about tenth row, center.

I say, "Hello, Rodgie."

He says, "Pah-wol? What are you doin' he-ah?"

He was born in Charleston, West Virginia.

I say, "You'll never believe this, Rodge . . ."

I launch into a full description of my detention at Orly and Marseilles, the Panthers and North Koreans in Algiers, and the upcoming Flash of Lightning.

When I finish, I say, "What are you doing here, Rodgie?"

"Oooh," he says, "I'm with Ahh-me Counter-Intelligence."

My idiot's chest pounds, but I do not have a heart attack.

I end this long journey home in the basement men's room, when I hand David Hilliard a manilla envelope with my cash.

At the Pressman Williams Enterprises office on the Pressman Toy Company floor of the Toy Building, our barely five-foot-tall young secretarial school graduate from Brooklyn is scared when she is notified by the FBI that they want to come to the office to interview her.

In the *Black Panther* newspaper that is distributed on the streets of Manhattan, the slim new issue features a centerfold, suitable for framing, "What We Want, What We Believe In." Cleaver had told me it is being published "so people will remember what we died for."

I call Uncle Stanley in Saint Louis who married bongo-bongo-I-don't-want-to-leave-the-Congo Aunt Sydel.

He says, "Make sure to have another person with the secretary when she is interviewed by the FBI. They're more careful if there's a corroborating witness."

I call the family office in the Chrysler Building and request fifty thousand dollars in traveler's checks. The largest denomination is one hundred dollars. My signature quickly becomes uniformly indecipherable as it takes me the resentful afternoon to sign them all.

I put my passport, cash, and some necessities in an attaché case.

I say to Elizabeth, "If there's a Flash of Lightning, don't look for me. I'll be going straight to Kennedy to Heathrow. I'll be at the Dorchester the next day."

Ed says, "I've got the Brooklyn Toy Factory guarded."

I walk on the streets of Manhattan ready to run, an enigmatic outlaw. I have no will to fight.

Then the victorious revolutionary Algerians offer Eldridge the luxury of the old French embassy. The Flash is called off. No sound or fury. Cleaver moves into the posh mansion. Visitors Timothy Leary and his wife, Rosemary, are put under "house arrest" when Eldridge gets fed up with their elitism. They pay to get out.

I have been glad to be of use but feel ridiculous. My bones need to be fleshed out again in a new way.

14

After the Revolution

1970–1971

1970

The phone rings in the middle of the afternoon. *The Revolutionary* has recently opened in a theater on Fifty-Seventh Street in Manhattan. I answer.

The caller says, "Is this Paul Williams?"

I say, "Yes it is. Who are you?"

He says, "Hello, I am Orson Welles. You know, I don't like many movies, but I loved your movie." Citizen Kane is on the line. He loves my movie.

Later, Sylvester Stallone says, "Your shots are too long. No shot should be longer than three seconds. That's how long a tiger looks at anything."

I say, "How's the audience going to learn how to fall in love?"

The critic Roger Ebert gives it a five-star review in the *Chicago Sun-Times*. He says, "There are things that I can't possibly describe, having to do with conversational nuances and the actor's small, unconscious movements, that make you realize how many movie actors just stand there and say their lines to you."

What role am I to play?

I am dressed for the awards night of the Sorrento Film Festival in a wide-lapel, four-button sleeve, double-vented white suit. Hans Koningsberger, my Communist screenwriter, says, "That is a fine suit."

I take it off and give it to the tall writer. He admires himself in a mirror. I put on blue jeans and a wife beater undershirt. My hair is down to my bare shoulders. Fashion is drama without a plot.

Marty (*Who's That Knocking at My Door*) Scorsese, Francis Ford (*The Rain People*) Coppola, and I walk together on the red-carpeted streets to the opera house. They are in black tie. The kids on the street cheer me.

I sit alone on a folding chair against a wall in the wings. In the center of the stage, a score of tuxedoed famous directors—including George Stevens, Elia (*On the Waterfront*) Kazan, Sam (*Major Dundee*) Peckinpah, Gillo Pontecorvo, Vittorio (*Bicycle Thieves*) De Sica, Francis and Marty—crowd around just one man.

In the thicket of directors, I can only see in the center a wide-brimmed black hat on top of the man's head.

Eventually Black Hat had enough adulation from the pie of Italian and American directors that surrounds him, and the crowd clears a slice to allow the man out.

He walks directly toward me as they all stare in tableau behind him.

Federico Fellini sits down. My new friend expounds about seeing, about expanded consciousness, about clowns. His films at this point include *La Strada*, *Nights of Cabiria*, *La Dolce Vita*, and *8½*.

He says, "Acid! Acid! All they want to talk about is acid! I never took acid! Who needs acid?" I second it, that perception can be extraordinary without any consciousness-expanding substances. I feel less alone. I like this guy.

Soon, the curtains open to reveal a sea of gowns next to penguins. The Eurovision TV cameras are live. The older directors are introduced and line up on risers on the stage.

Gillo Pontecorvo, the director of my favorite film, *The Battle of Algiers*, introduces me, "Paul Williams, for *The Revolutionary*."

I walk onstage dressed in my eccentric outfit, and Gillo hands me a gray-and-silver statue with what looks an olive with a pimento entangled inside a metal vine. As I walk to take my place on stage, I make a *V* with my right hand and walk it into close-up in the lens of the TV camera that's on me. Then I step onto the risers, Federico right behind me.

Frank Shakespeare, head of the US Information Agency, takes center stage after the awards are given, and says, "One of the films made by a young American director here does not represent the reality of the United States at this time."

I take my small suede jacket that I've been carrying all night and start to wave it over my head as Shakespeare continues his bullshit.

The audience of swells awakens with murmurs and then I feel a few fist-bops on my head. I stop waving my coat. I turn my head and look up.

Federico raises his finger to his lips and says, "Shhhhhhh."

I smile with tight lips at the Maestro, but I become still. We both don't know who I am.

That night at a private party on a hilltop overlooking Naples, I have a chat with a bright and beautiful Cliffie. She's a charming flirt. Scorsese and Coppola are inside the brightly lit villa with the host of Italians.

We lean against a low stone terrace wall, a short distance away. Kathleen is on her summer vacation from Harvard. I from Manhattan.

Soon, we jump into a cab to go to my hotel on the Bay.

As our cab pulls in, a long black limousine expertly cuts us off, braking hard to a stop.

A thin, well-coiffed elderly woman jumps out the far side. She is followed by two large men in dark suits.

She says, "Get over here, immediately, young lady. What do you think you're doing?"

She strides to us and I recognize Ethel Kennedy as she takes her daughter in hand.

The Secret Servicemen with the two Kennedy women disappear into the limo that backs away from my taxi and speeds away into the night.

And just who do I think I am?

As I walk toward the hotel I am intercepted by Sam Peckinpah—the director who changed the idea of the Western with the seminal bloody brilliance of his *Wild Bunch*. Before Peckinpah, when a guy on the screen was shot, he would grab his chest and die. Peckinpah introduced the cascading blood squib that Quentin (*Kill Bill*) Tarantino later made his trademark. At the screening of his film for the studio executives, Sam got up and pissed on the screen.

He says, "Kid, let's go for a walk."

We amble along the glistening midnight cobblestones and he heaps praises on *The Revolutionary*. I like him.

He says, "Welcome to the club."

I am considered a competent director by the best, but I don't like the movie business.

Who do I think I am?

Liz gives up full-time painting and goes to Columbia Business School.

One day, she invites another biz student, Harvey W. Wallender III, to our apartment and lunch, on our custom hand-decorated glazed plates that we had shipped after a visit to Biot, a medieval fortified village in the French mountains, above Antibes.

I ferret out that Harvey had been a Green Beret lieutenant in October 1967 and that he was a leader of the Eighth Special Forces Group in the unfortified mountains of Bolivia, and in a box canyon summarily executed Ernesto "Che" Guevara.

Please pass me the salt, Harvey.

Che said the revolutionary lives so dangerously, his survival is a miracle. I have an inkling. Perhaps I am delusional.

Che said, "Know this now, you are killing a man." And they shot him dead. Revolution is a dangerous business.

While I was editing *The Revolutionary*, I met a young American with strong hashish. I gave some of my stash to Danton Rissner, head of Warner Bros. in London. Young Danny has a great time hooking up European producers to the American studio for co-productions.

At the Cannes Film Festival a month later in an elegant hotel dining room, he turned on all the top Warner executives who smoked openly and joyously. Danny told them he had gotten the hash from me. He tells me that he was frightened that they would be arrested, but the executives blew him off.

Now, as the FBI interviews our secretary, I get a call from Warner's head of production in Burbank, John Calley, asking me if I want to direct a film about pot by ex-*Crimson* editor Michael Crichton. I say, "Yes. I'll fly out of here on the next plane."

I read the book, *Dealing: or the Berkeley-to-Boston, Forty-Brick Lost-Bag Blues,* on the airplane. It's really not my cup of tea. But I am in boiling water.

I am in his office on the lot. Calley's office is the size of a large living room—carrots, celery, hard-boiled eggs on the coffee table.

He says, "I have a big boat in the marina. Plenty of food and guns. Ready to go." His closest buddies are the directors Stanley (*2001*) Kubrick and Mike (*The Graduate*) Nichols. John Calley is the class act of Hollywood.

I say, "The Panthers think Los Angeles is the worst place in the country for an attack—too spread out, too many police spaced on a moving grid with quick response times—squad cars can be at any given spot in five minutes. The Afro-American community is contained in a ghetto—a Black in Beverly Hills is an easy mark. And LA cops shoot first, not like New York, where they first try to talk you into putting your gun down."

He says, "I've got a nice place in Hawaii."

I say, "I think LA is safe."

He asks what I need to direct the film based on the novel by Crichton and his brother, Doug.

I don't want a repeat of the enervating productions of *Out of It* and *The Revolutionary*.

I say, "At least twelve weeks to shoot and a professional crew, with a great AD. And soon. The FBI is starting to bother me in New York."

He laughs.

I say, "And Ed will be the producer."

He says, "How much can you guys make it for?"

How I answer will become a lock on the budget of the film. If it is too high, he will turn it down. It the number is too low, I won't be able to have a reasonable production. Not unlike Eldridge's question in Algeria.

I say, "Two million three" ($13 million today).

He says, "Okay, we're set."

Marvin Josephson is CEO of Warner Bros. and has to sign off on any green-lit project.

I walk to the appointed door. Inside is a duplex suite, a luxurious apartment with no indication of a workplace evident. It is air-conditioned cold.

I see a short man in gray cashmere pajamas and black slippers slowly descend the interior staircase, like Vivien Leigh in *Gone with the Wind*. It is the middle of the day. This clearly must be Marvin.

He sits down on a velvet couch. He smiles and is soft-spoken. The vibe may be sexual. I don't know. He makes no overt move. I dip a carrot in some concoction and chew. A secretary brings water.

He says he is happy to hear I am making the film. I thank him. I leave shortly.

I'm confused, but it seems okay.

Ed says, "They're going to cancel the film if you don't cast the lead in a week."

I say, "I can't find anyone." I am not enthusiastic about making this film, and certainly not without a good cast.

Ed says, "We've got to make a film, now."

I say, "I don't care. Hire the last guy who came into my office to read."

He says, "Who's that?"

I say, "I don't know. Call the secretary."

Ed calls the secretary and then the chief of casting at Warner, Nessa Hyams. He tells her to sign Robert Lyons, a good actor but not smelling of Harvard, who had recently played a supporting role in a film starring Elliott Gould and Candy Bergen called *Getting Straight*.

I continue to see actors in my bungalow at the Beverly Hills Hotel. The biggest pot dealers in North America have heard about the movie. They come visit me, tell me their best stories, and give me their best bud. It is so strong that I pass out in between meetings. I don't remember much.

A short actor comes in. We improvise wildly for an hour. At one point the actor is on his knees imploring me with clever words to do a dope run, when Ed comes in the door. He sees the young man on his knees in front of me.

Ed says, "What? Oh. I'm sorry."

He hurriedly turns to go right back out.

I say, "Ed! It's okay, come in."

He just stutters to himself.

The actor says, "What do you think is going on? I'm not giving him a blow job!"

I say, "Ed, don't be silly."

He walks out and shuts the door.

The actor says, "Jesus Christ. He thinks I'm gonna give a blowjob!"

I laugh, but am unhappy with Ed.

This flummoxed actor is perfect for the lead role of the Harvard pot smoker—as well as being smart, he looks like he's smart, and he's quick and funny.

I say, "Don't worry about Ed. You're a wonderful actor and you're perfect for this role. Unfortunately I can't remember anything right now. These dope dealers keep giving me their best stuff. I know you're an unknown actor and to you, I'm a big director, but please call me tomorrow and say, 'I'm the actor you saw yesterday who was just like Jon Voight when he came into the room on *Out of It*. You said to call you to remind you to hire me.' Say that."

I give him my personal telephone number.

Warner Bros. signs Robert Lyons before Richard Dreyfuss calls back.

I am still focused on getting Dreyfuss in the lead and fly with him to New York to improvise with John Lithgow (Class of 1967)—whom I've cast as his best friend, the dealer. Dreyfuss and Lithgow improvise brilliantly together. They sound like Harvard roommates. I know the film will work.

I fly back to Los Angeles and tell Ed we have our leads. I am finally excited.

On the Warner backlot, we climb up the steps of the big blue scaffold used in Clint Eastwood's *Hang 'Em High*.

I have a vivid premonition that I am swinging in a noose as we reach the high platform.

Ed says, "Look, if I tell Warner to pay off one little-known actor and hire another unknown actor—it's nuts. They'll call off the whole show."

I am stunned.

I say, "Dreyfuss and Lithgow will make the film work."

He says, "We've hired Robert Lyons. He's getting fifty thousand dollars."

I say, "That's nothing. The film is going to cost two million three."

He says, "We must make a film now. It's been over a year since we made a movie. They'll cancel the film! Pressman Williams must make a film, now."

I say, "The film won't work."

He says, "We have no choice."

I am doomed in muttering defeat by my expert. I am at fault.

1971

Barbara Hershey, the leading lady, stands with me, her director. Barbara and I wait for the lights to be ready for camera on a street corner in Boston.

She says, "Paul, you don't look happy. You don't look like you feel good about what you're doing. Are you?"

I say, "What does feeling good have to do with anything?"

She says, "I never do anything if it doesn't feel good."

I say, "That is such an alien notion to me. I do my job. I get it done. Fun is never a consideration. The question never occurs to me."

She says, "Really?"

I say, "I hardly enjoy anything, except sex."

She laughs.

I say, "You only do what feels good? That's it? No room for suffering?"

She has the most charming smile I've ever seen, which spreads across her face—and leaves an undying impression.

She says, "Yup. Don't do it if it doesn't feel good."

I never forget this concept either.

I walk along the busy streets of downtown Toronto.

Robert Lyons says, "Tell me what looks really real."

I say, "That building looks really real."

He says, "What else looks really real?'

I say, "That car looks really real."

"What else?"

"The sidewalk looks really real."

"What else?"

This catechism is unrelenting for two hours.

Then I say, "Nothing looks really real. Everything looks like props on a set!"

He smiles. I learn from Bobby Lyons.

Shakespeare said, "All the world's a stage." Gurus urge detachment, but shrinks might call it dissociation. It feels good to me.

Barbara says, "Can my boyfriend David come visit the set?"

I say, "Sure, why not?"

She says, "Most people are scared of him. Last week, he got arrested in LA for breaking into some mansion to play their piano. They think he's a madman."

I say, "Is he?"

She says, "He's cool."

I say, "Of course."

I have never watched his wildly popular TV show, *Kung Fu*, in which he plays the spiritual warrior, the monk "Grasshopper" Kwai Chang Caine. He has popularized the martial arts and Eastern philosophy in the West.

The day of David Carradine's arrival, the set is tense and excited in anticipation. We are shooting at the Toronto Zoo.

My arms lean on a low chain link fence behind a moat and, on the other side, a keeper who sprays a big hot bear.

I turn my lowered head and see his cowboy boots on the macadam approach. I straighten up, turn.

We look into each other's eyes.

Eventually, I smile.

I say, "I like your boots."

David's eyes twinkle.

He says, "I like your sandals."

I say, "Let's switch."

He says, "You want to wear my shoes?"

I say, "Yeah!"

He says, "Let's do it."

He laughs, takes off his boots, as I slip out of my sandals. My sandals slide right onto his feet.

Barbara smiles.

The monk's boots fit me.

In LA, David Carradine throws the mushrooms into a pot of water and picks up his guitar. He sings a song he wrote about me, "He Never Takes His Glasses Off." Then he puts on Robert Johnson's *Ramblin' on My Mind*. And we listen to Johnson's blues as he cleans out the strychnine from the well-soaked peyote mushrooms—my first consciousness-expanding drug.

Barbara and David and I begin to swallow them whole. They stop at six "buttons," but David says, "You can keep taking them until you start to feel nauseous."

I obey and stop at twenty.

After an hour, through the living room window,

[SPARE ME]

I see Native American bead-like patterns. On a giant screen that hovers in the sky over Hollywood, I watch a drive-in graphic art movie.

I look away but the screen does not move with my eyes—as my grandmother did in London.

Inside this wood cabin in Laurel Canyon, beyond the kitchen bar, I see a mattress on the living room floor. I look back into the sky—the geometric bead patterns still appear inside the floating rectangle.

So, clearly this is not a hallucination from my brain. It is a hologram of another simultaneous reality that I see.

I think, "It seems that I have gone psychotic. This is what psychosis is—I may be like this for the rest of my life."

"But, I feel happy. I feel good. I don't mind if I'm in this state, the rest of my life. It's better than my life has been."

I surrender to what is going on in front of my eyes. Peyote has put my mind at ease.

Then the pattern on the screen changes: bead designs or sand paintings follow one after another for an hour.

And then the empty space in the living room fills up with pink, yellow, and blue weightless, inch-long, floating, needle-sized lights.

I look at David and Barbara—a stream of needle-lights travel through the space from my eyes to reach their eyes, and vice versa when they look at me. When I speak, I see the flow of this rapid river of tricolored needles stream from my mouth to them across the room.

After twenty minutes, I look down and see nine short lengths of hose—about two inches in diameter—growing out of my body. Each hose lengthens and bends upward like thick stems. Then spheres grow from the ends of the nine stems, from the size of a fig to the size of a grapefruit. These grapefruits are pink or yellow or blue. They have no weight but you cannot see through them—their pigment is intense.

Barbara sits on the mattress fifteen feet away from me. I know that. But when I turn and look at her, I see only a swirling mass of "electrons" race in a six-foot oval path around the "nucleus," where she sits. The extraordinary electrons are pink, yellow, and blue and they swirl around and around at warp speed.

When I look back, an antelope stands in front of me. The hairless black snout is right in front of my eyes.

I say, "David . . . ?"

A voice says, "Yeah . . ."

I say, "I hear your voice, I know you're there, but I'm looking at an antelope with a big rack of antlers, fur, and the whole business. I can't see you."

He says, "Far out!"

I say, "What do you see?"

He says, "I see you, Paul."

I say, "Whoa."

I look over to the giant swirling atom on the mattress.

I say, "Barbara, what do you see?"

She says, "I see you."

Barbara wants to know what she looks like. She does not like the description I offer of the swirl of orbiting electrons. I think she wants to be an animal too.

At dawn the next day without sleep, we are outside the house. We stand on the lower plateau by a tipi. A tortoise shell forms in the sky above, a complete geodesic dome. Buckminster Fuller surely just copied it.

That night, back in the living room, a shape in the far corner near the door captures my attention. I focus. It is a man in a black cape and a large black hat who sits on the floor with his head down, his arms folded across his knees.

I think, "This looks to me like the Grim Reaper . . . 'Nevermore.'"

I ask David and Barbara, "Do you see a guy dressed in black on the floor near the door?"

They say, "No."

I say, "He's giving me the creeps. Let's move over here."

We move toward the kitchen.

The antelope with David's voice says, "Don't worry."

Suddenly, the man in black appears, rising behind the antelope's antlers. He looks at me from the shadows. I can't make out his features.

I say, "Whoa, this is getting a little too much for me. I really don't want to deal with this man here."

The man's eyes watch me for a few moments more before he turns and walks to the cabin door and out into the whisper of the wind.

I am glad I am still alive.

Months later from the peyote literature I learn that I should have asked him, Mescalito himself, to lead me through the door to give me my next lesson in the evolution of my spirit.

The next day, David says, "Stare at the sun. It's okay—it won't hurt you." I remember Jon's character in *The Revolutionary* quoting La Rochefoucauld, "Neither the sun nor death can be looked at steadily."

I know I will burn my retina and optic nerve. I take a quick look, then gradually longer and longer—and, lo and behold, there is no afterimage when I look away or when I close my eyes. The sun looks just like Van Gogh's—the licks of flame form a circle around the golden center. It shines into my eye and my heart. No damage done.

Later, the antelope morphs back into the corporeal David. And Barbara the giant atom turns back into Barbara the smiling beauty. The tortoise shell dome starts to dim. All the stars still stream bright trails in the hemisphere above.

At dawn, the stars fade away. The final remnants of the tortoise shell disappear.

[RESUME]

Peyote is a feast for the eyes and an education for them.

I feel cleansed and simply willing to be and willing to allow others to be, not so full of myself, humbled in my knowingness.

I later look at Native American peyote paintings. The grapefruits and the hoses and the tricolored "needles," the sitting man under the black sombrero—they are all there. It has been recorded for centuries.

A brain can tune in to holographic wavelengths of different universes besides the one that it has known as reality. Like a tuner, able to dial in different frequencies? How many more channels are on the dial?

Another opening, another show. Anything can happen.

When I fly back to Manhattan, I am full of wonder of this hologram beyond memory, beyond the legacy of the rational Age of Enlightenment. My mind may be far greater than my brain.

Liz gives the cook a few days off and we make no requests for the drivers. The novelty of my new, more awakened vibration is accompanied by the synchronous passion that is always so easy for us. We both have a good time. Just the two of us.

On the third day, however, Elizabeth sits down with me on our dark-yellow and blue living room couch by the sliding glass window to the balcony that overlooks Central Park.

She says, "You've been so happy since you got back, I didn't have the heart to tell you—I want a divorce."

I look down at the broad swath of green treetops that fill the two miles north from us to 110th Street. I look at her—what poor timing. She is not divorcing the same personality she loved and married. She has changed too.

A family life in Lakewood, in upstate New York, is now what she wants. She thinks my smoking pot has affected my potency. She is upset that she has not gotten pregnant. She needs to settle down and have a family. When she asks, I say I am not eager to have my sperm tested. Afraid of what it might reveal?

And she will not like hearing about my visions on twenty peyote buttons. How ironic—I humbly believe that now I can repair any earthly relationship.

But I know from Liz's certain tone that her decision had been vetted thoroughly with the family and the shrink and the lawyers. There is no compromise. She can't. I can't. But I can sacrifice.

I cry for a few minutes in sorrow not anger. This is my life. It is what's happening.

I say I will acquiesce. I understand how she feels, and I feel that I do not want to hurt her feelings any more than I already have. I know I have to go away.

Liz is concerned because at a Sunday brunch at her parents' a year earlier, her older sister, Nina, had laughed at her ex-husband for taking only fifty thousand dollars to let her swiftly out of their marriage. Everyone at the table joined in the laughter at this lowball demand. He was judged a fool. I know that she knows that I know. Not to mention the prenup amount.

I say, "Don't worry. I don't want any money."

She looks relieved. I will not call a lawyer. She is my best friend. But she is gone.

And I am not afraid that I will never walk anywhere again without two inches of carpet between my foot and the ground. I am sad and restless. I know I need something else. Give it away.

I know I have to go.

Before leaving Manhattan and its stone skyscrapers, I visit Jon Voight.

He says, "Don't go to LA. They'll eat you up alive. You're not strong enough."

Jon's warning corresponds to what I have intuited: ever since the beginning, I have developed a profound detachment—I have a tough core that usually outperforms when challenged but I have no real willpower to be paramount. I am no Nietzsche. All winds blow me—disaster after disaster, but there are so many it may look like a life lived dangerously. A woman's embrace is my default position.

Jon says, "What are you afraid of?"

I am silent. His instincts are accurate.

My childish task has been to achieve—but I am afraid that anyone will find out my real name. My task has been to make money—but I am afraid I will amass more than my father. Fame and fortune were falsehoods that channeled into the truth of uncertain revolution, but now that alternative is dissolving into the miraculous.

When I see my father briefly just before I leave, he says, "You know, money can take care of a lot of problems in a lifetime." But my successes to date have been so wildly beyond whatever he dreamed of for me that now he speaks tentatively to Goldberg's monster—as impotent as Doctor Frankenstein beholding what he made. Only this is not science fiction; this is my life untethered from the American rat race in which I believed. Going for broke. Peace of mind.

15

Into the Unknown

1971

I head south at the invitation of ATW, Andrew T. Weil, MD, to his farm outside of Washington, DC. Andy is based at the National Institute of Mental Health doing esoteric drug research. If I want to know, I must look.

His ranch house in the nearby countryside is adjacent to a large swimming pool and forest.

We fill beach balls from a fifty-five-gallon tank of nitrous oxide. Then we inhale and hold the gas in our lungs—and travel into the emptiness of starry outer space. The trip lasts less than four minutes, and the return is dependably safe, like the pendulum of a grandfather clock that swings out and returns back to the center. We practice the technique until it is comfortable.

On the third day, a group of Harvard classmates, now in coveted junior positions in the highest executive and judicial branches of the federal government, arrive with their young wives for an afternoon of the unobtainable wonder drug, MDA.

All swallow the tan granules in gelatin capsules with water. There is fruit by the poolside and the dozen initiates sit on the edge and dangle their white legs in the water.

After the first hour, I begin to feel warm all over. From acting workshops, I am familiar with a group that gets high naturally. These Harvardians at Andy's are new to it. I shine on.

One of the women walks up to me.

She says, "I want you to make love to me."

I look at her wide eyes and open face.

I say, "No, your husband is here."

Soon after, another's girlfriend makes the same request.

Their directness confuses me. I will not go off with them in front of their partners. This is dangerous. I just walk away into the forest (years later, a much less hallucinogenic version of MDA—MDMA—becomes notorious, known as Ecstasy).

I understand this: I can feel my heart. And it feels wide open.

My feelings about love have been the sum of totemic thoughts, not feelings. If a woman had the required faces on the totem pole—Intelligence, Humor, Beauty, Sensuality, Pleasant Speaking Voice, Good Grammar, and Strong Vocabulary—she qualified for love in my multiple-choice exam and I therefore loved her. But in this new realm of the pure feeling of the heart, there is no thought at all. The simplicity overwhelms me. A major refinement of my consciousness. I am Lazarus, as they say, come from the dead.

Alone in the forest, the pendulum of the grandfather swings up to its farthest extension and stops for several hours. My heart is open with no effort.

A huge tree with purely pigmented leaves and strong supple branches is in front of me—I hug the trunk of my new acquaintance in a serene love, deeply rooted in the ground. In the secret ministry of the forest, we communicate on a cosmic and cellular level. It's like some kind of cure for something that I don't even know I have.

I understand Hermann Hesse's perception, "In their highest boughs the world rustles, their roots rest in infinity; but they do not lose themselves there, they struggle with all the force of their lives for one thing only: to fulfill themselves according to their own laws, to build up their own form, to represent themselves. Nothing is holier, nothing is more exemplary than a beautiful, strong tree."

After two hours, time leaks into this transcendental high. I can walk now and wander the forest until I see a clearing that draws me near. The pendulum has descended, passed midpoint, and ascends to a lesser height. But it is potent.

I see Andy. He sits on a Navajo blanket as the sun rakes the tall grass. He eats fruit from a large wooden bowl. I sit down next to the big round calm being from the Animal Kingdom and, after a moment, throw my arms around him and start to kiss him. I'm a good kisser. I feel no inhibition.

Andy says, "Paul, think of the ashes afterward—not the fire during."

It is an effective tonic that cools my passion.

Pure love is more unconditionally pure than I could ever imagine before this day. Quietly amazing and pansexual. I have entered new territory.

Twenty-four hours later, I fly to LAX (designed by yet another Paul Williams, the first Black architect west of the Mississippi, who perfected his ability to render his plans upside down while sitting across the table from his bigoted clients who did not want to sit next to him in the 1920s so they could see what he had in mind, right side up). I check into the Chateau Marmont, rent a car, and drive for an hour up the coast to Malibu to Jennifer Salt's house on Nicholas Beach. Jon and Jennifer split up many months ago. I admire Jennifer.

I knock. A gorgeous woman with lovely eyes, who is not Jennifer, opens the door. My heart commences to palpitate wildly.

I take her hand and press it on my freakishly pounding chest.

I say, "Do you feel it?"

She says, "Yeah!"

I say, "Gee whiz. This has never happened to me before and I think I'm going to die. Right here, of a heart attack. My god. Maybe we should take a walk."

She looks at me wide-eyed and says, "Okay. Sure."

We walk down to the beach. The MDA is still manifestly in my system.

She says, "Are you feeling better?"

I say, "My heart is racing but I am alive. Thanks."

She sits with me on the sand looking out on the Pacific. We talk honestly of our experience and feelings about love, divorce, drugs, acting, revolution, and consciousness. Happily, as the sun sets, we are enough of one mind that we come to the certain conclusion that we should live together.

She is Jennifer's roommate, Margot Kidder—later *Superman* Christopher Reeve's girlfriend, Lois Lane.

Margot has a chronic breathing problem. After a couple of days I tell her to stop wearing the tight broad belts she cinches to accent her hourglass shape. Her condition is cured. We are in the full breath of love.

I am just in the first days of my brave new world.

I fly to Cannes for the Festival and have lunch with Jack Nicholson on the Croisette. He is there with his first directorial effort, *Drive, He Said,* with Karen Black and Bill Tepper, among others.

I say, "I like moments when a character appears foolish. When he breaks the expected pattern. He allows the cracks in his personality to show. It makes fresh how going as utterly competent is really a defensive act. He is vulnerable."

In his next film, Bob Rafelson's *The King of Marvin Gardens,* there is a shot where suave Jack jumps in his car and speeds away.

I see him again at a friend's house.

He says, "Did you see my coat? It sticks out of the door after I close it? That was for you."

I say, "I did! And I liked it. Yes, that was good."

He says, "But Paul, really, you should never step on your own dick."

I'm not so sure. What's the big deal?

I leave for Manhattan to meet with Ed, and I'm eager to see my peyote buddies again, Barbara and David. They ask me if they should do *Boxcar Bertha* with a young director named Martin Scorsese. A Boy Scout is helpful. I tell them not to miss the chance, even though it is a lowbrow, low-budget production of Roger Corman. Marty's next film after that is *Mean Streets.*

In Ed's apartment on Thirty-Fourth Street, Marty and Brian sit down with Ed and me to discuss Brian's new idea.

De Palma says, "Look, I'll keep ripping off Hitchcock, Marty can do his street movies, and Paul can do his sensitive films. We do it together as a New United Artists."

He's going the wrong way, for me. I don't like the idea of being even more of a product. I have difficulty with people every day—I feel pinned when they speak to some formulated idea of me. I observe them from a spot next to me.

I do not like "the business" of movies. I am uncomfortable with this plan to become more productive, more famous—a lifelong brand.

I am still not who I am. In this ruthless system, who am I? A detached entity with a public identity, the Boy Wonder, publicized recently in articles about Paul Williams in *Life, Playboy,* and *Time.*

I say, "It's too much work."

Movies are some kind of never-ending cycle, a trap of some kind. My new work is to get rid of this work that prevents me from doing my real work, whatever that may be.

I know who I am not.

Back in Margot's and Jennifer's living room on a weekend—weed, coke, and music—as usual, and the gang's all there: Susan Sarandon, Jill Clayburgh, Janet Margolin, Blythe Danner, and Brian, Marty, and his actor buddies Bob De Niro and Harvey Keitel; Steven Spielberg—doing TV at Universal during the week and infatuated with Margot—has yet to direct his first theatrical feature; and John Milius, who emerges for a day from his little room in Santa Monica where he is writing three screenplays at one time with the plan to present them as a slate to some studio to get a chance to direct. New albums play: Marvin Gaye's *What's Going On*, James Taylor's *Sweet Baby James*, and *Blue* from Joni Mitchell, whom I unobtrusively observe many mornings at the Colony Coffee Shop.

I sit on a mattress with Lorne Michaels. The brilliant criminal Richard Nixon is president.

Lorne says, "I'm doing a really new comedy show for TV. Our reality, our generation, not theirs. Would you like to work with me on it?"

I say, "Are you going to make jokes that will threaten the power of the oligarchy? Are you going to reveal what's going down with the military industrial complex? Do you have any idea how much power is exercised by the ultrarich?"

He says, "No. Not that far. It's network."

I say, "That's not what I want to do with my life. What's the point?"

Lorne's *Saturday Night Live* begins without me. Most Americans remain like the prisoners in Preston Sturges's *Sullivan's Travels,* who surpass their everyday preoccupations only at night when they laugh at Mickey Mouse on film.

I am confident *SNL* is a distraction business.

During the week, Margot stars in a TV series with James Garner, *Nichols,* at Warner Bros.

I cut *Dealing* on the lot. During breaks we rendezvous in her tiny dressing room. We can only barely lie down on the floor, on the diagonal.

Mike Medavoy, her agent, says, "Margot says you're the one. She's serious."

Ed has expropriated all of my directing salary for Pressman Williams expenses, but I have a huge weekly expense account from Warner Bros. which I don't get unless I turn in receipts each week. So, often during the week, Margot, Jennifer, and I meet up with friends and have expensive dinners at the Aware Inn and other posh eateries.

I am happy to pay for the dinners. Hungry? Eat. A real need is one that can be satisfied, after all. I have in mind a plan to form a commune with the regulars but long before that happens, everybody gets successful and goes off to burrow into their individual careers. Another delusion, but this barren effort lets a little more light into my soul.

I don't want to compete. This child needs to cooperate. I drift in a different direction.

A local female Native American shaman has made a wood-frame cradle; I am on my hands and knees with just my middle supported by the cradle's strong leather straps.

I follow her instruction. I exhale fully.

She pushes down sharply and powerfully at the bottom of my spinal column.

An electrical charge undulates up my backbone and I spin out the top of my head—and tumble into starry black emptiness.

I have no idea whatsoever of who I am. I am bewildered.

I think, "I am not here but I am here." This is someplace between what is me and what is not me.

Profound confusion as I spin in the dark, blown open, surrounded by the distant breathing stars. This is what it feels like not to have a self.

Out of thin air, I think, "Who is seeing this?"

Not "I" that believes, "I think therefore I am."

Usually my intellect watches me, the watched. Now there is a watcher of the watcher of the watched? Awareness of awareness of being aware?

I expand into something larger than I previously thought myself to be. Deeper understandings are coming one step after another. I am therefore I think?

Waldo Salt calls me, "I've been asked to do a screenplay of Carlos Castaneda's brujo, Don Juan. I'm at the Chelsea Hotel." Waldo knows about my peyote days from his daughter.

I am in midtown Manhattan and I head right down to Twenty-Third Street.

The fabled hotel has large rooms, high ceilings, old area rugs, and secondhand furniture.

I say, "This is wonderful timing for me, but the special effects will cost more than *2001*."

He says, "It's not that big a movie."

I tell Waldo about going with James Taylor to Hawaii for a concert he was going to give with Carly Simon. James and I took some MDA (he used it like aspirin) in his tenth-floor hotel room. At the living room table he showed me the old cigarette burns on the back of his hands—he tells me that it is his way of communicating to fools that their blather was causing him pain.

Then the MDA started coming on strong, and I walked out on the balcony.

I felt this could well be the moment to jump. I will ride the colorful band down to the ground—just like Castaneda in *Journey to Ixtlan,* into the Grand Canyon—and then ride it back up to rejoin my body. It is the ultimate step in the Way of the Brujo.

To Waldo, I say, "Before I make the jump, a voice came to me, 'Remember, you are on a drug.'"

I retreated from the balcony and sat in the farthest removed corner of James's hotel room until the grandfather pendulum came to rest, hours later.

I say to Waldo, "In any event, this Castaneda project will be expensive. Warren Beatty, who is canny about Hollywood, said to me, 'I'd trust you with maybe two million.' That's not enough. They won't let me direct."

I don't want the job. It's difficult being a spiritual man in the material world. I want to have fun. Later in the year, James lays down a brief track, "Mescalito has opened up my eyes, ah. / Mescalito has set my mind at ease, ah."

Margot and Brian restart their careers in an independent production of De Palma's wild knockoff of Alfred Hitchcock, *Sisters*—that I shepherd to Ed of Pressman Williams. I keep my distance from the production.

A song from the Lovin' Spoonful's new album, *Do You Believe in Magic,* is on my mind: "there's one with big blue eyes, cute as a bunny, With hair down to here, and plenty of money, And just when you think she's that one in the world, Your heart gets stolen by some mousy little girl . . . Did you ever have to make up your mind?"

Jennifer Salt, Margot's roommate, has a teenage sister, Debbie. She is a strong painter and works on canvasses bigger than she is. Debbie is bright as the sun, has a huge red Afro, and is full of persistent passionate energy.

We drive to Santa Fe and sit on top of a mesa. We eat magic psilocybin mushrooms. Consciousness expands to the sky and curving horizon. Nothing from the past reaches this present. I am united with the universe with no distinction between my personality and the rest of nature. Finally we float in the rosy clouds reflecting the setting sun. Unity and bliss. We are going the right way.

On the way back in the twilight, we see a young male Latino hitchhiker.

Debbie says, "Poor guy."

I say, "Let's give him a ride."

He gets in the back seat and pulls out a revolver.

He says, "Take out your wallet."

I say, "Are you hungry?"

He says, "Yes."

I say, "Well, why don't we go have a nice dinner before you rob us. Don't worry. We'll give you everything we have."

At the restaurant, he keeps a hand on his weapon under his jacket and eats with the other hand.

By the end of dinner, he trusts us to give him our money and to drive him to his home in a group of small cinderblock houses, miles off-road in the desert.

It is pitch-black scary, but we finally arrive alive at his house in the middle of nowhere. I empty my wallet. God's only money is God. God? In *Ethics*, Baruch Spinoza said that God and nature are the same.

He gets out and does not shoot us.

He keeps his word; we keep ours. There is light even in the darkness.

I am twenty-seven years old. Debbie is eighteen years old.

Debbie and I are together in my little house for six months. I have never met a woman with more enthusiasm and energy for sex. I try to keep up with Debbie but the effort finally makes me feel like I will die, soon. The relationship comes to its broken end.

Now, Waldo does not speak to me. I hurt his youngest daughter.

Decades later, Debbie forgives me. Her father is long gone.

She says, "I was on meth constantly, staying thin."

It was a life-and-death choice for me.

I decide I finally must investigate the consciousness expansion of LSD. Alone on a waterbed in my beach shack, I have a good setting and a positive mental set for my first trip—a large 500 mg dose of "window pane" acid. I am soon curled up in a fetal position under a sheet. I go further back than I did with the shrink in Brooklyn.

Slowly, slowly, I slide down a triangular tunnel—through the middle of three dachshund-long plastic pink balloons, filled with viscous liquid. They gently give way as I move along. These membranes push gently against my face, a perfectly slippery ride; suddenly, at the end of this tunnel, the pressure on my face ceases—there is a sudden radiant white light.

All is white. My brain is clean.

So far, so good.

On my back, on top of a soft surface: six dark ovals surrounded by dark hair, lean over my roofless cage made of wooden slats.

I see a limb appear and descend and tickle my penis—it is electric, focused. Then a stream of warm liquid releases pleasantly and fountains high into the air above.

The ovals shriek. I hear the sounds of laughter. They disappear.

The dark ovals reappear—another limb descends and pushes that same small part of me; another stream escapes and ascends again. And again I hear soprano howls.

This is more action than I've ever seen. My point of view is limited but so much is happening. Experience is added to my brain.

I sit in my highchair. My mother pushes yet another spoonful of soft food into my mouth. Yuck.

The next spoonful approaches. I clamp my mouth shut. The slop falls into my lap.

I have no mother tongue yet in which I can protest.

She lifts me out of the chair and transports me onto the speckled linoleum floor. On my back.

She puts her knee on my chest.

I only possess the language of feeling. There is no resisting this mother. A frightened child's psyche beneath her takes a traumatic step.

When the next spoonfuls come my way, I open my mouth.

I see the pretty Cliffie at the first Harvard mixer who mocks me, "No, I don' wanna' daynce."

I will no longer make an effort to speak perfect Mid-Atlantic English.

Fuck it, everybody comes from somewhere. I will speak the way I speak. Take a step back to go forward.

Do the strands of my brain's DNA contain memory of everything? Do my synaptic connections never stop changing as I develop? Can I reprogram any of this wiring, remove the blockage, change my destiny? By outgrowing it? Can an altered state become an altered trait? Quiet some networks, expand others? Stop rolling the stone uphill, Sisyphus?

Then I discover Fritz Perls's *Gestalt Therapy Verbatim*. Another giant step.

What am I feeling so guilty about? I follow Perls's simple procedure and speak aloud in my empty bedroom.

I say, "I feel guilty about—my brother Ted."

Perls says that behind every feeling of guilt is a feeling of responsibility, and that every feeling of responsibility is false—because, "Each person is responsible for his own evolution." How elegant.

"I am not responsible for—you, Ted." This is the first time I have said this notion aloud.

And Perls's next powerful premise in moving the internal world to the external world is that behind every false feeling of responsibility is an "unspoken demand"—a demand that is too awful to say, too calamitous to be allowed into consciousness. It is this demand that must be confronted and fully expressed.

"You have your own life to live."

"There's no contract here. You can drop dead—it's not my problem."

"It's over. You're on your own."

"I owe you nothing!"

I then wallop the pillow on my bed with a baseball bat.

"Nada. Zip. Fuck off. FUCK OFF, KID."

The forbidden words have been voiced.

The demand has been made here and now.

I am relieved.

How can decades of feeling guilty cease so suddenly? But they do.

Later, I call my brother and tell him.

I say, "If I do anything for you it is not because I owe you dick. The only reason that I will ever do anything for you, is for love."

He is confused and hurt by the call.

He says, "Why did you feel guilty about me?"

I say, "I felt that Dad and Mom were treating you in a really unhealthy way—Dad never wanted another child, he had dreams of travel, so he made your life miserable. And Mom could not tolerate your being so independent of her control. That's why I rented the house on Fourth Street for you to live in—to get out of that toxic apartment. I guess since that time, I felt my-brother's-keeper sort of feelings and that I should look out for you—I felt guilty that I had it better as a kid than you did."

Hard to believe, but true enough.

He says, "I see."

Subsequently, we have a sometimes testy relationship but without guilt. My ship is more balanced, drifting more freely on the journey.

I tell Julie Christie about Perls's powerful insight.

She says, "I walk around with guilt all day."

We spend an afternoon at the beach and run the procedure of quick catharsis until she, too, has run through her guilts. It is hard to believe it works. So fast. Free at last.

It helps a lot if you can deliver the unspoken demand with full emotional expression. Actors are simply ideal for this work.

16

A Childhood

1971

At a party at Margot's, Barbara Clarke dances with fluid grace and confidence. She shoots me a sultry penetrating power dyke-vamp stare. I am smitten. We chat.

I say, "You move so beautifully."

She says, "Are you gay?"

She speaks as clearly as my father demanded. With an English accent. She is perfumed with patchouli.

Barbara just completed a two-month road trip across the country with the Czech director Miloš Forman (later, director of *One Flew over the Cuckoo's Nest* and *Amadeus*).

She has a quick sense of humor. I am going to New York the next day and she asks if she can stay in my beach house while I'm gone. She seems free as a bird. I say okay.

When I get back, my small living room is filled by the low afternoon sun and a sculpture made of a discarded television antenna with warmly illuminated shells and shards of purple and red glass from the beach that hang from strings tied to the horizontal aluminum rods.

I also find a note: ". . . coming across the country with Miloš and going through Navajo country, I noticed pieces of brightly colored cloth (usually red) tied to the fences and when I inquired about them was told they were offerings to the gods. And that every time a piece of shell or material fell or was blown away, the sea gods were accepting the offering." Also, the note invites me to see her in New York the next time I am there.

I still go to New York because Ed still lives there. United Artists, MGM, and Columbia still have headquarters in Manhattan. The other studios are now all in Los Angeles.

Barbara and I stay together at her East Fifty-Seventh Street fourth-floor walk-up. We have an easy rapport and detachment from the norms of society. Her surrender and her skills in the realm of the senses are so beyond my prior experience, or Frank Harris's, let alone my adolescent dreams, that I am ecstatically imprisoned. She is an aristocrat of love, worth melting for.

While she is out one day, I find a NYC Police Department mugshot of her, full-face and profile. Cool and criminal. I fall in love with the astonishing waif in the two images. A reaction formation to Elizabeth? Barbara is unfettered by society and familiar with altered states. She is my new brave dream.

The mugshot was a result of her brief arrest after receiving some hashish mailed by a friend in Amsterdam.

Clearly, life can be beautiful.

The first week, we lie around, listen to music, drive for a late breakfast and newspaper reading twenty minutes down Pacific Coast Highway at the Malibu Coffee Shop. Later, she swims far out into the ocean, or sometimes we go for a horseback ride, or she draws—beautiful phantasmagoric visions of penis, womb, fetus, orchids. Every day we have leisurely mutual massages and a sunset walk on the beach.

The second tranquil week begins, and the same thing happens—I have walked into a wall of cotton. A zone of change. No ambitious work, just combed-cotton contentment—month after month. What a dangerous sensorial experiment.

One afternoon, I look at length into Barbara's eyes—her irises are cocoa but everything else in my field of vision is shades of white. I become her, she becomes me? We are one. How? What I know is not all there is to know.

My life has been lived out too fast at the demanding rhythm of the marketplace. Slow is good. Idleness is good.

I lie in the tall grass as radiant heat from the sun bakes and a brilliant red-orange hemisphere is everywhere with my eyes wide shut. I imagine my director friends movie-making all day on their sets and locations, becoming heroes of capitalist entertainment. Without knowing it, I am opening new doors of meaning for myself.

I wait for life to come at me, otherwise gone to pasture.

We walk in the hills of chaparral behind the beach houses. There is a long uphill dirt road that leads us to an old maroon cabin. The windows are dirty and we rub them with our hands to get a look inside. Simple, dilapidated, and abandoned.

She says, "This is a great place."

There are no neighbors in this box canyon that looks out at the Pacific from an elevation of about three hundred feet. We rent it for one hundred dollars a month and an agreement to feed the two Appaloosas in the field below the cabin. Utter luxury without swank comfort.

The unfenced fire trails of the Santa Monica Mountains cross our place and are open for long horseback rides. On one ride, Shawn's Lad grabs the bit and gallops at full speed along the narrow mountain trail. I hold on with my long legs and bend into the mountain as he charges around sharp turns, shod hooves pounding the clay. Incredible and scary and exciting to the boy from New York City.

We spend a couple of years improving the utilities—a potbellied stove trumps the fireplace, a charcoal filter makes the hard water potable—and get a deaf Dalmatian that we name Zoe. During the summer there, we often don't wear clothes, especially when taking LSD. Expanded awareness becomes the new normal.

After the tenth acid trip, I have no more hallucinations—only the vision of a vibrantly transcendent vibration. When a high lama takes 500 milligrams, it has little effect—it is not the drug, stupid, it's the place. There is there. You are there.

I am having a gorgeous second childhood. Horses and dreams and invisible worlds are now more commanding than the nervous hurry of the rational world.

17

Breaking Down,
Breaking Through

1972

But Standish Meacham has left Harvard and is chairman of the History Department at the University of Texas and asks me to travel to Austin for "A Convocation on the Year 2000"—a year that is three decades in the future. He has also invited a dozen other white males, including the French philosopher and political scientist Raymond Aron, author of *The Opium of the Intellectuals;* and the New York sociologist Daniel Bell, author of *The End of Ideology;* and the critic whose book *The World of Our Fathers* revealed to me my roots in European agnostic socialism, Irving Howe; and the futurist founder of the Hudson Institute and author of *Thinking About the Unthinkable,* Herman Kahn.

I think this might be an enlightening trip. On the face of it, the gathering promises too many great brains to miss.

On the afternoon before the convocation begins, the Texans throw a huge barbecue on the prairie. The host leads a spirited seventeen-hand black horse to me and challenges me to take a ride. They don't know I'm home on the Malibu range these days. I get on and he immediately whacks its rump and the steed bolts. I hear a big laugh from the Texan crowd as the horse races into the open flatlands.

No need for the Lone Ranger's "Hi-Yo Silver!"—we are at full gallop. I duck under low-hanging branches and pray the horse doesn't step in a gopher hole. I grip tight with my legs. After five minutes of running his heart out, the huge stallion decides to turn back toward home.

The Texans are surprised when I gallop toward their prairie party ten minutes later, still on top of the lathered horse. I pull in hard on his reins and skid to a stop, right in front of them, with a smile.

Except for Standish and the elegant Frenchman Aron, who is unanimously elected chairman, these intellectuals reveal themselves as academic narcissists. They present their brilliant ideas but don't entertain others'. Boors.

I offer that the conversation is failing because the participants are too strident in their defensive pride. As the *New York Times* reporter quotes me, "Maybe if we passed around a joint the situation might improve."

Aron asks me to have lunch with him.

I suggest that we don't eat but just sit opposite each other, relax, and for half an hour look in each other's eyes without any social obligation to entertain or to take care of the other. He is game. I stay in my heart—thoughtless, empty. After ten minutes, tears roll down Raymond's cheeks, and he keeps his gaze open as we continue to look at each other.

After the lunch break, he says, "Paul, I've had the most important visions of my life, especially of my childhood."

Aron tells the assembled group to listen up when I next speak.

I say that consciousness itself needs to change, to enlarge, that there is even a need to include interspecies understanding:

"The brains of dolphins and whales are much larger than brains of Homo sapiens. And the dolphins' evolution has been continuous for twenty-five million years—they were not interrupted by the five great extinctions of land animals. Land animals had to start from scratch every few million years. We would benefit if we enlarged our circle of inclusion."

One of the less frenzied elders, the naturalist philosopher and author of *Darwin's Century*, Loren Eiseley, smiles.

Standish introduces me to Lady Bird Johnson, President Lyndon Johnson's wife.

I say, "Wow, far out," Standish laughs out loud, and I shake her extended small hand. The former First Lady leaves the convocation, so I feel free to speak about extracurricular activities at the Human/Dolphin Foundation of John Lilly. Barbara is head of the Foundation. With a couple of her female coworkers, she often swims around in a large pen with male dolphins.

I say, "The ladies hook their knees around the dolphins' erections for the ride. Dolphins aren't fighters, they're lovers. That's the heart of the matter. They have figured out the porpoise of life."

Gray-haired Aaron Copland, the composer of "Appalachian Spring," sits next to me and has a congenial laugh.

In his 1960 book *On Thermonuclear War,* Herman Kahn laid out the hypothetical Doomsday Machine. His model rendered nuclear war unwinnable, and therefore unthinkable. Now with me, under a tree, the personification of "Dr Strangelove" himself tells me about his visions on his acid trip:

"The biggest industry of the twenty-first century will be the Meaning Industry. The Protestant Ethic will no longer be able to get people into heaven because there won't be enough productive jobs for a lifetime of good works. How can they feel good about themselves without worldly success?"

Kahn says, "There will be thousands of variations in the Meaning Industry: cults, religions, hobbyists, self-help movements, psychologies, philosophies, and messianic political movements—you name it."

"The other new giant industry will be the Planetary Food Distribution Business. Huge Malthusian events will require humankind to restructure the world economy with major economic rewards for a new food transportation infrastructure. A million people a day will start to die. The massive death will change human consciousness. There will be no problem growing the food but getting it to people will be a massive problem requiring vast numbers of new cargo ships."

In the eighteenth century, the first economist, Thomas Malthus, wrote in *An Essay on the Principle of Population* that the causes of economic change are population growth, disease, famine, war, and disasters in nature.

I feel better about the way my life is unfolding. Kahn is a futurist; I am becoming a presentist.

I watch the final cut of *Dealing: or . . .* in a Warner Bros. screening room in Burbank.

As I feared for a year, there is little chemistry between Harvard man John Lithgow '65 and Robert F. Lyons ("You can always tell a Harvard man"). The style is too European in its pace and sensitivities and will not work for pixilated Americans. It is an American failure.

I drive northbound in my van along Pacific Coast Highway. Electrical energy buzzes and shocks throughout my body. I must pull off the road and park on the shoulder.

I am paralyzed with nervous electrical overload.

I actually see in front of me a vision of the construction of my entire life from childhood to now—my choices, my efforts, my works. Each step is an interlocking small strut in an assembly of hundreds that create a geodesic cave where the windshield used to be—decades of accumulated adjustments, constructed strut to strut to strut, to avoid the wrath of my parents as I tried to fulfill their conflicting conscious and unconscious desires.

Then the synapses between these struts spark and break apart and fall like toothpicks.

The electric plug is pulled out of the socket—the shorting is over. I am burned out. All is still.

It is quiet. It is serene.

It is now afterward.

I am upside down.

The story is now up for grabs, not knowing it is magic.

The movie will have its first public exposure in a huge theater in Boston. I am high on LSD, in the bathtub of my suite high in the Hilton Hotel, when I hear a knock. Naked, I open the door and look into the eyes of a tall, buff Black man, and then look down at a white dwarf—I recognize the composer of the current ubiquitous hit of the Carpenters, "We've Only Just Begun." I invite him and his bodyguard into the suite and we josh about publicity and write our numbers in each other's phonebooks as "The Other Paul Williams." Another one! When they leave I get back in the tub. Vestiges of my old life are living me.

Later, I am at the opening with the cast, sitting in the packed audience when reel seven appears on screen after reel three.

The film makes no sense. Joy Bang (née Joy Wener), who had married Paul Bang and plays Lithgow's girlfriend, jumps up from her seat and says, "NO, NO! They put the reels out of order. It makes no sense. This is not the movie we made. Ask for your money back!"

The entire cast joins with her, trying to alert the crowd with frantic shouts. I stand but haven't the energy for an absurd shout. The lights go on, but the film continues to run in a nonsensical narrative. The lights soon go dim and the film unreels to its ending with no one in the audience leaving. Man composes, God disposes.

I find out the next day that the anti-hippie IATSE union projectionists deliberately sabotaged the counterculture pot film. A reality sandwich.

Later at a press luncheon for the stars and me, David Carradine covertly slips a tab of acid into my coffee.

I sit in a comfortable chair on the set of WGBH-TV in Boston with Elia Kazan (*On the Waterfront*) and Melvin van Peebles (*Watermelon Man*) with moderator Carl Stokes—the first Black elected mayor (of Cleveland) in the nation.

Kazan and van Peebles argue contentiously about the comparative merits of their films. I am quiet.

Stokes says, "Paul Williams, I would like to hear from you. What are your feelings about the influence of film on our current politics?"

I say, "I don't see why we are arguing with each other. We're just selling movies here and the only reason we are on the TV show here is to sell dog food at the commercial break. This is about making money, that's all."

The crew laughs in the dark.

Capitalism has little use for spirituality—the opposite of egotism.

An hour later I am on the radio.

The interviewer says, "You aren't yet thirty and have made three Hollywood films. What advice do you have to give to all the young filmmakers out there who are listening?'

I say, "If you're serious about directing, and you don't know anybody in show business—like I didn't—you ought to be speeding right now in a taxi with a copy of your script. You want to be ahead of everybody else to stop and accost me when I leave the studio."

I learn that an unruly mob showed up demanding to meet me. I was gone.

18

Alchemicals

1972

It is time to get serious and find an alternative to my still-greedy American ego. Andy Weil had given me a list of a dozen books. He feels that, for Westerners, the consciousness-expanding drugs provide an instant access to the East's extraordinary states of transcendence. Westerners would never postpone their frenetic professional lives to do the deep study and practice required to naturally get to these realms. The drug experience can be a sacrament to then motivate a commitment to study how high states can be reached without drugs. It is time to replace the distracting perfume of my personality with the essence of soul.

I read about how the human mind works beginning with Paramahansa Yogananda's *Autobiography of a Yogi, The Tibetan Book of the Dead*, and P. D. Ouspensky's *In Search of the Miraculous*. This wisdom beyond Western academic neuroscience.

There are more than a hundred people in the New York Arica Center of the authentic Sufi master Oscar Ichazo. A seven-day-a-week, full-time study of nine months cost $10,000 ($60,000 today) up front. This fee for Barbara and me drains my last dollars.

At this pretraining get-together, Ichazo catches my eye, walks straight over to me, leans forward, and whispers up into my ear, "I can give you hard-ons like you had when you were eighteen." These are the master's first words to me. I have never questioned my stiffness. Now, surprised, I wonder. What did he see?

The $10,000 is returned three weeks later, and Arica commences to pay us each $1,500 a week—an heiress of the Weyerhaeuser lumber family is in the training and has donated a large sum that Oscar shares with all. He must be for real.

When we start the work, the first meditation is the foundational key to altered states of high consciousness—the facility to freely move imagined golf balls of light anywhere on the fairways inside the body. No small task.

On my back on the carpet, I place my feet against the vibrating front baffle of two large speakers. As symphonic music pulsates against them, I let the sound rise as high into my body as it will go. I listen with my soles for twenty minutes each morning, for ten days. By the end I can hear the music everywhere head to toe. When the music stops, my entire body is a present empty void.

For the next ten days, I learn to use a golf ball of light in that void to make an *X* along the pathways of the nerves and ganglion of my physique—from left foot to right arm, from right foot, to left arm. I make deep body *X*'s until the twenty minutes are up.

After ten days, I can easily move my focused white golf ball consciousness. Meditation is not a prayer but a physiology. Fore!

Barbara and my new friend Artie Ross josh me for my dedication to the deconstruction of my ego as they often cut out for cappuccinos down in the street. Shall I die or have a cup of coffee?

I have learned to be passive, not to "go to work" when I meditate—there is light already in my mind. If I place the golf ball in from the bump on the back of the skull and let my eyes roll back and upward, I see pancakes of different colors roll up over the dome of my skull.

If I imagine the golf ball where the bones of the skull meet at the top—and place my tongue against the soft spot of my palette, I can let the ball travel down my tongue and onward to the solar plexus, and on downward to the center of the intestines and then on to the perineum. From there, the trip continues up the spine to the top of the skull. And again and again. The Sufis call this the snake that swallows its own tail, the *ouroboros*.

There is no hurry, but often I hear a small Murray drill sergeant positioned at the rear of my neck who obtrusively urges me to "Get an A." He causes effort. I create a second little drill sergeant behind him, and I have the second sergeant order Murray to take the day off.

I am in my best shape since the Lightweights as a result of the daily physical yogas of "holy gym." With a diet featuring ricotta cheese and lentils, my body rests lightly on my soul. After nine months of meditations, I am master of my breathing, able to inhale and exhale only once in a minute, rather than the six or seven breaths of low breathing. I can chant tones that vibrate each of my vertebrae with different musical notes, up and down the spine. I can stop all and any thought at will—to stay in the emptiness, the starry blackness of the Void.

This is the state one must have accessible in order to do the advanced Buddhist meditations—it is like the dark infinity refuge that I first discovered in my green bed when we moved away from home and friends in the Bronx.

Hollywood is far away. I am finally ready to start the highest meditation, the "Alchemical Transformation."

But Ed Pressman suddenly shows up at the Arica Center and pleads that I fly immediately to the Colorado location of *Badlands*, starring Martin Sheen and Sissy Spacek. He says the crew assembled by the production manager has refused to continue working for the first-time director Terrence Malick (Class of 1965) whom I had championed to Ed.

Ed says, "Terry punched out the production manager, Lou Stroller. The crew are with Stroller because they are dependent on him for their future work. You have to go and get them back to work."

I say, "Can't you go?"

He says, "No. What am I going to do?"

I say, "Talk to them."

He says, "No, I can't do it. You know how to talk to them. You must do it."

I arrive in Pueblo and schmooze with the strikers in the hot sun on the cloudless Colorado plain, as far as the eye can see. I repeat a mantra to small groups of the crew, "This is not a low-budget piece of shit, this movie is a classic! This will be the high point of your professional life. Work on!"

At midday, I walk back to a cheap two-story motel.

I bolt the door and lower the blinds of the small room. I follow the instructions for the ritual of Alchemical Transformation. I undress.

Naked, I sit down in the darkened room and assume a sitting yoga position. I light the candle that I brought from New York. I write my mother's first name, Mildred, on a rectangular card and lean it below the candle.

I meditate on the flame, an aid to "single-pointed focus." Soon, my eyes roll up and I am in dark outer space where the stars twinkle. (These stars are actually the phosphorous excitations on the ends of the receptor nerves which surround the eye's optic nerve. If I open my eyes in this state, I can simultaneously see these little explosions of phosphenes as well as the room in front of me.) The Buddhists call this seeing the *Bara Kath.*

I am in Void for several minutes.

Mildred emerges in profile in a tableau in front of me. She sits on a chair at her pink Formica kitchen table in the dining alcove of her Manhattan apartment. There are napkins in a holder on the table, some woodcuts by my sister on the cream wall behind her. She wears 1950s teardrop-shaped eyeglasses and a house dress and makeup, red lipstick. She is in her thirties.

Mildred is in her prime.

I look at her. She is still motionless. She is eight feet away.

Then, she turns her head to the right and looks straight at me. I look at her left eye. At first I blink a bit but then settle into the eye-to-eye contact that Oscar calls "*Trespasso.*"

Slowly, her makeup melts and slides off her face as her dress oozes off her body. Then the table dematerializes. Her eyeglasses too. Every manufactured detail of life falls away. Then the room itself is gone. She has emerged out of her everyday visible state into her true nature.

Then she stands and faces me, head to toe, naked.

We are together innocent in the Void.

I do nothing but look. She looks back.

A stream of white gushes from my heart across the divide to her heart. And then, from her heart back into my heart.

This stream is visible. I can see this horizontal track of white light between us. It pushes and pulls. It lasts thirty-seconds—and stops.

I start to cry.

I am sad. The white tidal energy is gone.

I will not be held close to her body anymore. I am no longer her darling baby. Tears run from my eyes. I feel alone.

I remember that Oscar had said, if you encounter your parents, "wish them the highest spiritual development they could possibly have in this lifetime, given their experiences of life."

I wish it for her, completely.

I feel free from my responsibility for my mother. My child inside saw her as an ideal, but my mother is only who she happens to be in her own life, a victim of her own parents, her own traumas. This is one woman with her own passions, excesses, and crazy idiosyncrasies.

It is still as we stand and look at each other. She is beyond my arm's reach.

Moments pass.

Then the white energy rises up my spine, up to the top of my head, out the top—it arcs high across the distance between us and then drops down into the top of Mildred's head.

A second later, the arc of light flows out from between her legs like a biplane crop duster that swoops toward the floor and then acrobatically climbs right up into my own perineum. And, in no time, once again out the top of my head. The light keeps circling.

It feels serene, perfect.

Like an actor who knows his lines perfectly—his next line comes out of nowhere—I remember the second instruction from Oscar, "Wish them love."

I wish my mother love—the best she could have. The oval of white energy flows around and through our bodies—not as a horizontal push or a pull.

And then, Mildred in the emptiness starts to shrink. She gets smaller and smaller and smaller until she is a miniature but fully formed human.

"Homunculus!" I remember a medieval woodcut of a tiny person at the controls inside a huge mechanical human being. No other thoughts. And before I can begin to wonder, this five-inch-tall entity rushes toward my heart, hits my chest, and passes right through into my beating heart.

I sit in amazement.

And in a moment, I am back—suddenly, fully present in the motel room.

I do a bow with hands pressed, and then blow out the candle.

I start to put on clothes for further labor-management mediating.

But three minutes after I blow out the candle, on the ratty bed, while I pull on a sock, my body starts to shake. It starts in my heart—heartbeat by heartbeat. The maternal homunculus grows bigger. Relentlessly it grows and slowly fills my left arm, my left leg. It fills the entire left side of my body, but it does not rise past my throat—it stays below my head.

This energy expands to the limit of my skin and then it begins to convulse in a turgid wash. These left-side convulsions last two minutes and then stop.

I sit on the bed in awe. I do nothing. I wait to see what else might happen. After fifteen minutes, I observe nothing else extraordinary.

I finish dressing and go outside into the summer heat and blinding sun, and look for the angry crew folk.

"There are more things in heaven and earth, Horatio, than are dreamt of in your philosophy."

To put it mildly.

The next day, the moviemakers begrudgingly return to work with a late-morning call. I visit with my friend Brian Probyn, the director of photography (DP). He tells me he feels ill and wants to return to London. Terry is eager to have the young camera operator, Tak Fujimoto, do the DP's job, but Steve Larner is senior and agrees to take over for two weeks. Then Tak will get his first DP job. We all agree.

I skip lunch with the company and go back to my motel room and undress.

I sit down on the floor. I light the candle. I write my father's first name, Murray, on a card and lean it against the candle. I concentrate with single-pointed focus on the flame and soon am in the starry Void.

Nothing happens. I am dismayed as I look into empty outer space.

Then I spot a man, far away—a football field away. I want to look him in the eye, but I just look at the tiny distant figure.

Suddenly, he rushes toward me faster than any mortal football player. In one second, he confronts me, stationary, a mere foot away—one big face; his big eyes stare at me.

For three seconds, I look intently out my left eye. And he is intense. Powerful. I am transfixed.

Then he quickly grows tall. I must look up to see the face of the giant that towers over me. I am a little kid.

And I start to cry—tears down both cheeks.

I say, "I'll be whatever you want me to be, just get your foot off my neck."

I say, "I'll be whatever you want me to be, just leave me alone. I'll be whatever you want me to be . . ."

I sob for some minutes.

I remember then to wish my father "as much spiritual development as he could have in his lifetime."

It is a new feeling. A good one.

He was born poor, then a child of the Great Depression, subjected to abuse and violence from the uneducated parents; to know that he was a flawed mortal, struggling to make his way the best he could in the world, is suddenly for me to know that he is not, in his essence, an autocratic monster.

This poor parent of mine is a bruised, damaged personality with a struggle. He made sure I had the skills to succeed in the difficult world as he found it.

I get to empathize with the villain in my life.

I wish him well and hope for his highest possible spiritual evolution.

A huge weight lifts from the top of my head and my shoulders. I feel that it is over—I will no longer be hurt by him. I am overwhelmed by love for him.

But I do not put this new feeling of love for him into words, to "wish him love with full intention," because I don't get the chance—he suddenly shrinks into a five-inch homunculus and—pop!—right through my sternum, Little Murray rushes into my heart.

I sit silently this time. On the bed, I wait for what I expect to happen next—after my experience yesterday with Little Mildred.

Nothing happens.

I snuff the candle. I do not go outside. I do not get dressed. I lie on the bed.

In three minutes, heartbeat by heartbeat the energy begins to fill my body. Same as with Mildred but only now it is the right side. This homunculus expands but also stays below my head. My body starts to convulse. It agitates my right—arm, torso, and leg. These surging convulsions last for a couple of minutes. Then it is over.

I start to dress.

In a few moments, I collapse backward onto the motel room bed.

The right side of my torso and the left side of my torso sashay in waves back and forth—a horizontal wash cycle in a bobbing washing machine that is me.

I just let it be, until the blending waves diminish and the turgidity calms.

In a couple of minutes, I feel a balance and quiet inside my body.

This is what a mystical reconciliation feels like. In a hologram of the second kind, the alchemical kind?

"Remember yourself!" is the Sufi's emergency warning to escape the control of your personality. Remember to visit your thoughtless serene place, remember your higher self, above the rushing tides.

At a mysterious airplane hangar in Pueblo, Marty Sheen's character, the serial killer Charles Starkweather, is taken in handcuffs by a crowd of troopers to a private plane for transport to jail, watched by his articulate teenaged nincompoop girlfriend, Holly Fugate, Sissy's character. These were the people that occupied Terry's imagined *Badlands*.

My head sits peacefully on top of Mildred and Murray within—awake on top of the world. I remember myself with just a slight smile on my face.

St. Paul and Freud plumbed having different parts; everyone has at least two personalities—the one you like and the one you don't like. What matters is the presence of spirit in a frequency beyond personality.

Later, in New York, I check with Artie and Barbara. They report no experience of any such parental encounter. I am disconcerted, so I fly to San Francisco to visit Oscar Ichazo one last time, and he says, "Well, that is the alchemical transformation. You're finished with the work. Now you can go out and teach." I tell him I am not interested in teaching, yet.

19

Whirled Like a Dervish

1972–1974

1972

I am on the path. I spend six weeks in Jamaica researching the practices of the mystical Rastafarians. So awake, Rastas create personal bibles with a new scrapbook page for every day—they mount mementos like a beautiful leaf, or write an important insight they have had, or a tear a picture from a magazine that has special meaning for them, to celebrate their present each day. This could be an acceptable context for a movie.

I take my last acid trip. Standing in a waist-deep lagoon, I watch distant lightning as the storm clouds approach and turn to walk to shore. But the sand beneath me starts to move and I jump up as a huge manta ray flaps its wings and swims off from under my feet.

Soon weeks after, I am in Paris. Raymond Aron, my new friend from the twenty-first century in Texas, is now president of the French Academy and sends a limo to pick me up for lunch. We sit in his luxurious booth adjacent to a wall of flowers under glass.

He tells me about his private conversation with his ex-student Henry Kissinger. Hundreds of academics in full-page ads in the *New York Times* condemn Kissinger's indiscriminate murderous bombing of North Vietnam. He advised Nixon to bomb them to force them back to the negotiating table— the Communists knew they had won the war and walked out of negotiations, not tolerating any talk of the USA's "withdrawal with honor." This becomes public knowledge a year later.

My headaches from Kissinger's realpolitik Harvard seminar are justified.

I report to Raymond the critical role of the Rasta musicians in the Jamaican revolution. Over the outdoor loudspeakers in the rural village squares, the candidate whose celebration in song get the most play, wins. Dance rules.

In *The Republic*, Socrates envisioned a citizen's education only after a completed preliminary education in music and gymnastics.

I do not say, "Music is the key to the dance—dancing is heaven."

A few months later, upstairs over the garage next to Francis Coppola's house in Mill Valley, California, Francis's young friend George Lucas shows me some scenes of his new high school movie, *American Graffiti,* on a flatbed editing machine.

In this scene, a young Richard Dreyfuss has attached an anchored chain to the rear axle of a parked police car, and a buddy races by in a souped-up old Ford. When the cop car peels out in chase without its rear wheels, the steel chassis rips up the street with sparks.

I laugh. George seems happy with the scene.

Francis now says, "How'd you like it?"

I say, "Oh, it's good, but too commercial for me."

George's film shall be the first high school film to take the market that my generation has been waiting for. *Out of It* remains a lox in the United Artists' vault. What can I do?

Francis teaches me how to cook bell peppers: place naked over the flame, turn until blackened, then pop into a brown paper bag, close until the pepper cools. Remove from the bag, peel away the blackened skin, cut open, remove the seeds, and cut slices. So tasty no olive oil needed.

As Orson Welles says, "Ask not what you can do for your country. Ask what's for lunch?"

A short time later, my drift from moviemaking gets halted at Margot's house, when John Milius gives me his screenplay *Apocalypse Now*, based on Joseph Conrad's *Heart of Darkness*. It is incredibly well-written, even transcendent.

Finally, beyond my last gasp, a great screenplay for me—about a man's failure to fulfill his destiny. My cup of green tea.

I hope that I can raise enough money for a low-budget to shoot it in a documentary style in the Philippines. I call Francis Coppola, who owns the material.

Francis says, "I have over $350,000 already into it with Warner Bros. I'd have to get more than that back to sell it to you."

Heaven must wait.

I say, "Well, then, I can't direct it, but I think I can get the money to produce it."

I give the script to Bob Rafelson, Bert and Steve's partner in BBS, who had invited me to Hollywood in 1971. One evening in New York, I analyzed why his film that he just showed me, *Five Easy Pieces*, was so great. It was daylight when I finished.

He said, "Come to LA and we'll produce any low-budget film you want." Their company had created *The Monkees* on TV, and the huge success *Easy Rider*.

I say, "You have to read it right away. It is *Heart of Darkness* in the Vietnam War. I've got to get back to Francis in a day or two at the most."

Bob says, "Vietnam?"

I say, "Yes. Vietnam. Just read it."

I call Bob the next day.

Bob says, "I haven't read it yet."

I say, "Read it today. Or forget about it."

The next day, I call.

Bob says, "Yeah, it's not for me. I don't know, you know . . . Vietnam . . ."

I hang up and call Francis.

I say, "Francis . . ."

Francis says, "Wait. Wait, don't you say anything. Just listen. I've been thinking about it since you called. I've decided to make it myself."

I say, "It will be great."

Some years later, it is nominated for eight Oscars and is a cultural phenomenon. The last act, though, was rewritten by Francis, and he avoided the spiritual climax of Conrad's book and Milius's screenplay, substituting intellectual idiocies for Dennis Hopper's character that made it clear that Francis had never been to real war—hell.

I am happily back at play in the fields of the lord when Edgar Scherick, head of Palomar Pictures, calls about *Stepford Wives*, a script by William Goldman, whose last screenplay was *Butch Cassidy and the Sundance Kid*.

This screenplay dramatizes the sleeping personality versus awake instinct. Another gift to me from Buddha. I can't put it down.

I write eight pages of notes on a legal pad.

Over the phone, I tell Edgar my approach, but he says it's a bit wild and Goldman will have to approve.

At the meeting of the three of us, I explain, "To play most of the automaton Stepford wives, we hire mediocre television actresses who are emotionally cut off. We hire three really great actresses who can change from sleepwalking to authentic wakefulness. Good actors will just play bad actors until it is time to transform into emotionally flowing beings."

William Goldman is delighted.

We spend four hours going over the script scene by scene as I describe how it will work. At the conclusion of the meeting I feel good. So does Goldman.

The next day, I get a call from Scherick, "Goldman is excited about your directing the movie. He thinks it will be great! So, are you excited? This is going to be a big hit, right?"

I say, "Edgar, I know this material. I know how to do it right and I will do a great job."

Edgar says, "Nah, I need you to be excited! We're going to make millions! Millions! I'll call you tomorrow and see if you've gotten excited."

What a nut job. I noticed he had a bite plate in his mouth during the meeting.

He calls the next day. The dialogue is much the same. This crazy man needs help.

On the third day, he calls again, and again the dialogue is not different except that Edgar gets angry and tells me he's "going to get someone else who is excited." And grinds his teeth as he hangs up.

Scherick hires a British director, Bryan Forbes, a man without sensitivity to the emotional tones that will create the transitional knockout power of the drama. I'm sure Forbes got excited about millions. He rewrites the screenplay and Goldman disowns it.

I, too, am disappointed—I can't say in a matter of seconds that I know it will make millions. But another internal voice simply dominates me at these critical junctures. The goal is no longer fame and fortune.

A few days later, Barbara and I exit the elevator at the Manhattan loft of Caron Smith (of the Metropolitan Museum of Art, Asia Department) and Jeff Steingarten (Class of 1964), now the *Vogue* food critic. All the New York white people are shrinks or writers. They pad around and speak in church whispers. Definitely weird. The dozen dark men in orange robes talk in normal tones to each other.

A robed dark six-year-old with a topknot plays with a hand puppet. I sit down next to him, pick up another puppet, and we play—our puppets hide, surprise, and chase each other. This kid laughs happily and often.

Pressure strangely builds against my left cheek as we play. After five minutes, the pressure is strong enough to push my head around to the right. No one is touching me.

I stare at a six-foot, nine-inch monk—into the brightest eyes I have ever seen.

I rest in those bright high beams.

I remove the hand puppet and thank my little friend with a smile and a bow, and walk over to the giant man.

He sits on a bed on a platform and he is so big that his head is not far below me when I stand in front of him. After several moments of eye contact, I slap him hard two times on the sides of his huge upper arms near his shoulders.

I say, "Hi, I'm Paul! Paul. What's your name?"

A modestly sized monk sits on the floor to his right and translates. The formidable monk listens; he looks directly at me.

Suddenly, his big arms and big hands outstretch and pummel my upper arms. "Dingo! Dingo!" is what I hear him say. He laughs.

Despite my shoulders' sudden pain, I smile, "Dingo!"

These Tibetans are traveling around the world to raise dough to save their sacred texts from the invading Chinese.

I say, "Dingo! How do you like being on the road, trying to raise money?"

Dingo's eyes are happy.

The translator translates. Dingo looks at me from four feet away; now pressure builds again on the left side of my face—an invisible hand pushes my head around to the right.

I look at the wall-to-wall, floor-to-ceiling book shelves filled with Jeffrey and Caron's books.

And then the entire wall of books dissolves.

I am stunned.

I stand at an intersection of two dirt roads that appear to be in someplace that reminds me of India.

There are different-colored one-story buildings on either side of the road I stand on that diminish to the horizon. Old people, children, and teenagers walk right past me.

A big brown ox lumbers by past me, a foot away. An ox.

I begin a hallucination test drill: first, my eyes are on the road that leads to the horizon. I tilt my head up from the view of the road and I see only the blue sky—in a hallucination, the road would rise up with my eyes (as my dead grandmother did in London). As I tilt my head down, the dirt road reappears.

Next, test the parallax conversion—when you stand in the middle of railroad tracks, the tracks appear to run parallel to a distant vanishing point. If you bend down and bring your eyes near the railroad bed, the rails appear to converge nearby. Stand up and the rails appear parallel again into the distance.

In a hallucination, standing up or squatting down, the rails will remain in a constant image. The brain supplies the vision, not the eyes.

The road I stand on is lined by one-story houses on each side. They appear parallel to the road and only converge at the distant horizon. I do a deep knee bend. They appear to converge nearby. When I stand up, they appear parallel into the distance again.

A final test: I slowly make a quarter turn to the left. I see a second long road run under me from the East. I am standing in the middle of a crossroads. When I turn left again another quarter, the first road continues its run under me to the south. I turn left another quarter and now I see the continuation of the second crossroad heading west. I turn left again—returning to the north, where I started: I see the first road lined by one-story houses parallel to the distant horizon.

One cannot look around the corner in a hallucination.

I surrender any doubt. I am certainly in India or a place that looks to me like India.

The muscles of my chest relax. I feel my heart warm.

And then the wall of books slowly fades in and hides any view at all of my India.

I know it lies just beyond the opaque bookshelves. Or not? Were my eyes in that distant country?

I stand for a few moments and turn back to Dingo.

He smiles.

I look in his shining eyes, put my hands together, and bow.

Dingo has responded to my question, "What it is it like being on the road trying to raise money?"

Dingo's teaching is all visual. But it involves neither a hallucination nor a simultaneous holographic superimposition nor any discrepancy from everyday sight—I just see from a distant place. Is this my road to Damascus? Saul was a Jew, blinded by a vision of Jesus—he later changed his name to Paul.

We embark on a two-hour conversation. Each time I have what I consider another bright idea about the perception of personality archetypes, he has a simple response that evaporates the thought into thin air and I am simply empty and present. Like a good actor. I decide right then to study the Meisner acting technique as soon as I get back to the West Coast.

This chat to nowhere is another of Dingo's teaching methods, called Tantric Theater. Dingo tells me when I smile that the tip of my tongue slightly protrudes through my teeth—it reveals that my particular avenue to enlightenment is not the way of the thinking head, nor the way of the instinctive gut, but is the way of the feeling heart.

Years later, a devotee, actor Richard Gere, informs me that His Holiness is regarded with awe by Buddhists of every persuasion for his vision teachings. He is known to all lamas as the great Teacher of Teachers. To put it to Westerners, if Einstein figured out how the atom bomb worked and taught everybody, and Oppenheimer built it, you could say that Dingo is Einstein and the Dali Lama is Oppenheimer. The current fourteenth Dalai Lama considers Dingo his principal teacher: His Holiness, Dilgo Khyentse Rinpoche.

"Dilgo?"

Dilgo!

Not "Dingo" (the name of the native Australian dog, an apex predator).

Dilgo knows his magnificent self, not swayed by anything from the outside.

Behind the name is the nameless. Beyond thought.

The Dali Lama says of this greatest lama of the twentieth century, "Once you control inner element, you can control outer elements. I am quite fortunate to see him, to receive his teaching, so therefore now essential, important to implement this teaching in daily life." He laughs. "I am very, very grateful to him."

Me too.

Dilgo listens to everyone he meets and usually responds with good humor, "I see, I see." I did not realize I was talking to the highest guy on the planet, at the time.

Home is where the infinite heart is. Remember.

"Haaaaaaaa...p." I look into Lisa's eyes in the small audience as Jon alongside me raps the spot on my spine where the sound comes from, and then a bit lower down—and the pitch of my voice lowers. "Peeeeeee...e." I look into David's eyes and Jon raps from this lower spot on my spine as the single syllable lowers its pitch again. "Birrrrr...th." I look into Susan's eyes, and Jon raps lower and now the sound of "day" resonates more fully from deeper inside.

David Proval, Lisa James, Susan Martin, and I meet every few days with Jon Voight to learn the acting technique of Sandy Meisner. After the Happy Birthday initiation, an actor sits on a chair opposite you and expresses what they feel utilizing only the words, "You are wearing blue jeans." Your required response is only, "I'm wearing blue jeans." The simple, "I am wearing blue jeans," occupies my mind and allows me to express what my body feels.

The volley goes on for twenty to thirty minutes. Emotions are released but not with thoughtful words, only within the repeated sentence that requires no thought. What a nice thing—switching from a director to an actor, you don't think when you're at your best.

In the beginning of these repeat exercises, I keep my eyes closed and concentrate on identifying on what's going on inside—emotional selfishness. After weeks, when I finally know my own feeling, I open my eyes to include the partner's emotional state.

After three months, as I repeat from deep within, I make "good sounds"—not upwardly displaced, higher-pitched wordy explanations. I can express love and hate and everything in between with just, "You're wearing blue jeans." That's why in verbal communication it's not the words but the tone that matters: I could say, "Goodnight, I love you," in a tone that reveals the opposite, or "I hate you," and communicate nothing but love.

And then we move on to, "You make me feel ____" and the response "I make you feel ____." No long explanation, just the simple word linked to the emotion you are having in that moment, as in, "You make me feel angry." It sounds angry.

Then your partner answers, "I make you feel angry," and reveals their feeling from the effect your expression has had on them. Scared? Hurt? Months of one-word identifications of each feeling as it occurs in the back-and-forth. There is a dramatic flow every bit as full as a scene with explanatory dialogue.

After months, we get up out of our chairs and do improvisations. But first, before we get onstage, we learn to do "The Check"—sitting silently with eyes shut for five minutes to recall the three most important emotional moments that you actually experienced within the last twenty-four hours. For example, you left your wallet in a store and only remembered minutes later in a panic as you went to get it back. Your daughter cried when you left for work and made you feel like a bad parent. Or you were dying to eat a hot dog, but the stand was closed. You pick one of these events of the day that is still filled with emotion and put it at "stake" in the scene to come.

In the scene, you say what you "want"—for example, "I want your shirt." And we have our private emotion at stake about "why" we want the shirt, but that is never spoken—it is your secret: "If I don't get the shirt off his back, I will not get my wallet back." You enter the stage with the want, and make the demand—and the other person always says, "No." They also have their private "stake" and never say "why" they must keep their shirt, only the "what"—that they will not let you have the shirt. A pure and intense drama ensues.

If you are shooting a movie, you will always have a fresh "alive emotion" that privately you can put at stake when you say any dialogue (supplied by the script). No problem of calling up ancient feelings when the camera rolls. The audience can feel you are never faking it, because you are not. You are pretending to pretend.

Jon, Dustin Hoffman, Al Pacino, Bobby Duvall, and Chris Walken made up one acting class at Sandy Meisner's Neighborhood Playhouse, in Manhattan.

Proval starts a weekly workshop in LA that I go to for a decade. Andy Garcia, Richard Dreyfuss, Teri Garr, Judge Reinhold, and Jon are among other regulars.

When I first start the Meisner work, I look forward to the high of the intensely present Friday-night workshops. After a while, the high lasts into Saturday, then even Sunday. Eventually it just stays. All the world becomes a stage.

A few shrinks and all gurus and actors are hip to the same emptiness—unlike most psychologists, neuroscientists, and philosophers.

One giant step for Paul.

1973

Producers Julia Phillips and her husband, Michael, live next door to Margot and me.

She says, "Scorsese is too much trouble; would you direct *Taxi Driver?*"

I read the script she gives me.

I say, "I don't think I could put my head around so much violence and so much degeneration for a whole year. Italian Americans are right for this project. Stick with Marty. He knows how to direct."

After that, Julia shows me the final cut of *The Sting*. She is worried it will be a flop.

I say, "It's great. I'll buy any share of it you want to sell."

I don't have much money, but she is reassured.

No sale.

Julia is the first woman to win an Academy Award for Best Picture, *The Sting*.

She dies early from a long and monumental indulgence in cocaine, after producing Spielberg's *Close Encounters of the Third Kind,* while in the midst of writing *Power Dykes of Hollywood,* a sequel to her successful *You'll Never Eat Lunch in This Town Again*—in which I get her only kind words: I relieve her head pain one day with my laying on of the hands.

No charge.

Liz remarries on the same day as our anniversary, June 23.

I remember Liz's favorite line of Prince Harry spoken to Falstaff, which she frequently quoted to me, "I'll so offend, to make offense a skill, redeeming time when men think least I will."

She marries a Yalie lawyer. A boring lawyer. I go to my human workshop.

About twenty of us who had been in the Sufi training attend a woman as she gives birth. Poor kid, what a hostile world he is about to enter. When the newborn appears, TIME STOPS. I am overwhelmed by the probability that there is as much good as bad. Everything, to exist, must exist in pairs of opposites. Just like emotions.

"For every loved child, a child broken, bagged, sunk in a lake," Maggie Smith, the poet, not the actress, versified, "This place could be beautiful, right? You could make this place beautiful."

Later, Barbara says, "I want to have your baby. You can come visit whenever you want, if you're gone."

That works for me.

I say, "I would like a child from you and me."

I would like to have a daughter. And with Barbara—hybrid vigor. Men have made a mess of the world. What would I teach a boy?

I say, "All right. Yes."

There's a part of me that likes the idea of helping develop what Che Guevara called a "new woman" in his book, *Socialism and Man* [sic] *in Cuba.*

Until the world focuses on nurturing children sanely based on moral rather than material incentives, and teaches them how to help each other, history will be an oppressive repeat. I hope it's a girl.

At Paradise Cove a short drive down PCH, I overhear two real estate agents talking at the bar, "Barbra Streisand bought the property at the end of Ramirez Canyon today." Coincidence redux.

Early the next morning I drive to take a look and see an adjoining empty three-acre parcel for sale. I buy it with a small down payment.

Within a year, Zoe the Dalmatian meets our new baby, a girl, whom we name Zoe—"Life" in Greek—new hope and love, in me.

I sell the Ramirez property for enough to buy our ranch, a city boy's fantasy come true. A homestead. I am a happy dirt-poor landowner with a pure-hearted daughter. Is this the City of God?

I am on a dimly lit stage with a dozen others in a small theater, far south on Robertson Boulevard in Los Angeles.

Anna Halprin, an older woman, says, "Close your eyes. See the thread of energy inside your muscle and let your body follow it."

In the darkness a golden current moves up inside my forearm. My arm moves with it, along the arm and shoulders and neck and then travels around my body. The body is dancing.

I am easily able to go deeply inside and now find I can coordinate my movement and posture in the external space with inner mindful realms. When I twirled in place with the Sufis for twenty minutes each morning, I had not applied their proverb, "As above, so below," simultaneous awareness of the inner and outer worlds

Now, bodies move gracefully in slow motion through the shadows. Imagine cells singing together.

Halprin understands the link between kinesthetic awareness and community. I go every week for a few months.

There is a unity of consciousness in this silent movement—a communion.

1974

Bert Schneider comes out to the ranch with Bob Rafelson. Bob smacks our Appaloosa, Shawn's Lad, in the head with a two-by-four to quiet him down enough to ride. Different folks, different strokes. Bob makes Shawn's Lad jump the log piles.

Bert wants me to meet his friend Huey P. Newton in Huey's penthouse in Oakland. I'm on my path, I'm postpolitical. I don't really want any more Panther adventures, but Bert is one of my best friends, and Huey is his. Why am I going to do this?

It is just too interesting. Temptation. Only those who resist know how strong it is.

I soon sit on a long couch at the end of a line of six attorneys. On the other end sits Lenny Weinglass, the renowned constitutional law advocate and defender of the Chicago Seven (Abbie Hoffman, Jerry Rubin, Tom Hayden, David Dellinger, et al.) Huey P. Newton sits alone in a big lounge chair facing us all. At the large window behind him, on a tripod, there is a telescope aimed across Lake Merritt into the courtroom of his ongoing trial.

Huey says, "Why is the Black foreman of this jury going to find me guilty of second-degree murder?"

An outlier in this legal mélange, I imagine I am the foreman of this jury.

None of the lawyers respond to the question. Huey waits.

I look at Lenny Weinglass. I wait. He is silent.

Not a word from the others.

I say, "Because he thinks that if you get a hung jury, the foreman of the next jury will find you guilty of first-degree murder. He believes he's saving your life."

Huey stares at me.

He says, "That's right. Who are you?"

I say, "I'm Bert's friend Paul."

Soon Bert and the attorneys and I start to leave.

Huey says, "Stay, I want to talk to you."

Bert leaves with the lawyers for LA.

I like this handsome Black man.

We stay up all night. There is a large bowl of cocaine and a big Bowie knife to use as a spoon. We are enhanced.

I say, "What were you talking about with Eldridge on the phone to Algiers?"

He says, "Murder. Eldridge was arguing with me that the Flash of Lightning would cause Nixon to impose a fully fascist regime that would then vitalize an American revolution."

I say, "Nothing about my wife and me? Who we were?"

He says, "No. I told him the Flash of Lightning was a counterproductive idea."

I say, "Is he still living in the French embassy?"

He says, "Yeah. He talks a lot."

We talk about mothers. And taking risks. His mother had showered him with an excessive amount of love when Huey was a baby. "I was the youngest one of seven. I was the baby, and my name was Huey, so everybody wanted to call me—don't say it, don't even think about saying it. Who wants to be named after a funny-walking, funny-talking cartoon duck?"

As toddlers, we both experienced the reality of an excessive instinctually unbalanced mother love that no other love can ever match. So in later life, we are always ready to move on from a healthy experience of love—to risk, to try to recover that bizarre feeling of excess. We agree that it's not healthy but that it gives you more self-confidence and forward movement.

Huey tells me about his conversations with Erik H. Erikson at Yale. What a coincidence. No surprise, they agreed about the need for a "positive identity" for Afro-Americans. Black is beautiful. Their conversations are later published as *In Search of Common Ground*.

I had learned about the Unitary Logic of Buddhism from Ichazo. In the West, we believe like Aristotle: if A is not B, and B is not A, then A and B cannot be the same thing. As in computer code, 0 or 1. In the East, however, they believe: that A and B always coexist, that only the equilibrium between them changes. That notion leads to reasoning rather than argument.

So too, Huey had done away with Marxist dialectic—thesis A gives birth to opposing antithesis B, and resolves in a synthesis, C. Huey gives me a yellow note card with a diagram of dialectic movement and below it a "trialectic" diagram.

He says, "In trialectics, there's oppression, point A, and there's revolution, point B, and then there's the balance between them at any given moment—that's the two-way arrow, equilibrium—C. Simón Bolívar said the fire of Revolution never dies—it just expands and contracts."

Huey says, "If Americans knew the disasters that lie ahead, they would transform this society tomorrow for their own preservation."

He tells me that he was in solitary confinement for three years, in six-month stretches. After each six months, he was brought before a judge. Huey lectured him on the racist system of perverted justice that the judge enabled. When Huey finished, he just cursed the jurist to his face, who then ordered him back into solitary for contempt of court.

In no danger of being raped, Huey survived on just enough food so he did not have to shit in his dark, bare cell. He exercised physically and mentally. Huey learned how to "stop the pictures in my brain"—to enter the Void. After he got out of jail, Tassajara's Zen Master, Dick Baker Roshi, acknowledged Huey's awakening.

I fly up to Oakland on the weekends that follow to hang out with this wise man. Huey tunes me into things I never would have learned on my own.

The readiness to die is not beyond revolutionary politics.

Huey is upset with me during another nighttime discussion.

He says, "Stop looking for heroes."

He picks up a copy of his recently published autobiography, *Revolutionary Suicide*.

He inscribes the title page, "To Paul Himself."

Think of that.

In the middle of the Oakland trial, Huey flees. On the night, he drives down to Big Sur. Artie Ross bulldozes a grave for the getaway car on Partington Ridge. After a few days, Artie drives Huey to LA to an apartment hideout in Watts. Sometimes we all meet late at night at Bert's, on top of Benedict Canyon, to plan his escape to Cuba.

A guy who flew into Wounded Knee wants $100,000 ($514,000 today) to fly Huey to Havana. The Mafia also is too expensive. A crazy Cuban, with a make-believe cell phone contraption, outlines a cheaper plan that ends when this psychotic takes a few gunshots at us in Cantor's Deli.

Artie then labors for two months to get his sailboat outfitted in Florida. When he gets it seaworthy, it will sail through the Panama Canal and then up to Marina del Rey to pick up Huey, then back again through the canal to Havana.

Artie is exhausted by the work and delegates two mountain men from Big Sur to set sail on the first leg of the voyage, at night. A few hours later, stoned-out Little John, who likes to wear women's underwear, is zonked at the helm. The vessel is on the wrong side of the channel buoy and powers over an underwater statue of Jesus Christ that rips open the keel. The two abandon the ship as it sinks and swim to shore.

Little John asks a passerby, "Where are we?"

The man answers, "Key Largo."

Bert, Candy Bergen, Barbara, and I visit Benny Shapiro in his elegant compound of jalapas in Yelapa, Mexico. Benny is an old Irgun Israeli terrorist fighter, ex–Bob Dylan manager, and successful smuggler. He is the racist who simply puts the "Schwartzer" Huey under an army blanket and drives him across the border into Mexico.

I turn down Bert's suggestion that I accompany Huey with a camera for the Caribbean leg of the escape. I refuse to enter into this danger for politics. I know I am over that line now.

On the east coast of Mexico, Huey buys a ride on a fishing boat with an outboard-powered dinghy put on board for the very last leg of the journey. In the surf of a beach in Havana, Huey crashes his little boat. He is arrested at gunpoint and held in jail for eight weeks until he is identified and then assigned jobs in a garbage truck facility as a repairman and in a school as an English teacher.

I have drifted away, floating above the hustle of moviemaking for some time, but a big payday is coming. I will pursue heaven with comfort. I go to Manhattan to see Ed to discuss our million-dollar profit on the low-budget film we produced, *Phantom of the Paradise*, directed by De Palma.

On my first film, I received nothing for co-producing, writing, and directing —any value went into our company, Pressman Williams Enterprises, Inc. On my second directorial effort, all my fees from United Artists go into our company. On my third film, all my fees from Warner Bros. go into our company.

Then Pressman Williams Enterprises produced *Phantom* for $1.2 million. Twentieth Century Fox picks up the film for distribution at a price of $2 million ($10 million today).

We parlayed our success for eight years.

Now I am a few years divorced, close to broke, and looking forward to taking it easy as a swell producing partner. I shall be the éminence grise in the background.

I sit down ready to hear about my check.

Ed says, "Brian plagiarized the entire script of *Phantom of the Paradise* from Universal's classic *Phantom of the Opera*, down to the commas and semicolons. Fox will only pay us our costs and give the rest to Universal as a settlement."

I say, "You are kidding."

He says, "No."

I say, "Jesus."

I sit stunned.

I say, "But our Errors and Omissions insurance will pay. That's what it is for."

Ed says, "I did not pay the last two monthly premiums, so we have no coverage."

I say, "What?"

He says, "I was trying to save money."

I say, "How much is the monthly premium?"

He says, "A hundred and twenty-six dollars."

I say, "Ed . . ."

I sit still.

I say, "We can sue De Palma."

He says, "Brian has no money."

Ed is the heir to his large family-owned toy company (his father brought Chinese checkers to America and pioneered knock-hockey), but Ed does not offer me any compassion or compensation.

When I tell my lawyer brother-in-law, Bob, about what has happened, he says, "Did he show you any papers?"

I say, "No."

He says, "You should sue him."

I say, "No. I trust him."

My partner is monumentally fucked by De Palma's crime. Another coincidence in my spiritual evolution?

The *Phantom* movie poster proclaims, "He's been maimed and framed, beaten, robbed and mutilated."

I know I am not that man I used to be.

"I'm making you two hot dogs with mustard and sauerkraut."

I say, "You don't have to."

She says, "Oh, yes, we can't watch a baseball game without hot dogs."

I sit on the couch in Apartment 10-F watching the Dodgers play baseball on TV.

I say, "I never seem to get any money from Ed. Sometimes I wonder if it's time to go off on my own."

The phone rings. Mildred gets up and answers the wall phone in the kitchen.

She says, "Oh, hello, Ed. We were just talking about you. Paul is thinking of dissolving your company."

Ed hangs up. She returns to the living room.

She got back at him for me? Or did she think she was just chatting?

I am stunned. It is not a dream. The cruel clambering bull has finally gored me.

Ed has a willful and flamboyant mother, Lynn Rambach, who has buried three husbands, including Ed's father when he was thirteen, and throughout every day wears haute couture Mister John hats, larger than a Mariachi trumpeter's sombrero, who dominates the Pressman empire she runs. Lynn carries excruciating weight in Ed's psyche. He never leaves out the *R* in Edward R. Pressman. Mothers' words have the weight to shock and awe. I know my mother's words will make Ed angry and vengeful in a massive defensive reaction.

Ed knows but cannot admit to himself that I had introduced him to all Pressman Williams's crowd of talent—De Palma, Malick, Scorsese, Avildsen, Coppola, Voight, Julie, Milius, Vonnegut, Bert Schneider, John Calley—and that would be the short list. Now he has his own standing as a unique young producer.

I have been his mentor and enabler. I still own half of Pressman Williams.

But I have uttered the wrong words to the neurotic Mildred of everyday reality.

I say, "That was just between you and me."

She might as well have screamed, "Murray, Murray, Murray!"

Soon, Ed summons me to our famed lawyer Sidney Cohn's thick-carpeted office to get my comeuppance—a settlement agreement that gives me next to nothing. Ed feels betrayed. And betrays.

I am responsible for creating this split. Is this the deep emotional frequency of the inner saboteur? Or the Big Bang of the superior self—creating a new beginning? What a privilege to fail. Most people would shoot themselves at this point, but it seems to me that this is clearly the next door to go through.

Yet my mind retains an edge—I remember Camus, "no matter how hard the world pushes against me, within me, there's something stronger—something better, pushing right back." Money is nice, but it is not the answer.

20

Life Upside Down

1975–1976

1975

Liz telephones.

She says, "You know, Paul, I've been out in the world now for a while, and I haven't met anyone who would have been as considerate of my feelings as you were when we were divorced. If you ever need anything, let me know."

I feel a deep sense of relief—understood and appreciated.

Michael Braun delivers a project to me that he knows aligns with my new ethos, *The Secret Life of Plants*, by Peter Tompkins (Class of 1940). My emerging self is willing to save the world, but not through materialism—the modern world is going whole hog for capitalism, as major department stores, for the first time in my life, begin to open for shopping on Sundays.

In Cannes on a Tuesday, I have a long talk with Gustave Berne, an owner of 20th Century Fox. Gus and I are in his rooms at the Carlton Hotel. He is in his boxer shorts when he agrees to finance the movie of *Plants*.

On Wednesday, Gus motions me to join him at his table on the Carlton terrace.

He says, "The bank where I have my line of credit just failed." He is a victim of the Sindona-Vatican bank scandal (later dramatized in *Godfather III*). My god. What a coincidence.

I call Michael.

He says, "We must secure the rights immediately. *Plants* is exploding with popularity. I don't know how long Peter will stay with us."

I call Elizabeth in New York and explain my urgent need.

She says, "I'll talk to my father and get back to you."

She calls back five hours later and says, "We no longer invest in retail. If you wanted the money to buy a company that made the film stock, we would look at that kind of thing."

I say, "What did you mean when you said, 'If I need anything, just ask?'"

She says, "I meant, if you needed an operation or something."

I say, "Thanks for trying. I do have Blue Cross."

I am The Hanged Man of the Tarot, upside down. All coins fall down from my pockets. "Our gold is not common gold," the Fool said.

Barbara gave birth to Zoe a few days ago. It was a harrowing long delivery of new life. I implored Barbara to have a natural childbirth. But finally an epidural had to be given to get her out of the pain. Our child emerged sunny-side up, feet-first, from the womb with her umbilical cord tightly wrapped around her neck—thank god we were in a hospital.

The infant is at her breast for a few days when Bert calls and asks me to go to Cuba with him to visit Huey.

He says, "I told the State Department that the purpose of our visit is to investigate potential USA-Cuban film co-production." Cuban-American relations are warming—there has been talk of a baseball game in Toronto between the two countries' All Stars, like the ping pong game that was the prelude to Nixon's opening to China.

It is not easy to leave Barbara and tiny Zoe for a few weeks, but I do. Zoe has far less interest in me than I do in her, and it is clear to me that my role comes later.

We head for Cuba with friends from Los Angeles—Candy Bergen, Terry Malick, editor Lynzee Klingman, Jane Fonda's producer Paula Weinstein, and my director friend from San Francisco—Francis Ford Coppola.

All the LA people are in Bert's hotel room in Mexico City. None of the others know Francis, so I am delegated to bring him into the group for the first time.

When I get to his room, he is eager to join the others.

I say, "Hold on. I want to meet Fidel. Listen to me. Suppose you were Fidel. Imagine? What would you most like from us?"

Francis pouts his lower lip and slightly shakes his head.

I say, "A Spanish subtitled print of *The Godfather: Part II*—if you get the reels here, we will meet Fidel. He's a hero of the film."

Francis gets on the phone and locates a print in Madrid. We all wait two days until *II* arrives in Mexico City.

I walk around the now-dowdy Havana Hilton Hotel that Fidel expropriated for his first headquarters after the revolution from Meyer Lansky and his US Mafia, who had bought it for a bargain price from Bill Rosenwald, who had sold it dirt cheap to them rather than take their offer of partnership.

We finally meet Fidel in the empty parking lot behind a huge public square after he finishes a speech to five hundred thousand people. It is an annual celebration of their block-by-block, grassroots electoral process of Municipal Assemblies.

Prime Minister Castro had implored the throng, "Don't believe in me. Believe in yourselves, in our revolution!"

The half million responded in unison, "Fidel! Fidel! Fidel! Fidel!"

Now, Paula asks, "Why did you kill all those people in the sports stadium?"

He says, "Revolution is a serious business. We took over the country. We gave them a chance to leave. They didn't. They wanted to kill us."

Fidel looks down for some moments. He looks at us softly.

He says, "They wanted to stop the Revolution."

Fidel shakes our hands as he makes his way around our circle. When he is in front of me, he leans close and whispers in my ear, just like Oscar Ichazo when we exchanged our first words.

He says, "Do you play basketball?"

I say, "Yes. I do."

I played center for the Cambridge University basketball team in 1966 against Oxford (Brits never played basketball then) and their six-foot-five American center, who out jumped me on the tip-off, dribbled down the court, switched the ball from his right to his left hand for a layup as he used his right elbow to smash my eyeglasses into my skull. I left the game in an ambulance. That Oxford Rhodes scholar Bill Bradley later stars for the NBA New York Knicks—and becomes a US senator from New Jersey.

Fidel says, "Okay, bring two guys at nine o'clock tomorrow to the school-yard by the beach and we'll play."

I say, "Okay. You got a game."

He says, "Okay, we got a game."

Francis stands to my left. Fidel shakes his hand and says, "I hope you don't mind, but we have stolen the print of your movie from your room and are copying it now to show our people."

Francis throws his arms up in the air and says, "It's not mine! It's Paramount's!"

Mission accomplished.

The next morning, the three-on-three basketball game pits solid Fidel and two buff Cuban soldiers, all in fatigues, against rotund Terry, hefty Francis, and skinny me. There are no other Cubans there—Fidel needs no additional security in this land where he is so adored.

Castro fouls me hard as he elbows his way into the post and makes an easy layup.

We get the ball out on the next play, and I back him into a deep post and give him a hard elbow in the ribs.

Fidel says, "Foul!"

I say, "No, that's the same as you did."

He says, "Foul, foul, foul."

He takes the ball out of my hands, walks to the free throw line. He takes two shots.

On the next play I am careful not to foul him, but I guard him so tightly that he has to stop dribbling. I quickly fall off him to help my two chubby directors guard their two fleet soldier-athletes.

Fidel can't find a passing lane.

Castro simply begins to dribble the basketball again and heads straight in for another easy layup.

I say, "Hey, hey! That's a double dribble."

Fidel looks at me.

I say, "That ain't basketball. You can't do that. It's our ball."

Fidel holds the ball and looks at me. I look at him. I see he is serious—he just must win.

He says, "This is my country. I can do whatever I want here," and laughs with a smile.

We laugh too.

Some egos are so big they can cradle a nation.

Before we fly away, Huey says, "Cuba is still racist—Black Cubans are victims of discrimination by the lighter-skinned Cubans." And he says he misses American hamburgers.

Fidel says, "I find capitalism repugnant. It is filthy, it is gross, it is alienating because it causes war, hypocrisy, and competition."

Huey wants to make a deal to come back to the USA of Richard Nixon and Gerald Ford.

And so goes politics. Give me some more of that New Age religion.

Back in the Santa Monica Mountains of Malibu, I do much of nothing and read *Enchiridion* by Epictetus—born a lame slave, died a philosopher, the disabled Stoic, "Demand not that events should happen as you wish; but wish them to happen as they do happen, and your life will be serene."

My daughter is six months old when she sits next to her mother in the back seat of a friend's car as we head down PCH past Zuma Beach. I am in the front passenger seat.

I see a tan body in a bikini dart into our path. My friend slams on his brakes, the car swerves. It hits the woman's hip with a powerful but glancing blow.

Our car skids across the opposite lanes. I see a telephone pole get closer and closer in slow motion.

I look back over my shoulder and see that my daughter lazily floats through the car's cabin like a weightless astronaut, toward the front windshield.

I casually raise my arms, put my hands around her, and pull her down into my chest as I curl around her. Finally, our car hits the pole with a bump.

This accident happens in less than three seconds.

Ted Williams, not my brother, the last baseball player to hit over .400 (.406 in 1941), allegedly could tell a pitch was a curve by watching the rotation of the laces on the baseball.

Time can expand.

A few months later, a dream assaults me at five o'clock in the morning. The ground shakes. I see a herd of angry elephants stampede directly at our one-year-old child.

I bolt up from the bed, wide awake.

I say, "Where's Zoe? Where's Zoe?"

Her mother, Barbara, wakes up and I ask again.

She says, "What?"

I am on my feet and dash into Zoe's bedroom. Empty. The living room and kitchen too are empty.

Barbara runs up the hill to the three hippie families, each with toddlers, that live on upper plateaus in a trailer and a Quonset hut and a school bus. Zoe is not there.

Now everyone in our community is out of bed and running galvanized in different directions over the landscape. It is frantic.

I run straight down the dirt road across the natural damn and up sixty yards to the crest of the south hill of our box canyon.

In the dawning light, I see a patch of blonde on the right side of the dirt road at the edge of the tall grass. I run.

Zoe sits on her little ass two hundred yards away from me.

She is twenty yards from the cars and trucks that race down Pacific Coast Highway from Oxnard, filled with low-paid hourly workers imagining they are NASCAR drivers as they rush to their construction and garden work in Los Angeles.

When I pick her up, she is happy and calm.

I carry her back to the house. She had made the trip on her hands and knees.

The Hindus' dancing elephant deity—Lord Ganesha, clears away obstacles and paves the way to go forward in life.

Young millionaires Isaac Tigrett and Peter Morton propose to join me on *The Secret Life of Plants*. I now plan to make the documentary film as a vehicle to dramatize the progressive stages in the development of highest consciousness.

The first plant investigator will say, "I believe the plants have emotional feelings—'That man is truly ethical who tears no leaf from a tree,' and that's what Albert Schweitzer wrote a long time ago."

His ego is attached to *belief*, like the out-of-it kid when he starts high school—the lowest level of consciousness.

The second investigator says, "I have performed measurements and have seen that plants have electrical reactions to Beethoven and have other cognitive capacities."

His ego is attached to the professional's *ethics*, like the radical kid who becomes a revolutionary—more liberated for action than the man stuck in belief.

The third says, "Step right up. I can sell you a ticket to my unique plant exhibition."

He has *sainted* his ego, like a Harvard student who becomes a dope smuggler (or like Donald Trump). He is just about himself, not constrained like the believers and ethical professionals.

The fourth investigator says, "I have studied the spiritual works of the East, cosmology, and even quantum physics, and I can tell you, of course plants have consciousness."

His ego has hidden itself inside his *brilliant ideas*, like the director planning a movie about crypto spirit in Brooklyn—but he has more freedom of imagination than the ruthless ego saint.

In a desert location, we find the fifth investigator: "I and everyone else who thinks that they know plants have consciousness are nuts—see that cactus? Sit on it."

His ego is his enemy—he's become fed up with his own thought and become a spiritual *hermit*, like the young refuge from Hollywood isolating in the mountains—but he has fewer constraints than the person with their brilliant ideas.

The sixth investigator says, "I, I poisoned myself, with oleander."

His ego has destroyed him, a *suicide*, like the cocaine adventurer ending up on the wrong side of a gun—no more ego limitations, call the coroner.

The seventh investigator says, "I almost died when my ego crashed down from its tower, but now after a couple of years of accepting all my experience and living with the plants, I can see their essence. They struggle to survive, to reproduce, and to live, just like me."

He has become *objective*, as my daughter, bless her heart, says I am. His ego is transformed into a servant of love.

In the coda of the movie, we see a man sitting still with his eyes rolled up. He has left the filmmakers a note, "I am empty. I am in the dimension of the perfect forms of plants. We have common origins."

He is referring to his extra-ordinary state of connecting the pure mind, pure heart, and pure experience. Like Dilgo.

Expecting difficulty from the various investors, I have explained to Tom Pollock before the meeting how to make a formula that could change depending on each investor's contribution over time. Tom fears it is too complicated a calculus to communicate.

The parties around the conference table argue about how to maximize their individual profit participation in a traditional partnership contract. It grows contentious.

I say, "Just be quiet." A philosophy teacher teaches philosophy. A philosopher lives his philosophy. I get out of my chair and stand on my head in the center of the table.

But Tom gives up on the meeting and walks out.

During the break that ensues after I get down, Peter Morton says, "Do you want to partner with me and Isaac on a hip hamburger joint in Paris? They are so ready for it!"

I say, "I'm not really interested, no."

The Hard Rock Cafe does fine without me.

A year later, Isaac tells me that Morton says, "Paul's the laziest guy I ever met." I understand his point of view. Am I good for nothing? I have no audience—ahead of my time? I just confuse people. Do I just atrophy?

I am seeing more and more clearly now, as far as I am concerned.

I call Rodgie about a legal matter that he quickly lets me know is outside his current purview. No longer with army counterintelligence, he is H. Rodgin Cohen, chairman of Sullivan and Cromwell, the preeminent New York law firm and, according to the *Wall Street Journal,* "The country's leading banking lawyer." Army war profiteers are far in his past.

I say, "By the way, Rodge, when I told you about my adventure with the Panthers in Algeria, why didn't you turn me in?"

He says, "We were both really on the same side. I was in the army just to catch war profiteers—and we caught some!"

Rodgie is good.

New and unusual adventures keep presenting themselves. It's what's happening now. We start a weeklong whitewater trip down the Snake River in Idaho—two guides, Bert and Candy, Artie, and Steve Blauner (The S in the production company BBS—Bert, Bob [Rafelson], and Steve). We all climb into a long, inflated rubber bucket raft.

We push off. The river flows gently, moves between the mountains like a big viper. But soon after a wide bend it narrows and the raft picks up speed, the foam churns around us, and we are in a current that rages high.

The raft is about twenty-five feet long and, as the rapids propel us over the first huge swell, the front of the raft rises up and then flexes down the wave—only the back of the raft is held down by Steve, who weighs more than 275 pounds.

As the raft slides well over the crest, the shortening back end suddenly catapults up like a seesaw and big Steve flies above us through the air like a Macy's Thanksgiving Day balloon and then plunges into the broiling Snake.

The others are stunned, paralyzed. I move quickly to the back of the raft as it approaches the man ahead.

I manage to hold onto a rope with my left hand and lean over the white-water to grab the back of his life jacket with my right. I manage to hold onto Steve as the river sprays around him.

Finally, we round into a calm eddy.

The guides paddle toward shore. Steve finds footing on the hard bottom.

He says, "Give me my stuff, I'm going."

The guide says, "It's a two-mile hike back."

He says, "No problem."

Bert says, "Come on, Blauner, it's going to be a great week on the river!"

Artie says, "Steve, it's just the beginning—Big horns. Mountain goats. Bears!"

Steve says, "Bye, Candy. See you in LA. Thanks, Paul."

He heads back toward our origin.

I am calmer in crisis than in everyday life.

Back from Idaho, I'm baby-proofing the cabin, nesting with Barbara and Zoe. A quiet time.

Bert calls and says, "Can you hide Abbie up there?"

I say, "Yes, what's the story?"

Bert says, "He's on the FBI's Ten Most Wanted List."

I say, "Hah. *Venceremos.*"

Abbie Hoffman is one of the founders of the Youth International Party, the Yippies. As one of the Chicago Seven, he was found guilty of inciting the 1968 Democratic Convention riots. He was the most vocal, dramatic, and funny of them all and later wrote *Steal This Book*. I thought he was the smartest of the Seven. He understood political theater, that laughing at authority is the blasphemous, ultimate social weapon.

Abbie skipped bail and starts to go by the name "Barry Freed." He has a surgical reverse nose job to make it big. Abbie left his wife, Anita, for Johanna "Angel" Lawrenson, his "running mate."

Johanna starts the "Save the River!" organization, and Barry Freed testifies at a Senate Hearing in Washington, DC. His argument motivates Senator Daniel Patrick Moynihan to block funding of the Army Corps of Engineers' ecologically destructive plan to keep the St. Lawrence Seaway open in winter.

Barry Freed exits Washington, DC, only to resurface in Las Vegas, where Angel says he shouted in a crowded hotel elevator, "I'm Abbie Hoffman, I'm Abbie Hoffman. Arrest me."

Abbie Schnozzola can't get arrested.

They arrive at our place in Malibu. Manic. Barbara and Zoe like them. He has a sometimes charming ego the size of a barn. He is not the least interested in any Sufi experiments to transcend it. Angel and Abbie take up residence in an old Quonset hut up one plateau.

Bert calls to say he wants to come out to see his old friend.

Barbara finds a cowboy hat and chaps, and we send Abbie up the mountain on an Appaloosa. When I look up and shade my eyes, that will be the signal for him to gallop down to Bert.

Bert arrives. He says, "Where's Abbie?"

I say, "I don't know where he went." I look up the mountain, shield my eyes.

A gray-and-black horse bursts onto the dirt fire road and heads downhill.

Bert follows my eyes, shakes his head. He says, "That would be Abbie . . ."

In the Chicago US District Court trial, the defendant Abbie first appeared dressed in judicial robes.

Abbie asks me to get him a date with Julie Christie. He suggests that he can meet her at a motel on Pacific Coast Highway.

I call her. She agrees to a rendezvous.

He's gone for an afternoon.

When he gets back, he says, "She gave me a shoebox with $10,000. And when I asked, she agreed to roll around on the bed for a minute, but that's all."

Artie has pressed me into working with him on a screenplay, *West Coast*. One of the characters is based on Abbie. Rick Dreyfuss wants to play the role. He comes out to meet him. They're both impressed with meeting each other.

Abbie starts to abuse Angel in the mornings. That takes me by surprise. Artie gets some Thorazine and strong-arms him to swallow it. Angel is okay.

Now Freed starts to make phone calls every morning from our kitchen. He wants to produce a movie based on the memoir *Stranger at the Party* by Johanna's late mother, Helen—a model and *Vogue* editor who concurrently dated its publisher, Condé-Nast, and the Communist founder of the NY Longshoremen's Union, Jack Lawrenson.

Producer Freed's three weeks of careless manic phone calls to Hollywood contacts are about to reveal the Most Wanted Abbie's whereabouts. There is no way he will let me help him diminish his ego. It rules his whole being. I am ready for him to leave. He is a diversion. It's time for him to change hideouts.

I tell him it's time. I give him my last prized possession that possesses me—a Dutch, hand-painted belt buckle that Liz gave me. He and Angel drive away down the dirt road to the highway.

Abbie's personality will soon kill him.

The screenplay *West Coast* is about a raft trip down the Snake River with four macho guys and one liberated woman—who saves them all with clear right action after their various macho egos fuck things up. Artie and I finish writing.

My old friend Dyanne Asimow, says, "You guys should be writing a screenplay about two crazy guys writing a spiritual screenplay in a goat shed about the man on the Ten Most Wanted list while they try to keep him hidden."

Bob De Niro is shooting *1900* with Bernardo Bertolucci in a rural town north of Milan. I fly to Italy. I take a seat on the aisle of the cinema that, I've been told, Bob is going to on his break this afternoon. I sit alone in the repurposed antiquated church.

Twenty minutes later, Bob and Diahnne Abbott walk down the aisle.
I say, "Hello, Bob."
He says, "Paul, what are you doing here?"
I say, "I'm here to talk to you about a movie."
He says, "We have a house near here. We can go there."
We spend a couple of days in the rustic house in the forest with a huge fireplace and stacks of wood and kindling.

I try to explain the spiritual and womanly virtues of *West Coast*. He is unimpressed.

Finally, he says, "Why did you ask me that question at Cannes last month when I was onstage?"

I say, "You were uncomfortable, so I figured I'd lob you an easy one to talk about."

He says, "I hate being onstage to talk. I just want to get off as soon as I can. I hated you for asking the question."

I do not understand that women's lib's heyday is still a long way off. And he does understand that the more he indulges his personality, the less he just observes from emptiness, the more he jeopardizes his pure actor's instrument. It hits the heart.

In Malibu in June, my phone rings and wakes me up.

Steve Blauner says, "Artie's dead. I just found him leaning against the staircase from the kitchen in Pressman's house. His face is frozen by the nitrous oxide. He still has the breathing mask tied on and the tank is still turned on." Artie was promoting a De Palma film, territory by territory with a dozen prints, and was using Ed's Hollywood pied-à-terre.

I go into shock.

The crust of terra firma under me disintegrates—I free-fall, rushing downward through black empty space, free-fall in a black silo, free-fall for nearly a minute. I fear the landing, but it never comes.

Seven different times this day, the earth under my feet opens and I fall, and fall, and fall.

The next day, I plummet six times into the blackness.

The next day, five. These toppling black waves plunge me into black free-falling descent—but every day, one fewer wave—until they cease when the week ends.

He lived his twenty-nine years and that's it? Now eternity?

At Artie's funeral in Westchester County, New York, his casket in the ground in front of me, I address the mourners.

But I look down at the event from fifteen feet above my head. I am not in my body. I have lost my best friend in this world.

Floating in air, Artie's syntax and vocabulary suddenly fill my mind. I don't think about it. I speak his words in his cadence and in his tone of voice.

These words galvanize and unify the mourners. Does Artie live again in these utterances? In or from a mystical dimension? Or not.

When the mourners begin to disperse, I descend into my body in Scarsdale.

The higher self knows everything, including its own source?

1976

I sit on a big pillow in the living room. Zoe walks over to me. She looks at me.

She punches me in the shoulder. I look at her, and then punch her shoulder with just an equal force.

She looks at me. She punches me harder than the first time. It hurts a bit.

I look at her. I hit her back again just with the same degree of force.

She hauls back and punches me hard. It hurts.

Strong little girl.

She looks at me. I let her see that I am in pain.

I hit her hard enough to hurt her, but no more than that.

She cries softly for a moment.

I look at her.

Zoe looks at me and smiles.

In *Toward an Ecology of Mind*, Gregory Bateson (coincidentally, a friend of Professor Ray Birdwhistell) ridicules insights of shrinks, not to mention actors or gurus, because he deems their perceptions subjective. But I still find him useful to expand the mundane matrix of being.

I say to Barbara, "Bateson defines mental health as, one: the ability to properly identify a context, two: the ability to communicate effectively in that context, and three: the ability to shift from one context to another without difficulty. Home is a context of openness, a restaurant of social rituals, grandma's house or something else. They each require different behavior and expressions."

She says, "I get it."

I say, "The hippie Perfect-World we are creating for her is the wrong paradigm. We must stop creating an idealized world for Zoe."

She says, "We live and learn."

Warren Beatty's new movie *Shampoo* is in the theaters. In a scene on a hill-side, Julie tells Warren that that he is not serious enough and that she will not marry him. In real life, Warren collars me at a party at Bert's.

He says, "Julie is in love with you."

Surprised, I don't take my time.

I say, "I love her, too."

Two days later, Julie swims toward me.

I stand by the edge of the pool of her rented house on top of Benedict Canyon and watch the naked star approach.

She gets out of the water, walks up close, and kisses me.

My dream girl.

We go into the house.

We talk. Later, she walks across the room on her hands, with her legs up, feet tucked behind her head.

I am long back from the year with the Sufis. Julie now clearly also pursues the yogic path.

She says I should walk out on Barbara.

I explain that I cannot leave baby Zoe because it takes a couple of years for Erik H. Erickson's "First Stage of life—Basic Trust" to be solidified. Once Zoe has that trust of love and can depend on her effectiveness in her world, it will be hard to lose. A lack of basic trust will last for a lifetime.

Julie is the one. I understand James Joyce's "Love loves to love love." But I can't leave Zoe. Not taking what one desires is the hardest thing in the world.

Julie is hurt.

She will not try again.

This is a remorseful conclusion to bad timing with, as Al Pacino calls her, "The most poetic of actresses."

In a corner of my heart, I resent my little baby Zoe, not to mention her mother.

I have introduced attorney Tom Pollock to our gaggle of young talent—that Pollock, Dekom, Rigrod & Bloom now represent.

He is appreciative.

In his office in a tall building on Sunset Boulevard, there is a life-size, framed color photograph behind his desk of a strikingly beautiful red-haired actress with an extended bare leg—smiling at me with a powerful gaze.

I say, "Wow. That's a terrific picture. Who is that?"

Tom says, "Karen Black."

I say, "Do people ever look at you when they're at your desk?"

He says, "I have a great project for you to direct. It's from the *Harvard Lampoon*—they have ten million subscribers—there's no way this won't be a hit."

I say, "What's it about?"

He says, "Fraternities. Parties. Sex. Very funny."

I say, "There are no fraternities at Harvard. I know nothing about them."

He says, "Read it."

I do. It is a hilarious, spiritually bankrupt, absurd drama about fraternity life. Something I know nothing about. I do know that I don't feel like making movies—especially not an unwitting celebration of ego, like this.

I call Tom.

I say, "I am certain I am not the right director for the film. You need somebody who knows something about the subject."

Later, this low-budget film, *Animal House*, is well directed by high school dropout John Landis and makes $143 million in domestic box office receipts ($418 million today). Tom eventually becomes president of Universal and later a picture-maker for them.

I introduce Pollack to David Odell, and David eventually directs a few films for him. I will not. I am headed somewhere else. But I will let it come to me.

Bert calls, "I'm having a party up here at the house tomorrow night for the Weathermen to meet Hollywood. I invited everybody. We have lots of copies of *Prairie Fire*. Come on up with Barbara."

This is exciting history. *Prairie Fire: The Politics of Revolutionary Anti-Imperialism* is printed in book form with a soft red cover. This book is the collective statement of the Weather Underground, ready for sub-rosa distribution.

Mark Rudd says, "It is an attempt to influence the movement that we abandoned back in 1969. It says, 'Don't despair, we're all part of the same thing.'"

The Weathermen took credit for twenty-five bombings—including the US Capitol, the Pentagon, the California Attorney General's Office, and a New York City police station. How will all the entertainment business liberals behave? I am so interested.

The next night we drive up Beverly Glen and walk into Bert's. The Weather Underground is represented by eight comrades. They outnumber the Hollywood attendees—Bert, Candy, Jack Nicholson, Huey, Barbara, and me.

That's it. No one else shows up.

The Last Tycoon opens, starring Jack and Bob De Niro. In their only scene alone together, Jack includes not only what is going on between the tycoon and union boss but also what Jack Nicholson is feeling about playing for the first time with another great actor of his generation—Robert De Niro, and also what Jack is feeling about the cast and crew on the set at the moment watching the championship match. Bob is focused on his imaginary circumstance, surrounded and swamped as Jack includes everything.

Then the Western *Missouri Breaks* opens, starring Jack and Marlon Brando. They have one scene alone together, and for the only time in his career, Jack acts stiffly on screen. He does not allow his real feelings of awe for Brando to be included in the expression of his character's feeling. Brando sits comfortably in his saddle. Jack fails to admit Jack's veneration of Brando and we can see him make an awkward effort to convince us, the audience, that they are mano a mano equals. He loses his full flowing power.

At fault? "Never step on your own dick." The heel of Achilles?

Jack and Brando gave Helena Kallianiotes the third house in between theirs in a gated Mulholland Drive compound overlooking LA. Helena belly danced at a place in town and regularly glided out the door, dancing out onto Hollywood Boulevard followed by a crowd of cheering celebrities. She has a monologue in *Five Easy Pieces* where she plays an aggressive, lesbian hitchhiker. Jack and Karen Black sit in the front seat as Helena, in the back seat next to Toni Basil (who created the very first music dance video, *Hey Mickey*), explains how this filthy world is filled with nothing but crap.

Helena calls me and asks me to work with her on a screenplay that I think we can turn into a story about significant evolution beyond ego. I drive up to her house several times a week to improvise with her, playing my version of Elizabeth. Helena writes a screenplay about her own character—a street prostitute—and my heiress, whom she wants Julie to play.

I say, "These two have to learn from each other. They are both caught in their limited personalities. Let them both evolve to something higher."

She says, "The rich girl is so full of shit."

I say, "Everybody is a victim."

She says, "Bullshit."

I say, "How about a waterscape by Monet? Or a novel by Virginia Woolf? Something where she enlarges your point of view?"

She says, "That's not what it's about."

I say, "It should be."

She says, "No, she has to learn how to be real—from me."

I say, "Anyway, the story is lopsided. Julie won't want to play that role. And she knew Elizabeth."

Helena allows a clear moment or two in the screenplay for the heiress, but it is no spiritual awakening for the characters. I know Julie will not find it interesting. I don't.

Still, I get on a plane for Lima, Peru, to meet Julie after she returns from her climb up magical Machu Picchu on LSD. I have never been to South America. There are only two flights a week from LA, so I will arrive days early for our meeting.

I check into the Gran Hotel Bolívar built on the huge Plaza San Martín in 1924. There are photos on the walls of Orson Welles and Ava Gardner in the 1940s. There is a message at the front desk for me that Julie will arrive in three days. I drink pisco sours.

I walk around town to score quality, cheap cocaine. Unfortunately, I am a foot and a half taller than the Peruvians and an obvious target for police and a mark for sellers. In a crowded basement bar, I nevertheless skillfully negotiate the purchase of a white powder ball the size of a grapefruit, covered in Saran wrap, before I slink out onto the street. Back at my hotel room, I am unhappy with my large supply of expensive talcum powder.

The next day as I walk through the plaza, I am unsettled as a score of short, barely teenage boys besiege me with sexual offers of themselves. I find it hard to believe. And disheartening. I decline.

Julie shows up at the Bolívar in love with a new boyfriend, Duncan, a left-wing English writer. I am disappointed. We drink in the hotel bar.

She reads the script. I chat with Duncan. It is not for her—too one-sided.

No coke, no romance, no casting. But I enjoy the time.

No movie. I am lazy. It feels good.

21

Holy in Hollywood

1977

David Proval drives out to Malibu to give me James Andronica's screen-play *Nunzio*. I have no enthusiasm for work and don't read it right away. When I do, I think it is a perfect metaphor of a "normal" society of egos mis-understanding a man of pure essence and compassion.

A crypto holy movie. I might be able to attend to this revolt of the soul against intellect. But why do I keep going back?

The head of a major studio makes only a salary. But after four or five years of stressful stewardship, they are rewarded with "picture-maker" status by their studio. They make three or four or five pictures a year—and get a producer's piece of the profits of the movies—that's the switch from paltry income to real capitalist. My old champion Jennings Lang is a picture-maker at Universal.

He wants the star, Robby Benson (*Ode to Billy Joe*), to play the lead in *Nunzio*.

I say, "You must see my actors who brought me the project."

He says, "Okay, bring them up and do a couple of scenes in my office."

I rehearse the scene in which the delusional Nunzio is confronted by his brother for refusing to take gratuities for his grocery deliveries and explains simply, "Superman don't take tips."

They do the scene for Jennings in his office. He cries.

But we do not get a start date with this cast for this movie ostensibly about a lower-class, mentally challenged Italian in Brooklyn.

The Academy Awards are a week later. At eleven o'clock, John Avildsen's *Rocky* wins Best Picture. He wins Best Director. The movie is about a lower-class, dim, challenged Italian in Philadelphia.

I am at the wood-burning stove in the cabin when the phone rings. It is Jennings Lang and MCA-Universal CEO and president Sid Sheinberg on the line.

Jennings says, "Can you start shooting *Nunzio* in early summer?"

I say, "Yes. Not with Robby Benson. With David and Jimmy?"

He says, "Yes. Okay. Come in tomorrow and we'll start."

The most important thing to understand about Hollywood is, as Tom Pollock said to me, "We want to make a picture just like the last big hit—only a little different."

Yes, Brooklyn, not Philadelphia.

The next morning, Jennings tells me that my fee for directing is $150,000 ($624,000 today). My "unknown" actor friends, David Proval and Jim Andronica, will get $35,000 each. I tell Jennings to pool the fees and give us each one-third, $85,000. The actors will be happy. And I have communized and mommy-ized my wealth.

I walk into Jennings's office on the tenth floor of the Tower. Walter Matthau sits in a high-backed plush chair in front of a black-and-white English hunting print. Jennings sits behind his English antique desk with an open bottle of scotch, half-empty. I visit with the two of them in the mornings during pre-production of *Nunzio*. Jennings finishes his daily bottle by noon.

He takes a phone call—he's also producing one of the *Airport* sequel movies.

Jennings says, "James Mason wants what? Tell your client Mr. Mason that the movie is a piece of shit. He can read the script when he gets here. We start in three days. It's two hundred and fifty thousand—yes or no? Today. I'll get somebody else tomorrow."

Walter is the most centered American I have met. He is as awake as a Buddha. He is famous for *The Odd Couple* with Jack Lemmon, and his Oscar-winning performance in Billy Wilder's *The Fortune Cookie*. Even Jack Nicholson relaxes onstage during the commercial breaks at the Academy Awards—when the countdown to the back-on-the-air moment occurs, everyone gets ready to be "on"—except Walter. He's the same sitting in Jennings office or in front of a billion people with Jack. He is one powerful Jew.

Sid Sheinberg, head of MCA-Universal, orders me to have lunch with two young men about to direct their films for Universal: Steven Spielberg and Michael Crichton.

I know Spielberg from weekends at Margot's house, and Crichton from afternoons in the newsroom of the *Crimson*. I am happy to help them.

I say, "I know Sid made you come here and you don't need to hear anything from me. You are directors."

They nod.

I say, "One thing I wish I had known before I shot my first feature: I did not know exactly what rhythm I needed—within scenes and the pace between scenes—to make the movie swing. And I did not appreciate how unimportant entrances and exits are."

They both pay attention.

"Make sure the actor enters an empty frame at the beginning of each setup—even if there is no dramatic reason for the entrance. A clean entrance into the frame works—regardless of location, even if the character isn't speaking. Same at the end—exit the frame.

"Then in the editing room after the entrance of the first actor into his frame, you can cut to a shot of a second character—who you want to seem to 'start' the scene (allowing you to cut the second's prior undesired blah-blah that you did not like), and then you can go back to your first character wherever you want in their dialogue (allowing you to cut any of the first's prior unwanted blah-blah).

"If you do this, you can start a scene where it gets good, and end it when you decide it is done—using the same cutting technique for the clean exit.

"You will have control of the internal rhythm of the scenes. You will also have control of the pace between the scenes in the movie. You will also be able to throw out unnecessary shots of people coming in and going out doors."

Spielberg smiles.

I say, "Your final cut can be smooth."

Crichton nods.

I like helping people.

Jennings says, "Your budget is two point three and the production department budgeted it out at three. You've gotta cut seven hundred thousand."

I say, "Let me see the budget."

I see there are thirty Teamsters in the budget for the entire length of the show for close to $700,000.

My writer and now best friend, Jimmy, calls his brother in Brooklyn who is "connected" to one of the warring Mafia families. Jim was a boxer in New York and resembles Rocky Marciano in his murderous compactness and speech.

Later, Jim says, "Can you get Jennings to come to a meeting in Brooklyn? There's four lieutenants, just below the *capo*—Sammy runs one-quarter of Brooklyn—he can fix things, but he needs a sit-down."

Jennings, Jimmy, and I approach an Italian restaurant in Brooklyn. Two big guys stand outside the front door. They usher us in and return to their posts. The large dining room is empty but for one dark man, who sits in the back in a half-oval booth.

Jennings enjoys the drama and sits down comfortably. He knows the mob rules the unions in The City. I sit on the other side of our host and notice a white-handled revolver in a holster on a belt. He had been a key member of the late Crazy Joe Gallo's crew.

Jimmy introduces us.

Sammy "The Syrian" Zahralbam says, "So, you got a problem." His voice is low, raspy, and accented with the speech of the borough.

He says, "Jamsie says you got thirty Teamsters?"

Jennings says, "That's right, Sammy. We can't make the movie if there are that many."

He says, "Okay. You know what? You know how many Teamsters you're going to have? You're going to have one Teamster."

He holds up a finger.

I say, "One?"

He says, "That's right. One."

I say, "That's great."

He says, "But there's one thing. You know that film that was here with the Travolta kid?"

Jimmy says, "*Saturday Night Fever?*"

Sammy says, "They got firebombed the first two weekends. Then we got the job to be location manager, and it stopped. We can be your location manager and everything'll go right. No *moulinyans*. No trouble. We'll have a couple of guys there and some baseball bats in the car. Mistah Lang, can Universal do that?"

Moulinyans in Italian is an eggplant, slang for a Black human being.

Jennings says, "You can have whatever is in the budget for location management."

That is thirty-two thousand dollars.

We eat and chat. When Sammy gets up, I see that he has a second white-handled revolver in another holster on his other side.

Jennings gets in a cab and heads back to JFK.

I am going to make my spiritual movie.

Joel Wiley had been a California surfer before he lived with the Montagnards in Cambodia, and then become a monk in Tibet. The lamas had told him he had gotten too far out, "Go back into the world and rebalance."

He wanders up the road to our little house in the box canyon. I like him.

I plan to take Joel to Brooklyn to sit with David Proval in his trailer while we shoot *Nunzio*. I want to show an empty man (albeit mentally challenged) with little ego who interacts with egocentric Western people—but do it without any mystical references. This will be subtextual transcendent pedagogy.

David does not want to follow my plan—to look into Joel's thoughtless pure monk's eyes in his trailer between takes. He says he will not do it.

We go to Manhattan for preproduction and rehearsals.

A week before we shoot, Joel and I introduce David to Joel's old buddy, the 16th (Black Hat) Karmapa, Rangjung Rigpe Dorje, who now visits in an apartment on Park Avenue.

The Karmapa's translator informs him that Proval is in fact mentally challenged. The Karmapa asks David to walk back and forth in the living room. David does his well-practiced Nunzio shuffle. The Karmapa, a completely enlightened Buddhist master, has David sit before him and bends him forward so he can blow repeatedly over the back of David's neck. When the Karmapa finishes blowing, he gives David a blessing and we leave.

Out on Park Avenue, David says, "Fuck you, Paul. No fucking lamas in my trailer."

I return to my parents' apartment in Manhattan and Proval goes back to Brooklyn.

My whole purpose is to show the world beyond personality. I am stymied. Principal photography is just days off.

At eleven o'clock, I hear the wall phone ring in my parents' kitchen.

Proval says, "Paul, I went back to Brooklyn and played basketball under the lights in the playground—all night, until about half an hour ago. I-never-missed-a-shot. You hear me? Never. Not-one. I-did-not-miss. Joel can sit in the trailer."

Jimmy and David have scored a supply of heroin. They arrange for three junkie supermodels to join us in our suite on one of Universal's floors in the Essex House—located on Central Park South only a few doors east of where Elizabeth and I lived five years earlier.

This is my first experiment with heroin. Jimmy expertly shoots me up.

I am on my back and she is on top of me. She slowly undulates with the swells in my imagined ocean. Just say yes. She makes enhanced endless love on a harmonious cellular level. I am global, nearer God.

She emits a staccato series of fast, deep gasps that sound like a foghorn of a tugboat, followed by short exhales. After nine of these calls, she topples off me and onto the plush carpeted floor.

Jimmy jumps from his tryst quickly and is on his knees at my comatose lover's side. He holds her nose shut with one hand and puts his mouth over hers and blows. He is focused.

I immediately see that we shall be arrested with a big story in the *Post* and the *Enquirer. Nunzio* will be canceled. The old, forty-nine New York City warrants for assault that Jim ran away from when he moved to LA will be revealed. This is foremost in my mind, not this poor dying woman.

Jimmy keeps perfect rhythm as he breathes into her. After two long minutes, she comes back to life.

Jimmy is a good doctor.

And actors are often reminded that what they are doing is not that important—like saving a person's life or something.

We are into the fourth week and I have shot all the easy scenes that I scheduled to be sure I was on schedule and on budget. I start to fall behind now, but I know the studio will not pull the plug—there is too much money already invested.

Sammy the location manager blames the problem on our production office. Sammy has the local funeral parlor place an empty casket in the office of our production manager, John Nicolella, who finds it when he arrives one morning. John is nervous when he informs me.

Later this day on the set, we shoot a long scene between Jimmy and Morgana King, Nunzio's mother. Morgana, otherwise a jazz singer, played Marlon Brando's wife in *The Godfather*. She has trouble remembering her lines. They argue. It goes slowly.

Sammy walks onto the set, right into the shot.

I say, "Sammy, you ruined the shot."

He says, "I want to talk to you." He points. I follow him behind the wall of the living room set. I can see from the bulges on his hips that he has his guns on.

He says, "You're behind schedule. You're going over budget."

I say, "So?"

He says, "So—you're over budget."

I say, "Sammy, what? Are you workin' for Universal?"

He looks at me.

I say, "They're not going to stop the movie. It's too late."

He says, "But you're behind schedule."

I say, "Is it your money, Sammy? Huh?"

He looks stern. I don't know if he's going to slug me or whack me.

He laughs.

He says, "You don't give a fuck?"

I shake my head.

He says, "Holy shit, you don't give a fuck!"

I smile.

Sammy turns and walks away laughing, "He don't give a fuck . . . He don't give a fuck . . ."

Richard Dreyfuss asks me to hire his girlfriend as my assistant on the film. I agree. She is an actress and accustomed to sets, most recently, Spielberg's *1941*.

Lucinda Valles arrives from Los Angeles and walks around the Brooklyn locations with a walkie-talkie on her hip and her shining eyes wide open. She looks directly at everyone. She is in her early twenties and in full bloom. Her openness convinces Sammy, unused to actors, that Lucinda loves him.

On a Saturday morning two weeks after Lucinda's arrival, one of the "location staff" asks me to invite Lucinda and to escort her on Sunday morning to their boat to go fishing. We will head out of Sheepshead Bay with Sammy, two location guys, and me. He adds, "Sammy's going to rape her."

I call Rick in LA.

I say, "The Mafia boss asked me to bring Lucinda out on his boat tomorrow with two made guys and they told me they're going to rape her. I'm going to bring her to JFK and fly her away tonight. It's not safe for her here anymore."

Rick says, "My god. Okay."

I do not tell Lucinda about the danger. Mafia fishing trips have returned with fewer on board than at embarkation. I want her quickly out of the way with no drama that might involve police, much less our location team. She is upset at being let go. After shooting all day, I drive her to JFK and I see her off.

The next morning, I appear at the slip to find Sammy with the two bodyguards on a dilapidated twenty-foot pilothouse inboard. More modest a vessel than I expected.

One bodyguard says, "Where's Lucinda?"

I say, "She went back to LA last night. Richard Dreyfuss called her."

The four of us head far out into the bay. It is hot. And quiet. They give me a fishing rod. After some hours at anchor, I catch an ancient invertebrate. I am impressed with my starfish, but my companions morosely toss it back into the water without a thought of adding it to their pasta dinner.

On a phone call with Richard on the line the next day, Lucinda says, "How could you tell Richard and not me what was going on?"

I say, "Okay, I was insensitive to the matter of women's equality but I did not want to take any chances. Maybe you would have called the cops. That would have been a real mess. My father always said, 'All this could have been avoided.'"

Richard says, "That wasn't right."

I say, "I understand your point of view."

They do not speak to me for two years.

It's okay. Her life is saved.

I shoot all day in Brooklyn. A car picks me up, exhausted, and delivers me to the new Broadway show *Annie*. Jennings wants me to direct the movie version for Universal.

I say, "I don't know anything about musicals."

The show begins and I fall asleep in my third-row seat.

After we finish shooting *Nunzio*, he asks me to direct the next film in the *Airport* franchise. I know it is important for my career to make a commercial movie but my career seems to be my enemy.

I say, "There's nothing to direct. That dialogue?"
He says, "Telegrams. Easy."
I say, "What do I know about shooting airplane action?"
He says, "You just sit in a screening room and pick takes that the second unit shoots during the day."
I say, "It's not something I want to do with my life."
Jennings says, "You're not a director. You're a rabbi."
I like Jennings.
He's right. He's more than right.

It is seven weeks into the shoot. I plan the wild garbage truck scene when Nunzio careens the truck along the neighborhood streets and over the sidewalks. The kinetic emotion of this scene sets up the final scenes of compassion.

Jennings says, "We are too far over budget. We wrap next week."
He opens the script. He turns to pages at the back.
He says, "The garbage truck sequence?"
He rips out the pages.
I am dumbfounded.
Jennings says, "We're back on schedule."
He don't give a fuck, either.

Nunzio is scored by Lalo Schifrin (*Theme from Mission Impossible*, and *Cool Hand Luke*, and many more Oscar-nominated scores) and is the closing-night choice for the Toronto Film Festival. In a huge theater, our movie receives a standing ovation from the entire audience. The Canadians identify with the mentally challenged hero who triumphs over the greater egos of the USA. The film has deeply touched their national chip on the shoulder. They go wild.

In New York, *Nunzio* gets a tepid reaction from the critics when it opens—a minor work, dismissed by serious critics as too sweet and syrupy.

Book Four

How to Get into Heaven

22

Upheaval

1978–1980

1978

Joel says, "The Dalai Lama is coming for the first time to Hollywood. Can you introduce him to the community?"

The goat shed that I live in is too small for His Holiness's audience, so I call Julia Phillips's ex-husband, producer Michael.

Weeks later, Joel runs up my hill to the shed, "You forgot?"

He hustles me into my VW van. When I pull in to Michael's Beverly Hills hilltop mansion, I see dozens of LA cops and motorcycles and ear coil–wired Secret Servicemen.

I plan to introduce the Hollywood people to the Dalai Lama with a demonstration of Detachment meeting Expression.

We do the Meisner repeat exercise.

David Proval sits opposite the highest lama and begins to express his feelings but only with the words, "You're wearing orange robes."

The Dali Lama is detached. He says, "I'm wearing orange robes."

David's voice reveals a changed feeling as again he says, "You're wearing orange robes."

The Dalai Lama repeats, "I'm wearing orange robes."

David is on an emotional ride, "You're wearing orange robes."

The Dali Lama repeats, "I'm wearing orange robes."

The volley repeats again and again and again. David's feelings continue to roll. But the Dalai Lama is not prone to engage in "the wheel of the passions."

The pitch of his voice, however, does rise higher and higher as his energy is displaced upward in his body. The opposite of the Happy Birthday exercise. Finally, after a particularly falsetto "I'm wearing orange robes," His Holiness ignores Proval.

Now, in deeply resonant kath tones that vibrate every molecule in the air, he says, "I am Rainbow Body. I am Rainbow Body."

Proval says, "You are rainbow body."

"I am Rainbow Body." His Holiness does not "include" Proval's meek reaction.

His Holiness continues in a strong, cadenced rhythm, "I am Rainbow Body. I am Rainbow Body. I am Rainbow Body." He stops.

The living room packed with two hundred stars and starlets is fully present, full of his energy.

He says, "Om Mani Padme Hum . . . Om Mani Padme Hum . . . Om Mani Padme Hum . . ." (the mantra of the Buddha of Compassion—each spoken phrase lasts six seconds; the traditional chant of Om takes six seconds with a pause of about six seconds to inhale).

All repeat his chant in unison. All now breathe in this natural rhythm.

I chant, "Om My Money, My Mommy . . . Om My Money, My Mommy . . . Oh My Money, My Mommy . . ." An unprofitable, mindless mantra.

In the West, the actor maintains emptiness by expressing the changing emotions, the tensions in his body, moment to moment. In the East, the lama maintains emptiness moment to moment in thoughtless detachment, or a focused chant. This emptiness is where the East meets West—the twain have met, Mr. Kipling. No future, no past.

One of the cardinal rules of acting onstage is the prohibition of actual physical violence—the readiness must be all. But I was raised to use my brains not fists. With the fearsome actor Vincent D'Onofrio (later, in *Full Metal Jacket*) and another time, with Andy Garcia (later, in *The Untouchables*), I force myself to stand toe to toe, ready to fight, to take a punch or throw one. In the moment. It's intense.

Soon after, I meet an Italian American gangster from Brooklyn at Jimmy's apartment in Hollywood.

The guy says, "So I paint a dishwasher shipping carton silver and cut out a rectangular slit near the top with a sign, 'Out of Order. Deposit Here.' Then I put it in front of the night deposit box in the drive-in lane of the bank. I park down the block in a station wagon until 2:00 a.m. When it's dead, I speed back to the drive-up and throw the carton in the back. Later I sit on the curb and throw all the checks down the sewer. I just keep the cash."

I laugh.

He says, "You Jews don't have the guts."

I stand up from the couch. He stands up. Jimmy watches. He must have told the guy I was a Jew.

I'm ready. My heart beats—I am not just a piece of meat. I'm a standup guy.

The Italian guy laughs. He says, "Okay. You're okay."

Jimmy says, "Calm down, Paul. Sit down."

He laughs. Goldberg sits down.

My heart pounds.

I stand alone in the Imperial Gardens when Steven Spielberg notices me from some distance and says, "Williams—I didn't know you were a sushi man! Come have sushi with me."

Spielberg is the now the prince of Hollywood with *Jaws*. The biggest hit Hollywood has ever seen. And now he is open and friendly.

I cannot speak. The hackneyed wisdom is that you're only as good as your last film. I am depressed about my film *Nunzio*. I feel unworthy and insecure. He has given birth to the summer blockbuster.

I say, "It's okay, no, thanks, I'll be all right . . ."

I am paralyzed, as I was when Elaine invited me to play doctor when I was ten. I cannot tell him that the Jew, Goldberg, is in my attic.

1979

I read Sigmund Freud's *Cocaine Papers*. He had been an ophthalmologist but gave it up when another ophthalmologist published a paper on the same topic that Freud had been researching for years—six months before Freud would be ready to present his work. It was clear to Freud that he would not be the number-one ophthalmologist in Germany, and he had to be number one. Ego.

Cocaine is the anesthetic of choice for the eye.

Freud writes about his subsequent cocaine explorations. I follow the procedures and dosages he used to investigate his unconscious. Injecting two-tenths of a gram, it is as astonishing to me as though I myself have discovered the id. I connect to my spinal column's forceful undulating energy into my sexuality. My movement mainlines into my lizard brain, my medulla oblongata.

I repeat the procedure many times with no restraint from my superego to box me in. I undulate wildly on the mountain whenever the moon is full, naked in my African dance, accompanied by a boombox that blares Bruce Springsteen's "Dancing in the Dark."

The feeling is sexual but not orgasmic; the energy stays within.

John Lilly lives two canyons south on PCH in Malibu. His pioneering work with dolphins and consciousness exploration are featured in the movies *Day of the Dolphin* and *Altered States*. John also studied with Oscar Ichazo. I had years earlier implored Barbara to respond to Lilly's ad in the *Malibu Times* for an associate. She was reluctant, but I insisted that he would jump at the unique opportunity to employ a bright local ravishing someone who also coincidentally has studied with Ichazo.

She became his main associate in all his activities and global travels— and enhanced the rest of her life. After decades as head of the Human/ Dolphin Foundation, Barbara's explanation in her funeral oration about John's work was brilliant, moving, and clear as a bell.

I introduce John, B.Sc., M.D., Ph.D.—he only used COU (Center of the Universe) and MIB (Master of Inappropriate Behavior)—to this then little-known book of Freud's. He travels to England to review Sigmund's papers in Anna Freud's house (the Anna whom Erik Homburger worked for, in her Vienna art school for kids). John decides to write *Cocaine Papers 2*, excited about explaining coke's role as an "enhancer" of other drugs taken in concert.

Cocaine is an amplifier of the moment, whatever the now is.

In Malibu, I now live up the hill in a sixteen-foot-long, eight-foot-wide wood shed. Estranged from Barbara, I sleep alone as she and Zoe live on the plateau below in the main cabin with Bruce—the handsome carpenter with whom she fell in love while I was in Brooklyn shooting.

There is a four-foot plywood wall between me and the six goats that share my austere dwelling at night. Chilled, their milk in the morning tastes good. All is good.

With the hinged wood window propped up by stick, I look out the rectangular opening of the shed at my friend Joel.

He says, "*Conan* is a big hit."

I say, "You're kidding me. How do you know?"

He says, "It's in the newspapers. A hundred million dollars, worldwide" ($466 million, today).

On Andy Weil's recent advice, I do not read newspapers or watch TV.

Years before, for Pressman Williams Enterprises, Ed bought the rights to the Conan comic books. He could not manage to finance the film with the young unknown weightlifter Arnold Schwarzenegger, and sold the rights to Dino DeLaurentis for $250,000 ($865,000 today). Ed had given me only a 5 percent interest in the continuing *Conan* rights when we parted company.

I call Ed in New York to find out what is going on.

Ed says Dino had neglected to ask for sequel rights in the contract when he bought the original *Conan*. Now Dino plans to make *Conan 2*.

Ed says, "He paid $4 million for the rights" ($14.6 million today).

I say, "Fantastic, Ed. Congratulations. Finally. It's good for me too—I have a small piece. You know I'm living on three hundred dollars a week."

Ed says, "Sue me."

He hangs up.

I ransack my cardboard file boxes that are stacked in the corner on the goats' side of the plywood partition.

The boxes have been munched but the intruding goat teeth have only been able to bite off the edges of the Pressman Williams Enterprises Settlement Agreement. In the center of these serrated pages, the text and signatures remain intact.

I call Elizabeth in New York and recite the disheartening facts.

She says, "That's just terrible. What's wrong with Ed? If what you tell me is true, I will back your lawsuit. Send me the papers."

The next day, I leave for the Cannes Film Festival.

A few days later, I stroll on the Croisette near the Palais des Festivals. As I pass the Carlton Hotel veranda, I spot Ed at a table.

I am surprised that I am genuinely happy to catch sight of him.

I say, "ED!"

I walk onto the terrace and smile as I sit down. He is nervous.

I say, "Look, Ed, it's really good to see you again. I feel fine. Let's just have a good time. Forget about the *Conan* lawsuit. Pretend we're in a Louis Auchincloss novel. I spoke to Liz and she said she'd back it, so let's just leave it for the courts. How are you?"

The blood drains from Ed's face, and he suggests we meet the next morning and settle the matter. I surmise that the quiet Ed does not want to challenge the power and deep pockets of the Rosenwalds.

At breakfast, Ed says, "A lawsuit will take five years. You will lose interest and legal fees."

I say nothing about my loss from his forgetting to pay the errors and omissions insurance premium on De Palma's *Phantom of the Paradise*.

Ed says, "Present value is fifty cents on the dollar. I will give you $125,000 next week." He thinks me a heartless hind?

I say, "Okay."

The trick is not to mind being an idiot. Or, sigh, as the Sufis say, make your room full of rubies inside your heart, not outside in a bank.

Back in LA, it is two in the morning. I sleep naked in the arms of my new girlfriend of three months—with whom I'm certainly and deeply in love.

At the sound of movement in the room, my eyes open. Without raising my head, I see a man walk in the darkness from the bedroom entrance door around the bed to the other side—he seems to know the layout.

He kneels down in the dark and extends his hand onto my nearly hairless, silken-skinned leg. He gently runs his hand up and then up somewhat higher—and his hand is on my junk!

His hand pulls back as if shocked. He stands up and stomps into Carrie's large adjoining bathroom. He flicks a switch that turns on theatrical lights spaced around the perimeter of the huge mirror, and reaches into the small of his back and pulls out a black semi-automatic 9 mm pistol from under his jacket.

I am wide awake. The lights from the bathroom flood into the bedroom.

He turns toward me and walks straight to the foot of the bed and points the gun directly at my chest.

Carrie looks at the man. She obviously knows this man and is desperate to remove herself from the line of fire and jumps more than eight feet through the air, diving behind an elegantly covered couch in the sitting area of her large bedroom.

The author of "The Expressive Meaning of Body Positions in the Male-Female Encounter" notes that the gunman's head is higher than mine—the "Acrotropic" position. Without thinking, a baboon would see the posture of the new guy as dominant. In this dyadic confrontation, I am clearly in the inferior position—naked, legs and arms akimbo, torso exposed and passively inclined on a hill of cushy pillows. In this quintessential "Unaggressive" position, no ego feels proud to die.

I am rooted in this mortal moment, near certain death. The madman shouts something at me as I look into the black barrel, but I hear no message.

I am now conscious with full cognition, but somewhere else.

I have launched up and away, through the roof.

As I lift off from Hollywood, I watch the state of California recede. Then the entire West Coast of North America diminishes.

I am a giant white bird. I travel faster than a speeding bullet but feel no wind. I belong to the cosmos.

I stop on a dime and then turn east at warp speed. I instantly cross the mountains ranges below and arrive above the East Coast.

I stop and zoom down, down into the Bronx, touch down onto Tenbroeck Avenue by the old redbrick row house, and zoom back up miles into the sky and zoom down to Massapequa Park, Long Island, our split-level suburban house, only to return up to the ionosphere for a flight of a few seconds to reach Boston.

I zoom down to the newspaper kiosk in Harvard Square. No time to say hello-goodbye, I ascend miles up and cross the Atlantic in no time; then straight down toward England, toward Cambridge, to Trinity Hall.

And then back up, back across the ocean again to the airspace over New York, and dive down toward Manhattan, to 210 Central Park South, where I had lived with Liz; and shoot back up above the atmosphere again, heading west, across the USA and into a steep, speedy descent to Los Angeles, to Hancock Park—inside the bedroom, now corporeal—I have yoyoed back into my body.

A dwarf of a sweaty ugly man shakes with a gun pointed at my chest.

He says, "Get out of here. Get out of here. Get out of here."

I hear him. I remember the neighborhood mob guys in Brooklyn, "If a guy has a gun, run, and not in a straight line. Come back when you have a gun." I jump naked out of the California king bed and dance, herky-jerky from side to side on my toes, nevertheless an easy target.

I say, "I'm outta here. I'm outta here." I spasmodically dance to the door.

He says, "Get your clothes."

I dance left to right, right to left, left to right and pluck my pants and socks from a chair.

"All of them!" His voice slurs and his gun hand wavers.

I grab a shirt and shoes and zigzag to the exit.

I run down the hallway and the steps to the ground floor and then out the front door, across the residential street, and duck behind a parked car between the house and me. I put on my clothes.

It is two o'clock in the morning. I run three blocks to a nearby home of friends. Emily lets me in. We sit at her kitchen table with her husband, Berthold.

Quickly, I explain what has happened and use their telephone to call Carrie's live-in bodyguard.

I say, "There's a guy up in Carrie's bedroom with a gun. You better go up there right now. She's in danger."

The bodyguard says, "Oh, that's just Jack. I know Jack. Don't worry. I have a shotgun and a rifle. If there's any real trouble, I'll take care of it."

I am dumbfounded.

I call back a second time and reiterate the lethal danger.

He says, "It's a game. Relax."

My love betrays me and almost gets me murdered. Echoes of my earliest trauma.

Yet now, death is not so frightening. Can I go astral traveling without a gun at my head? Beyond normal sensorial systems? Can everything in the universe be only thought—some of it in physical form? After his NDE (Near Death Experience), the British logical positivist A. J. Ayer told his doctor: "I'm afraid I'm going to have to revise all my various books and opinions."

This is the first test case of the California "rape by instrumentality" law—just passed after a public outcry about a television show, *Born Innocent*, based on a female inmate of a juvenile delinquent prison who was sexually assaulted with a broomstick, but there was no legal way to prosecute for rape.

Under oath in the courtroom, I identify Jack, who looks back at me with the same eyes as Charlie Manson. He is such a pipsqueak and I am so tall that the fact that I ran out of the house does not play well visually.

After I departed that night, the Oscar-winning composer Jack Nitzsche (*One Flew over the Cuckoo's Nest, The Exorcist*) threatens to kill Oscar-nominated, Golden Globe–winner Carrie Snodgress's (*Diary of a Mad Housewife*) and famed musician Neil Young's little sleeping son, Zeke.

And then Nitzsche uses his gun barrel to rape Carrie. His addled brain is abused by Percodan and alcohol. The bodyguard never leaves his quarters.

All the networks feature the trial for three evenings on the national news.

Then Nitzsche quietly pays Carrie $400,000 ($1.4 million today). The next day on the stand, she withdraws the sensational pistol-rape charge. The national press vanishes.

Rolling Stone reports simply that I ran out of the house. They could have mentioned I was unarmed when I deserted my dearest one.

If you google the gunman today, you read in his 2000 *Rolling Stone* obituary: "Though Nitzsche had a stellar reputation as an arranger and composer, his private life was a bit more spotty. He was arrested for pistol-whipping then-girlfriend actress Carrie Snodgress and threatening to kill her and Neil Young's son in 1979. He was consequently fined and sentenced to three years' probation for assault with a deadly weapon."

If you weren't there, Charlie, you don't know what happened.

And not just in this dimension. Another holographic universe encounter, of the near-death kind?

What do I do now?

1980

I drive to North Hollywood to visit Jimmy.

I knock on the front door. It opens wide.

He stands in front of me with a revolver pointed right between my eyes. I can see the gray bullet heads in the chambers.

I stand mute, stock still.

He puts the gun down.

I say, "Why did you do that?"

He says, "I wanted to see how you'd react."

He thinks I'm strong.

I know I have no will. The Sufis have provided me with a satisfactory excuse—the pure strength of the action of nonaction. I continue to stay in this plane of reality.

I walk in. Jimmy sets up two shots of cocaine. Much more cocaine in a syringe than Freud's usual two milligrams.

We shoot up.

In fifteen seconds I hear high-pitched bells ring.

They get louder and louder.

I say, "I'm hearing bells and they're getting loud. Really loud."

Jim pulls me out of my chair, hooks his arm around mine, and strides us to one end of the room, then quickly turns, and we stride back. Again and again.

The blaring bells of Saint Mary's Tinnitus feel extraordinarily wonderful, but I know the tunnel out of this life is about to appear. I am about to permanently lose my body.

Jim says, "Heroin hot, cocaine cold."

He leads me into the bathroom, shoves me under the shower, and turns on the cold water. In a few minutes, I step out alive.

It is time to leave this place, Los Angeles.

Clearly.

Getting into heaven is no straight line—it's a zigzagging spiral to a more spherical life that changes the focus from needs and fears to values.

23

Roman Holiday

1980–1981

1980

Candy Bergen has left Bert. She has begun to live with producer Ibrahim Moussa. Years earlier in Rome, fresh from Alexandria, unemployed Moose jumped the walls of the Cinecitta Studio and charmed the European actress Sydne Rome (Polanski's *What?*), who happened to walk by. In no time, he became her talent agent and soon agent to all the great beauties of Europe.

I am at sea in a sieve, and hang out some evenings sitting on the floor at a two-foot-high round table and a bowl of cocaine with Moose's friends and his Egyptian producer buddy, Dodi Al-Fayed (later famous for dying with Princess Di).

Charles Bluhdorn owns Paramount Studios and hired Moose to be a vice president. He gets Charlie great dates but has not, after a year, gotten a single film green-lighted. Ibrahim asks me if I can go to Rome to make a film on a very low budget for him with Italian money and European talent. Still traumatized by loaded guns aimed at my face, I am at this time perfectly willing to get diverted by a job four thousand miles away.

I suggest to Moose that we can fashion a low-budget movie out of improvised scenes.

Before I leave America, I hear a woman speaking wonderfully expressive Italian at Michael Phillips's second wedding. I need a bilingual assistant. Michael gives me the number of the tall, dark-haired Claudia.

She says, "Sure! I be your assistant. Yes!"

I say, "We are on a low budget. Do you have a place to stay in Rome?"

Claudia says, "Yes, I have a place."

221

I fly to Rome with actor Bill Tepper to work on the screenplay, *Miss Right*. As we walk along the narrow cobblestoned *via* toward our hotel the first night, a squad of twenty bulletproof-vested, helmeted, federal *carabinieri* round the corner. Their automatic weapons at the ready, they run toward us. Still halfway down the street, I put my hands up, high, five fingers spread.

I say, "Turistas. Americanos."

Bill stands still.

I say, "Turistas. Bill, put your hands up."

He says, "No way, this is bullshit."

I say, "Somos turistas. Turistas."

The police column approaches.

I say, "Put your fucking hands up."

He slowly raises his hands about halfway. Macho actor.

The police halt ten yards from us. I repeat my Spanish words. The Italians run back down the street. We are alone and alive.

During the night I hear three distant bombs.

I keep in touch with Julie to play a role, but the scriptwriting takes too long and she disappears into the Cambodian jungle on a spiritual journey.

We rehearse for two days in my cramped chrome and fabric apartment close to the Tiber River.

I say to Claudia, "Do you live near here?"

She says, "Yes."

I say, "Is it bigger than this place?"

She says, "Oh, yes."

She writes her address and invites us to come the next day.

A few blocks down the Via del Corso from the Spanish Steps stands the block-square Palazzo Ruspoli.

I enter the large inner courtyard through a heavily doored archway. On the second floor, I ring the bell to Claudia's apartment.

Inside, I am in a hall fifty yards long and twenty yards wide with a ten-yard-high arched fresco-covered ceiling.

Perched in a corner of the great hall, Principessa Claudia Ruspoli has built for herself an open open-topped working movie set on stage risers—she lives in this two-bedroom, modern, all-white Roman apartment. We rehearse comfortably.

Claudia introduces me to "Roma Crema"—the aristocrats of Rome.

I fall in love with Claudia's friend, she-who-must-remain-nameless—talented, sweet, brilliant.

She accompanies me to tea at the home of my casting director, Paola Roli, who had cast *Casanova* for Fellini.

Afterward, we stroll on the cobblestones across town to spend the night in Nameless's rooms over the Piazza Navona. Naked, she is still perfect.

I am naked too, excited.

This shall be a coupling of my atavistic totems and heart-open pure love.

But I hear loud sounds—pounding sounds of a blitzing linebacker, sounds that get louder and louder as he bulls closer to a bone-crushing tackle.

A full-volume audio hallucination.

She smiles, on her back, on her bed.

I lean in close, intense.

I say, "Look, I have to ask you one question. I know it's weird. This is not usual for me."

She says, "Ask me."

I say, "Do you have a boyfriend?"

She is still, then bursts into tears. Sobbing.

I watch with despair. In a minute, she still sobs.

She says, "You don't have to worry. My boyfriend is in jail—for the rest of his life."

I say, "Really?"

"Yes. He will never get out."

I say, "Why is he in jail for the rest of his life?"

"He committed a murder."

"Really? Who did he kill?"

She says through her tears, "Aldo Moro."

Aldo Moro? The late prime minister of Italy. The Red Brigade kidnapped him for fifty-five days and tried to negotiate with the highest authorities before he was executed. Brigate Rosse! His death doomed the First Republic and changed the course of Italian political history. That was her boyfriend.

My boner disappears.

I say, "I'm sorry, but something's going very wrong with my life here. This is not where I want to be."

Upset and confused, lost. I get dressed.

I am downstairs in the ancient square near Bernini's seventeenth-century sculpture of the four great rivers, a fountain financed with income from unpopular taxes on bread, meat, and salt. Funny. Is this part of the trip?

Dante likened humility to the sea because the sea's lowest place means that everything flows into it. The beginning of a divine comedy?

One evening, I meet Virna Lisi at her townhouse in Rome.

Virna and Sophia Loren are the leading actresses in Italy. Virna played opposite Frank Sinatra in the American movie *How to Murder Your Wife*.

The security is high-tech in this time of Brigate Rosse. Many clicks and buzzes before one is inside the site and at the front door. The interiors are marble, glass, and chrome.

She is forty-four years old without any pretension. We sit in a small pit in the sunken living room.

Soon comfortable, she tells the security guard and maid that they may go home.

I talk about my most personal views on love and relationship, and she responds intelligently in heavily accented English, with an open soul. I say Bill and I could write a sequence customized for her. She is quick and anything seems possible in her present.

She says, "I am married."

I say, "Where is your husband?"

She says, "He is in Spagna, he hunts with my son."

I imagine them as they come through the front door with their shotguns threatening like Nitzsche's 9mm and the idea of a promiscuous encounter evaporates.

I tell her about Carrie Snodgress. Virna listens. The hours pass without notice. It is clear that her heart is larger than any I have ever encountered—certainly mine. Her understanding moves me to tears.

I say, "You are so beautiful."

She smiles at me. She is heavenly.

I say, "And your features are so proportionate and balanced."

She says, "Yes, see how the top of my ears line up with my eyes?"

I say, "I see. I see. So what happens when this frivolous egomaniac, fifteen years younger than you, wants to end your relationship on this evening?"

She says, "He is just, just a dalliance. But my character, she pretends that she is not perfect enough for him—if I have plastic surgery, then he will still want me. He thinks I am serious. He says, 'Please, please, please, don't do it.' He begs me to let us end without the surgery. Finally, I say okay."

I say, "That would be very funny."

She says, "My son loves American football. We cannot find the pads for the shoulders anywhere in Italy. Or an American football. So he can learn to throw it. Can you find them?"

I say, "I'll have them on a flight from California tomorrow."

She gives me a warm hug. She is a smart, wonderful artist.

She says, "This will be fun. Give me pages as soon as you can because I have to memorize every word phonetically, so I sound like American."

The next day, Moose tells me we've been invited by a marquesa to a dinner party that night at her small palace on the elegant via Margutta.

He says, "She just ended an affair with Fellini."

Several times we hear distant bombs exploding in the night.

I find myself seated to the right of the refined, multilingual hostess, Giovanna, who looks about the same age as Virna.

I say, "Last night, Virna Lisi told me she would do our movie, but I have to write about an affair with an older woman. I don't use my imagination much when I write. And I've never had an affair with an older woman."

Giovanna says, "Oh, then I will have an affair with you."

I say, "Would you mind if I stop and write down what you say while we are together? I don't want to forget any dialogue."

She says, "That would be fine."

I say, "We have to start right away."

She says, "I will come to your place tomorrow afternoon."

She does. We do.

The scene is written in a few days but on the last day she snorts some cocaine for the first time and evidently has exceptionally enjoyable feelings.

So we continue to see each other until I leave Rome. She tells me she is "a descendent of the Renaissance rulers of Siena."

Princess Claudia says, "A direct line from pope . . . I think, Leo the Tenth."

Six months after I return to Malibu, USA, a yellow taxi drives up the dirt road to the cabin and the marquesa emerges.

She says, "It is good to see you."

A kiss on each cheek.

She says, "You know, I have no idea how to get any cocaine in Rome."

I have a great assistant director for the first time—Gianni Cuazzo.

He could have worked for John Huston. He did work on Elizabeth Taylor and Richard Burton's *Cleopatra*.

He knows his job, he knows my job. He is great with the Italian crew, and he speaks fluent English.

On the first day of the shoot at De Paolis Studios that Mussolini built, I feel like I finally have top-of-the-line professional support.

A production assistant walks continuously around the studio with a tray of *espressos singolos* for all.

I need to communicate with the cameraman who only speaks Italian. I call out, "I need Johnny Cat-so! Cat-so!"

Everyone stands still. I hear a muffled laugh or two.

My elegant AD walks past the smirking Italian crew and approaches me with a kind smile.

He says, "Paul, it is pronounced, 'caught-so' not 'cat-so'—'cat-so' is a prick."

I say, "I am so sorry, Johnnie."

The phone rings in my apartment near the Tiber, Fiume Tevere.

Barbara Clarke says, "Joel died in a car crash down in Malibu at two in the morning. Janice from Oceanside wouldn't let him stay, so he had to drive home. He fell asleep at the wheel, crossed PCH, and crashed into a telephone pole."

Joel was crazy in love with a woman who had no interest in sex with the awkward emeritus monk. He never stopped trying.

I lie face down on my bed.

I go into the Void.

Joel smiles at me, looks down, and rubs his curly hair.

I smile at him with my eyes closed.

Soon he fades away.

A real friend is gone. I go to my open balcony and face the river.

I say, "Oh, Tiber! Father Tiber! / To whom the Romans pray, / A Roman's life, a Roman's arms, / Take thou in charge this day!"

I repeat these lines from Macauley's "Horatius" that my father declaimed downstairs every Sunday in loud chorus with a haberdasher, Mister Ash, who had retained my father to polish his English. I could hear them clearly from upstairs with the door closed in the Bronx row house.

Now, I am in tears.

I laugh through them when I remember Mister Ash's straining Yiddish accent murdering the Macauley.

I will miss Joel's funeral.

My second best friend is gone from Earth.

Twenty-five-year-old Angela Molina is a Spanish actress in demand and the daughter of famed flamenco singer and actor Antonio Molina. Moussa invites her to meet us in Rome. She is a supersensitive and turned-on free spirit. She and Bill hit it off, and he writes a ferociously wild scene for them—after he tells her their affair is over, she grabs his character's prized porcelain Buddha and places it on her crotch as a surrogate member and uses it to humiliate him. She ends up smashing it in a powerful feminist exit.

Unfortunately, at the last minute, the feral Molina gets a leading role in a big spy film in Germany that pays money. She flies away from our expenses-only arrangement.

Moussa somehow produces the fragile English actress Jenny Agutter (who starred in Sidney Lumet's *Equus*) for the first day of shooting. Jenny has no idea how to bounce her boyfriend's porcelain phallus between her legs while she insults him. Jenny is *gentille* to her bones. This scene is going to be a train wreck.

It is a long day on the set. I try to use long hand-held takes to shoot twelve pages of script in one day. It is not possible. And the miscast Jenny is in tears after most takes. There is only one more day scheduled with the febrile Agutter. I doubt we can get her sequence filmed in any reasonable way.

But the European star of *Cousin Cousine*, Marie-France Pisier, is in town to audition me that night to see if she wants to donate her services to the movie. She made three films with François Truffaut and had an affair with him.

I am exhausted and smelly. I walk to the Hotel d'Inghilterra, where she has a room.

Upstairs, Madame Pisier opens the door. She is a petite beauty and speaks English with a wonderful accent.

I say, "Can I use your bath before we go to dinner?"

She says, "Of course." She flutters her hand in the direction of the bathroom.

I leave the door slightly ajar, hopefully enticingly. I get in the tub. Unfortunately, she does not bother me for almost half an hour.

She says, "Come on, already!"

We sit at a table for two in the middle of the room at a nearby restaurant frequented by the movie crowd on the via Condotti.

I say, "We will write the scene to reflect your true feelings about love."

I tell her stories of my own tragic romances and ask her about her deepest feelings and experiences. I am not impressing her. Marie-France is preoccupied by someone she sees across the restaurant.

I look over my shoulder and see Clio Goldsmith, a voluptuous, young star of sexy Italian B-movies and the daughter of the Anglo-French financier Sir Jimmy Goldsmith (who had arranged for Elizabeth to attend the Slade, many years ago).

I know Clio from dinners with Ibrahim and his stable of female stars while I worked in Rome with Bill on the script.

I say, "Would you like me to introduce you?"

She says, "Yes, I would like that."

We walk to Clio's table and the two women chat for several minutes.

Back at our table, she wants to know all about Clio.

Later, we walk for an hour after dinner on the dimly lit deserted cobblestone streets. It is a romantic setting, but sex is not on her agenda.

I say, "You know our lead male breaks up with his four girlfriends on one night. In your scene, he sees you are deeply upset and knows, of course, it is because of your deep love for him. Actually, you broke up with your girlfriend earlier in the day. You are distraught. He is oblivious. You finally tell him that he doesn't really matter to you—he was just a sporting event. And you race into the bathroom and slit your wrist with a scissors, slightly. You cry over your lost love. He consoles you and bandages the wrist before you leave him, with a mercy smile."

The next morning, the second impossible day with Agutter, Ibrahim comes to the set, beaming.

He says, "I just dropped Marie-France at her plane. She's coming right back and will do the movie. She said that you were the 'Maximum!'"

Karen Black, the stunning ingenue in the huge poster behind young Tom Pollock's desk when he offered me *Animal House*, has now been in thirty films. She got an Oscar nomination for *Five Easy Pieces*, with Jack Nicholson, and a Golden Globe for *The Great Gatsby*, with Robert Redford. She played the crazy libidinous model, Monkey, in *Portnoy's Complaint*, with Richard Benjamin.

Bill and Karen acted in Nicholson's *Drive, He Said*, and she is now an old friend. Tepper persuades Karen over the telephone to play one of his girl-friends in the movie. She flies to Rome.

I go to her rented condominium on a Sunday to meet Karen Black.

The door is open and she is naked on the phone and argues like a sailor with her ex-husband in New York.

I say, "Excuse me!" I turn around to leave and give her privacy.

She says, "Hi! Stay. I'll be off in a second."

I say, "No, no, I'll come back."

She says, "Don't worry. My life is an open book. No secrets!"

I sit down, surprised by her complete openness. A female Allen Ginsberg. She radiates energy and has a wonderful throaty laugh.

The camera dollies back as Karen enters the stark set of Bill's apartment. When the rehearsal move is finished, she comes close to me.

She says, "Can you put a light right above the lens? My eyes are close together. One light right there," she points, "will fill them both and I guarantee you that I will look much prettier."

I say, "Sure." I ask my AD Gianni to instruct the DP to set a light.

Karen looks at me, eyes sparkling.

She says, "Thank you. No other director has ever been responsive."

I say, "I don't understand. I want you to look beautiful and I'm sure you know your face better than anyone."

She smiles with joy.

Later in the day, we are about to shoot an intimate shot of her with Bill.

While the crew sets up the camera and lights, she takes my hand and leads me around a wall on the set to a private spot with a chair.

She says, "Sit down." I sit. She sits on my knee.

She says, "Okay, now kiss me. Let's make out a little."

I say, "Oh . . .?"

She says, "I have to get in the mood for the scene."

I believe her and take this directorial duty seriously.

After a couple of minutes, she gets up, and smiles.

She says, "I'm ready now."

Julie is long gone into the jungle in Cambodia. We have no one to play the ultimate woman for the end of the film.

Zoe runs into five-year-old Maggie and her mother, Margot Kidder, in the Trancas, Malibu supermarket. My five-year-old tells Margot that I need someone to replace Julie. Margot agrees to come to Rome for expenses if she can bring Zoe with Maggie.

Margot, flush from *Superman*, inadvertently tips her taxi driver five hundred dollars (a couple of thousand today) when she arrives from the airport. It doesn't mar a happy Roman family reunion.

Later, when I must leave to go to the set of *Miss Right* and Maggie's mom has the day off to play with them, Zoe bursts into tears.

She says, "It's not fair."

I love her.

After a minute, I cry too, with her—and soon, Zoe is fine.

"I've been shot," John Lennon says in front of the Dakota, on Central Park West, next door to Ed's building.

When he dies, his last words are, "Yeah."

I am walloped. He and Yoko Ono had progressed beyond commercial entertainment with a spiritual vision. *Imagine.* Love is all you need.

I find it hard not to think of JFK, MLK, and RFK.

Many years later, the head of the CIA, Robert M. Gates, says to me, "The CIA and the Soviet's NKVD use the same method in assassination. We find some nut case who wants to kill the person we want to eliminate, and he suddenly finds himself with new friends who can easily get guns and passports and cash. We're the best friend he ever had. And we make sure he gets the job done."

I meet Claudia's uncle, Principe Dado Ruspoli, in his apartments in Rome. His friend, Fellini, created the Marcello Mastroianni character in *La Dolce Vita* based on Dado.

The principe greets me kindly and shows me a collection of scores of opium pipes, some a meter long, made of silver and glittering precious stones. They are in glass containers on the bookcases.

He says, "Salvador Dalí and I smoke a bowl every morning and every evening, when he is in town."

I mention to Dado that in Los Angeles, I live in the forest estate of Lady Victoria Hamilton, a psychoanalyst author and her husband, Nicholas Tufnell, who had been a teenage lover of Dalí's. Nicko asked me to consult on his novel in progress, *Taboo*, about a heterosexual couple in analysis who have misplaced their sex organs.

He says, "There are many shrinks in Rome, but most of their patients are priests."

I say, "It's a shame that the rational psychoanalysts' understanding of the personality, on the one hand, and the mystical priests understanding of the higher self, on the other hand, are not shared in a common model. That's the wonder of the Sufis."

Dado smiles.

He says, "A fine wine has the elegance derived from the combination of all the various trace ingredients, but spirits are just a jolt of alcohol. Compare complex opium to distilled pure heroin, or psychedelic mushrooms to synthesized pure LSD? Opium and mushrooms are transcendental but heroin and LSD are blows to the nervous system."

I say, "You know, I found out by accident one day at a desert spa that soaking in a mud bath takes away the deep bone pain from the withdrawal after three days of smoking opium."

I stay in Rome for many months to edit the film at Fono Roma, just off the Piazza del Popolo. I plan the climactic special effect: our hero ends all his affairs in one night of serial dinners—the total reduced to four by one Jenny Agutter on the cutting room floor. The next morning, the very first woman he sees—*miracolo!*—is Miss Right, herself. A huge bubble of pure white light will be added in postproduction to surround Margot and Bill—the infinite reality behind what they experience in their everyday world. All will be white, a poor man's *2001* transcendental ending.

Just as we send the final cut negative to Technicolor in Rome, Moussa and I duck into a screening room to check the special effect. Bill staggers around Margot on the set, imagining the mystical shine—but now with the effect added, they seem to be surrounded by an upside-down bowl filled not with white luminescence but with what looks like dark yellow urine—magically suspended. The suspension is not one of disbelief but one of pee-pee that never responds to gravity. This will not transport any moviegoer.

I say, "It's a bowl of piss. Now it's a disaster movie!"

Moussa says, "I have no more money. Paul, I can't even pay to get the negative out of Technicolor."

I say, "It's supposed to be a love-of-my-life story."

He says, "Paul, you have to go to Technicolor tonight at midnight. I bribed a man there who will give the film to you. Then get on a plane to LA and bring it to the lab there, immediately. You must get it there before it dries."

It is my last day in Rome. At Leonardo da Vinci–Fiumicino Airport, I buy one seat for me and one for the five cans of wet film, and fly away before daybreak.

I came, I saw, but I did not conquer. *Arrivederci, Roma!*

24

The Bells Toll

1981–1991

1981

Low on funds, preoccupied, oblivious to my surroundings, I shuffle up Main Street toward the Irving Thalberg Building on the MGM lot in Culver City. Are my lower instincts jeopardizing my sincere heart's spiraling effort to transcend my ego?

"HEY, WILLIAMS!"

Francis Ford Coppola hollers at me from forty yards away as he walks in the opposite direction with a group of his Zoetrope executives around him.

I say, "Francis."

He says, "Do you have any film you're dying to make now? I'll do it."

I have been thinking a lot about a modern Americanization of Dostoevsky's *The Idiot*—Elizabeth is Aglaya, the rich general's daughter, and Barbara Clarke is the wild Natasha, and Jimmy is Rogozhin the killer, and I am Myshkin, the saint who ends up in the insane asylum.

I think about how to explain it quickly in a shout. How Freud claimed *The Idiot* was the key to his work on the unconscious.

Francis says, "You took too long to answer. If you had a film, you would have answered right away."

And he turns and walks on toward the Buster Keaton Building with his entourage.

Just as well—after all, the ultimate state of happiness is the annihilation of the individual self.

Karen Black is back at home in LA and calls to say she has money to do a film. I tell her about *The Idiot*.

We have complex conversations. She is insightful and wise. She is a gifted writer. But there is no money for a movie.

She says, "You're such a sucker for a pretty face."

I start spending my weekdays at her Fremont Place mansion. She was born with the name Karen Blanche Ziegler ("Ziegler?" "Oh!" "German." "Oh." "And Czech and Norwegian." "Oh."). Before she starred in Francis's first and her first film, *You're a Big Boy Now*, she married a guy named Black for a year. No name trauma, there.

I learn from her extraordinary instinctual way of being alive and awake. She is always present and focused. I feel best when I am around her.

I discover this in her journal, "Paul is a river stopped—but in his presence and because of it solely, meanings are found which were there in the air above, now captured for examination. He allows and produces large intricate beautiful effects on those around him. His heart is very full. I wonder what would happen should he release it onto that dangerous stream?"

She is a great friend going the right way.

I get a small acting role in some production.

Karen says, "Say your lines."

I say them to my satisfaction.

She says, "No, you don't know them. Repeat the lines aloud twenty times and say them without any expression in your voice—absolutely, flat tone."

I do as she says and learn.

She says, "Now you can put all of your attention on what's going on in the scene. A hundred percent. No mental energy required to remember your line."

I say, "Yes, yes, Marlon Brando pasted his lines on Maria Schneider's forehead for their scenes in *Last Tango in Paris*."

One simply can't act and think. You get in your own way—you lose emotion.

The dehydrated face appears when a gray metal shield rises suddenly and reveals a man stretched out on a gurney behind a long horizontal glass window. A white sheet covers his body but is turned down to exhibit his head; the paramedics' clear plastic tube still protrudes, taped to the side of his mouth. I do not recognize my sixty-eight-year-old father.

I fog the glass with my breath as I press as close as I can. I gradually recognize the skull bones under the grotesquely taut, dry flesh. Whatever had been my father's life force is gone; I begin to hyperventilate. I nod to a silent morgue worker behind the glass, turn and walk to the gray metal door, and exit. I am out; the huffing and puffing gradually subsides.

New York law requires that the identifier of the body at the morgue must be the same one to confirm it at the funeral chapel.

The next day, a thin mortician in the basement of the Riverside pulls a blanket down and reveals my father's face—the fulsome spitting image of my living dad.

I say, "What did you do? My father explicitly ordered that not a penny was to be spent on any fakery."

He says, "I didn't know who was coming down here to identify him. Can you imagine if your mother came down here and saw him the way you saw him yesterday?"

I remember the white flesh stretched to near tearing at his nose, cheek, and chin bones, just like the gruesome Albrecht Dürer drawings hidden in the Prado—we were granted special permission to see them on our honeymoon in Madrid.

I say, "She'd have had a heart attack."

He says, "We only put in some fluids. Don't worry, I won't put it on the bill."

I say, "Thanks." I feel the compassion of this stranger, and love him for it.

Like Gristedes' grocery deliveries on Ninth Avenue, the corrugated box holding his corpse proves the impermanent nature of all things as it slides along the horizontal ladder of rollers into the flaming furnace.

Murray more than once admonished me that "proves," used in this way, means testing, not proof.

I remember when I once arrived late at an assembly in the auditorium of his elementary school, I noticed him in the back of the hall standing at attention. His eyes were shining as he watched his rainbow-colored student body put on a play. Tears rolled down both his cheeks. That was the only time I saw him cry.

Murray made me read. He insisted that logical reasoning is the highest human faculty. He made me write. Murray made much of my life.

His death brings more lightness to my being. Less urgency to time.

Oliver Stone spent the day struggling to get his next film financed, *Platoon*. We sit one late night snorting coke in Claudia's villa above PCH and Will Rogers Park.

I say, "I knew that when I did not go to Vietnam, I would not be the one to write our generation's *Naked and the Dead*."

He says, "Yes. That's why I knew I would not miss it."

Oliver reminisces.

He says, "Some nights, I sit on the Mekong River bank with my sniper pal, watching the Viet Cong silhouettes. They're green through the sniper scope when they walk along the opposite bank, like ducks in a shooting gallery. Every so often, he shoots one. The impact of the bullet catapults the guy off his feet and slams him into the ground—but the dust that had been on his clothes stays in place in the air. It looks like a ghost. Then it slowly fades away in the evening breeze."

Karen's son, Hunter, is seven and regularly torments Zoe.

One afternoon, he throws a small rock at her head at close range. I know Karen would be upset if I slugged him.

I squeeze his biceps with my hands. I come as close as I can to causing great pain with my grip without maiming him physically.

I remember my father's words.

I say, "Don't ever do that again."

Karen and I stand on a busy street corner in Bucharest, Romania, leaving a film festival event. The shelves are empty in the dry goods store behind us. As the traffic light changes, a wave of Romanians walk past us and I suddenly feel a kinship with them all—and a separateness from Karen. Her glamorous face suddenly looks odd. All these Indo-Europeans look like me.

I say, "Look at these people. Right here, you don't look like a human right now. You have a bizarre dainty little face that looks like it's made out of white Dutch porcelain."

She says, "Yes, yes."

I say, "Really, what planet are you from?"

She smiles.

I say, "Beauty is so culturally determined. If we were giant slimy insects, I would lust for your thorax and mandibles."

She says, "That's so true."

I say, "I feel better-looking here."

There is rest in union.

I stay with Karen in the penthouse of the Carlyle Hotel and often visit my grieving mother in Apartment 10-F, downtown.

At the Martin Beck Theater on Broadway, I watch many rehearsals and then many performances of *Come to the Five-and-Dime, Jimmy Dean, Jimmy Dean.*

Karen plays a transexual in Robert Altman's production, in an ensemble with Cher, Sandy Dennis, and Kathy Bates. Karen is a sensitive and bold handsome man. Egomaniac Cher has a genuinely slow brain but is a clear acting instrument, and Sandy Dennis is a demon—moving around the stage to force whomever she is talking to, to have their back to the audience. Altman manages Cher and Sandy Dennis well and protects Kathy and Karen, who are beyond their egos and shine in their roles.

One day, I run down to refurbish our supply of Winstons. On the way back, I step into the elevator to discover the six-foot-nine, slightly stooped John Kenneth Galbraith, who escorts a coiffed, gray-haired, attractive woman. The elevator doors close and J. K. Galbraith pushes the button for the third floor.

I say, "Professor Galbraith, I was your tutee in Winthrop House in 1963 when you introduced me to Angie Dickinson. Long story, but I became a movie director. Karen Black is waiting for me in the penthouse. I owe it all to you. Thank you."

As the doors slide open, the woman laughs, and the professor says, "You're welcome."

They walk away into the elegant hallway.

Twenty years later, Galbraith writes in his last book, *Name Dropping*, "Reminiscence and anecdote, as they tell of one's meetings with the great or the prominent, are an established form of self-enhancement. They make known that one was there. This is not my purpose; my aim is to inform and perhaps, on occasion, to entertain."

The ego is a part of our psyche that consistently leads us off the spiritual path.

Karen writes in her journal, "It is not a normal love-affair with Paul. We can't go bowling. I have almost never bowled, but I can see us there toiling and telling the idiosyncrasies and mannerisms of the folk who would be gathered there, laughing at the clumsy ball rolling time after time into that little alleyway next to its bowling perversion. He stands, in my imagination, tall and lithe, his noble, indecent profile to me, standing laughing with the little dark lands eye line out into the tiny horizon at his feet, whilst lumpy ladies in red sweaters with dyed blonde hair and their holding males argue and attempt with great seriousness to knock over the pins at the end of the alley. Or to a picnic. Or on a drive in the country. Fucking under the maple tree, an activity which I have heard tell about only on sheet music. Instead we lie in the dark and labor over the changing glints in one another's eyes."

I am the only sentient being on the acres of chaparral. The other residents of the ranch go to work or school during the day.

I sit in a trailer at my typewriter. I stare at the page. I am writing a screenplay, *After Death*. The main character leads executives along a catwalk high above steaming vats of steel while walking backward demonstrating the perception of causality, by banging his fists with robust exaggeration as I did at my first Sunday brunch with the Rosenwalds. The character gets so excited when he invokes Schopenhauer's conviction that stupidity is the failure to understand causation, and so demonstrative with his clashing arms, that his momentum carries him over the railing and he drops down into a gigantic lethal cauldron.

Suddenly, the front grille of a 1951 Studebaker, its center a rocket-like nose encircled in chrome, knifes through the page in the typewriter at high speed. It is on course to slam into my face.

In a fraction of a second, my body instinctually hurtles me out of my chair eight feet onto the single bed at the far end of the trailer.

I am in shock. I am a heap on the bed for several minutes.

I say, "What the hell was that?"

I get up slowly and walk outside to take a look. There is nothing unusual to be seen. Cactus. Chaparral. Yucca.

When folks return that evening, there is a hubbub because one of the uphill renters' two elegant Afghan dogs is missing.

After a couple of hours, they discover the dog near our dirt road entrance on Pacific Coast Highway about 250 yards as the crow flies from my green writing trailer. The dog was run over and killed.

I do not put the Studebaker and the Afghan together until later in town.

Karen says, "Since dogs get run over because they do not see cars until the speeding cars are too close, the Afghan looked up, saw the Studebaker for an instant, and its spirit (like yours did when it exited in the face of Nitzsche's gun) fled his body and rushed into the nearest sentient being—you!"

I say, "And why do you think I saw the Studebaker grille?"

She says, "You saw through his eyes at his last moment."

I believe her.

The next day, as I drive south on PCH toward Point Dume ("Point Doom," as the locals say), I see a 1950s Studebaker speed north. I marvel at the coincidence and wonder if this is a local commuter.

But then I see a large Afghan dog in a slow-motion trot, head across the north lane. The dog is smacked on the left side of his head by the front bumper of the oncoming car, hits the macadam highway, and bounces up again—and is smacked a second time by the bumper, thrown down again, and run over.

I see this all in slow motion.

At twenty-four frames per second, it could not have taken more than a second.

Somehow, I see it at ninety-six frames.

I keep driving.

The next day, I drive north on PCH from Point Dume. When I pass the spot where I saw the dog's slow-motion death, I suddenly find myself crying, sobbing.

Classical physics, unlike quantum physics, holds that the everyday reality of three-dimensional space is absolute and that time must be seen as a linear progression. It again appears to me that the fourth dimension, time, can be out of sequence. If consciousness connects everything to everything in some kind of transdimensional hologram . . . ? I am one step over the line.

John Lilly and Barbara's friend Richard Feynman (whom NASA will pick to figure out why *Challenger* blew up, and he does) says, "If you think you understand quantum physics, then you don't."

1984

I retreat to the small guesthouse on the wooded Brentwood estate of Nicko Tufnell and Vicko Hamilton, who immigrated to the USA several years ago.

Barbara sends Zoe to live with me when the twelve-year-old is too big for her to discipline. I am suddenly a single parent—a devoted Mister Mom, as well as launderette and chauffeur.

When teenage Zoe and a friend jump up and down on the L-shaped couch in the living room, they persevere in their insult just learned from *E.T.*, "Mister Penis Breath! . . . Mister Penis Breath!" Not knowing yet the derivation of their new vocabulary, I go outside, grab the garden hose, return to the living room, and spray their fire. No corporal punishment.

My teenager is supposed to hurt me. Alienate my love continually, so she knows what it feels like to be on her own—when I die.

One day Vicko the shrink and I are in the laundry room.

I say, "I have the awareness of my death in mind every day. It makes everyday life more precious. I think it is some sort of Buddhist wisdom."

She says, "Oh, you know for certain that you're going to die. But from one day to the next in your crazy life, you never know what's going to happen, so you obsess on your death."

I say, "Oh."

I know my body is dying every second. I accept that every day is doomsday so the light gets brighter. "I heard a Fly buzz - when I died - / The Stillness in the Room / Was like the Stillness in the Air - / Between the Heaves of Storm -" are Emily Dickinson's words for it.

1988

I get the role of a Vietnam vet with post-traumatic stress disorder in the ABC-TV film *To Heal a Nation*. Eric Roberts stars in the story about the building of the Vietnam Veterans Memorial wall in Washington.

One hundred fifty real army combat vets sit in front of me.

Now they listen to my perfectly memorized tearful speech about my debilitating war experiences as I stand facing them all.

But my tears for the veterans are of this moment. Pretending to pretend. The bells toll.

1989

We drive down to PCH to alert the firemen of our existence, hidden from their point of view in the hills above. We park and start to walk to the firetruck. A nearby cop spots a baggie of mushrooms on the back seat.

He says, "Those yours?"

I say, "No."

He says to my brother, "So, they're yours?"

Ted says, "No."

He says, "Yours?"

Haim says, "No."

He says, "Turn around. Hands behind your back."

I sit alone on the floor of the Malibu jail. There are no windows, just institutional glossy walls that remind me of PS 108 in the Bronx.

It is silent. I meditate and am soon in the Void.

I see three police cars surround the two sedans and a station wagon that sit on our ranch's dirt exit road. Each vehicle is jam-packed with everyone's stuff. The cops cuff all the people that flee the ranch.

As the Great Malibu Fire blows in from the northeast toward the ocean, I see the officer's hands that discover my big stash of cocaine—wedged amid the piles of personal treasures hurled into the back of the wagon.

This is not a hallucination. Not a hologram. Not a dream. It is as immediate as the visions of far-off India imparted on me by Dilgo Khyentse Rinpoche.

In the early morning, a paper plate with three MacDonald's pancakes and a small cup of maple syrup is served with a pint of milk through a rectangular opening in the solid door.

I ask this jailer cop for my one telephone call. In an hour, he returns and leads me to a counter in the main room.

I call Steve Blauner, who lives in Malibu.

He appears within thirty minutes and bails me out.

Big Steve says, "I put up my house to guarantee the bail."

The cop is not happy.

I say, "I want to bail out all the others that you arrested at my place."

He says, "What others?"

I say, "Barbara Clarke, Linda Bell, Barb Cooke, José Ramos . . . and Theodore and Haim."

He says, "What are you talking about? You've been in solitary."

I say, "You arrested them. I want to bail them out."

Steve says, "If they are in jail here, I am here to bail them out, now."

I say, "Thanks, Steve."

Soon, the others are released and we are reunited. The charges are dropped because no one admits to owning or abandoning the contraband.

I am in wonder at this variety of extraordinary seeing occurring again. The Buddhists call it "distant seeing." It seems that power visits me—that transcends space and time.

When I return to the ranch, I find my small tin storage container melted and burned. I had put my past in there: all the LPs made by the Beatles, Rolling Stones, and Cream; a selection of bespoke clothes—an alpaca bespoke overcoat, white tails, a tuxedo, and jackets for each season; framed posters from all my movies. The ashes are another step in the path of liberation?

Just before this great fire, the mortgage bank insisted I double my fire insurance. Now everything on the property burned except the cabin. The tin shed and the Quonset hut—melted; the decks and trees—ashes.

I buy the new user-friendly Mac 512K computer. Every single item in the thirty-page, small-print insurance policy has its own page in my loose-leaf book. A restatement of the particular coverage, a Polaroid photo, and a receipt—they are mounted and neatly described with an impressive font. I approximate receipts utilizing the software for those items missing them. I take Polaroids of detritus that could well be the remnants of the item claimed. A maximum of five trees at a hundred dollars per tree could be claimed, so I find five eucalyptus stumps.

One day, a State Farm insurance adjuster meets me on the property. He looks sad and exhausted. I offer him some coffee and we sit and chat. He loves movies.

Finally, I suggest he take a look at the loose-leaf. He opens it and looks at the first three or four pages. And starts to cry.

He says, "I walk into eight houses every day of the week and these people come walking out with big cardboard boxes filled with jumbled piles of old receipts. What am I supposed to do with them? What are they thinking?"

I say, "My god."

He shudders. I give him a box of Kleenex.

I say, "This will be easier. I promise you."

He says, "What do mean? You did all my work for me. You claim is approved."

We drink some more coffee before he leaves, feeling happy.

The insurance check for $125,000 (twice that today) arrives in the mail. Lordy, just in the nick of time. It's been a long time since I've made any money.

1990

Zoe says, "Teen age boys fool around, they're 'amazing'—a girl does it, she's a 'slut.'"

I say, "Boys are sex-crazed lunatics."

She says, "But I want to."

I say, "That's okay, but never believe a word they ever say about love and sex."

She says, "There is no such thing as a slut; guys are sluts."

I say, "They're all just trying to get in your pants."

She says, "But they're all so creepy. What am I supposed to do?"

I say, "Just do what you want to do. Never do it to satisfy anyone else."

She says, "That's it?"

I say, "When you get older you will meet some great people."

She says, "How old?

I say, "Twenty-five . . ."

She says, "How will I know them?"

I say, "Just look in their eyes for a while. You can tell. Don't listen to their bullshit. You will recognize each other."

She says, "That's years from now."

I say, "Have a good time now but don't fool yourself—they're all boy toys."

After an extraordinary day of sexual indiscretion, I am profoundly nervous when I admit them to Karen in the evening. She sits me down at the dining room table, and directs me to look into her eyes and tell her all the things I've done and withheld, which I thought hurt her. Tears frequently roll down her cheeks during the long hour, but when we are finished, she smiles beautifully—intimacy has been restored. It is hard to believe. The air between us is clear again. It is simply one of the most amazing moments of my life.

These times, they are Roman. The USA uses most of its treasure to fund vast legions to fight endless wars around the world while only the wealthy citizens participate in the government of a broken capitalistic system—that eliminates a real progressive tax, eats the middle class, and burps up its savings to the one-percenters.

Most Americans are like frogs in water brought to a boil so slowly that they accept their despair: the ruthless process of shifting working people to the working poor; the incarceration of millions; the withering of social services and public education that crushes young people with debt and makes social mobility feel like a joke; the yearly cowardly compromises of the conservative courts; the militarization of the police, and the bought-and-paid-for congresses that legalize corporations' greed.

Abbie Hoffman dies in April. He commits suicide with barbiturates at fifty-two.

In August, Huey is shot dead with a bullet from the back by a kid intent on making a rep on a street corner in Oakland. Huey is forty-seven years old.

These noble friends saw the bleak future of phantom democracy but will not get to see more of the decline and fall.

They saw no way out.

1991

I sit in the waiting hall of United Airlines at Denver International Airport for a flight to Los Angeles. It is a two-hour layover.

I look up and see a gigantic twelve-foot-by-twelve-foot opaque apparition—the immense smiling face of Dilgo Khyentse Rinpoche looks right at me—his eyes are shining clear.

Why?

This is certainly a hallucination of another kind, an out-of-the-blue kind.

I turn my head, but the image does not move. I look up—it stays where it is. This is not a hallucination but more of a holographic presence.

I look at him and feel serene—a heart essence teaching from the great master.

After a minute, the image dissolves and I can see again the waiting crowd sitting where he had appeared, and beyond. It is September 28, 1991.

I find out a decade later that Dilgo died on that day in Bhutan. He had written:

"Even if, bright as a flash of lightning,
Death were to strike you today,
Be prepared to die without sorrow
Or regret, giving up attachment to
What you are leaving behind.
Without ever ceasing to recognize
The authentic view of the real,
Leave this life like the eagle
That soars into the blue sky."

I remember seeing Dilgo and the 14th Dali Lama receive fearful terminally ill Tibetan Buddhists, take their hands in a reassuring grasp, and burst into laughter and say, "It's going to be all right."

25

Beyond Eccentric

1991–2009

1991

When I arrive at Jon Voight's rented beach house, he says, "You want to play cards?"

I say, "Poker?"

We sit on stools at a low table. Jon wins the first few hands and gleans that I am playing my cards so he will win.

He says, "All right. I see what you're doing. Whoever loses, wins." There is a large bell jar of candies on the table. We each get a pile to bet.

The game is intense, but his daughter, Angelina Jolie, toddles over repeatedly and steals the candies from our piles. No way to keep score. We give up.

I tell him about Ishi, after the nineteenth-century massacre of the Yahi people, living alone in the mountains for twenty years before encountering civilized California in 1911, at the age of fifty. I know Jon will love to play the anthropology professor who studies Ishi, and I suggest we do the film together. It can contrast the competitive Western industrial ego with a Native American consciousness that reveres nature.

He says, "Sounds wonderful!"

I give him a paperback copy of *Ishi, The Last of His Tribe*, by Theodora Kroeber, and leave.

Match.com does not exist. Lonely, I drive down the 405 Freeway to an industrial park in Torrance, to be videotaped for a service that libraries many thousands of VHS cassettes of singles neatly organized on rows of tall shelves. I sit on a chair opposite a few lights and a cheap camera as an interviewer asks,

"Where would you go for entertainment on your first date? What kind of movie? A Lakers game?"

I say, "One evening chatting with me and you're a goner. If she looked to the entertainment industries for her interesting times, she'd be inappropriate for me."

The interviewer stops the camera and turns off the lights.

She says, "We have thousands of women here, and I can tell you that you wouldn't be right for any of them."

I say, "Oh."

She says, "But, there was a woman who came in recently who I think would be perfect for you. I'll try to find her application form."

When Susan Emerson sat down and saw the harsh lights, she said, "I'll look terrible in this light! Get somebody in here that understands light, for god's sake. I wouldn't go out with anyone who looked like they would look, photographed like this." And she walked out.

She is the best woman to stand with near the tree and watch the sun sink. After that, she points out the undulating line of black that demarcates the night sky from the silhouette of the hilltops. We help each other to see better. During our year as lovers, I urge Susan to add representations from the animal kingdom to her still life paintings that uniformly present only minerals and vegetables. She adds a scurrying chicken to a still life centered on the green doorway of a rustic house in Mexico. Then she adds a black-and-white dog looking at the viewer, but the dog has no eyes.

Whatever shadows compelled her, Susan's singular need to create in order to be happy makes her my muse. She's a worker. She gets me to work.

1992

Zoe has no idea that real Democrats had once existed (Bill Clinton gave up the masquerade and became champion of the oligarchs, Republicans happily diminished their taxes—invisible behind mean but popular cultural propaganda). Because I had stupidly enrolled her in the expensive private Brentwood School, she thinks Reaganites are sane role models, not existential economic criminals dooming society. The destroyers of compassion. What can I do as a responsible parent?

I start to plan to kill the sitting President of the US, George H. W. Bush. I call Jimmy and ask him to join the conspiracy.

His wife says, "You're not allowed to kill the president. It's against the law." They fight about it.

After a month, I realize I shall have to exchange my life for Bush's and that I am a coward.

It would be difficult for Zoe, too.

I sell the Malibu ranch, except for ten bare acres on the other side of the hill, to pay for a gorilla-budget movie in which I shall play a left-wing assassin. Jim begins to write the screenplay.

The first scene in the screenplay is my calling Jim and his argument with his wife.

I write the POTUS and ask permission to shoot him. I get a gracious but firm refusal on White House stationery.

We film Tom Hayden of the Chicago Seven (now California state senator from the Twenty-Third District) lamenting the coincidental deaths of JFK, MLK, and RFK.

Watts erupts in days of rebellious fiery violence after Rodney King is beaten. The TV news announces that Bush will fly to Los Angeles to make his presence felt. A useful coincidence. I call the Secret Service and ask them how to shoot the forty-first president. They tell me to go to Remote Terminal 3 at LAX by 7:00 a.m. with ID and an explanatory letter under a corporate letterhead.

I fabricate "World Wide Communications" picture IDs for my cameraperson, Susan—a tall, slim, blonde, blue-eyed aristocratic Republican ideal—and me to hang around our necks. I wrap them with Scotch Tape. I mount "WWC" placards on the back windows of my car.

I memorize my lines for the assassination.

As day breaks at Remote Terminal 3 and the gates are unchained, our WWC is the third vehicle in line, behind ABC and CNN, ahead of NBC and CBS.

We drive to the first staging area, where the Secret Service checks our car and WWC corporate letter. Then we walk to the second area, where they open our cameras and inspect.

Finally, we walk toward the metal detector arch through which the accredited White House journalists enter. On the other side is a metal-fenced corral in front of a lectern with the Seal of the President of the United States of America.

As we reach the detector, an agent stops Susan and me.

He says, "Look around, only accredited White House Press credentials—these here are no good."

I say, "Oh. I'm sorry."

I reach into my breast pocket and pull out my refusal letter from the White House.

I say, "The White House has okay'd us."

The agent glances at the one-page letter with "The White House" in neat black Helvetica letters at the top and a signature from an executive staff person on the bottom.

My gaze is steady.

The agent says, "Okay, go on."

Humongous, thundering Air Force One arrives on time.

George H. W. Bush emerges and stops at the base of the stairs. He begins his speech to the press pool and us—twenty feet away.

In one continuous shot, Susan pans off the speechifying president and swings around to me. I move my lips quickly with Jim's dialogue—without making a sound:

"They killed our guys, now we kill theirs. It doesn't matter who pulls the trigger. Sarah Jane Moore missed because somebody pushed her arm. And Squeaky Fromm, she didn't know how to cock the gun . . ."

My right-hand pistol threatens just like Sarah and Squeaky, who attempted, seventeen days apart, to assassinate President Gerald Ford. My thumb cocks my extended index finger, that sits atop my three-finger fist grip.

Three perplexed-looking Secret Service agents in dark suits move deliberately from three directions toward me, but I continue my silent diatribe.

The agents slip through gaps in the partitions of the press corral and push their way forward through the crowd of reporters in front of me.

I finish my lines before they reach me, just as George walks right past and waves to me. Assassin and president are captured together in continuous camera frames—one shot.

I lower my flesh-and-bone pistol and shut my mouth.

I am not arrested.

Later in the sound studio, I lip-synch my voice.

The November Men begins with a title card that reads, "All cinematography took place in strict compliance with the Laws and The Constitution of the United States of America as they stood in the Spring and Summer of 1992."

Not true after the USA Patriot Acts pass in response to 9/11/2001—after which it is illegal to depict the shooting of a sitting president.

Got it. Good boy.

From my driver's seat, I look up at the passing huge billboard on Sunset Boulevard, "HBO Presents Jon Voight in *Ishi, The Last of His Tribe*. Coming soon."

Nearly forty years later, Voight has the Medal of Arts placed around his neck in the White House by Donald Trump. When I was leaving Manhattan after Liz divorced me, and Jon told me I'd be eaten up alive by sharks in Hollywood, I did not realize he would be one of them.

1993

I show the finished film to the acquisitions VP at New Line Cinema.

He says, "That film is irresponsible and seditious."

I say, "It depends what side you're on."

Bob Shay is an old friend and founded New Line. He agrees to watch the film. We eat sandwiches in a small screening room.

He says, "We're too big now. This is a kind of *Reefer Madness*. You need us twenty years ago."

Another friend, critic Len Klady, in *Variety* writes, "*The November Men* is the ultimate in conspiratorial presidential assassination films . . . The very edginess of the story, combined with appropriately off-kilter performances and cinema verité techniques, keep the audience off guard and riveted. Up to the very last moment, one remains unsure whether the movie's assassination script is only a movie or some horrible extreme of ego and dementia."

Oliver Stone sends a note, "I always knew you were crazy. Brilliant filmmaking."

Roger Ebert invites it to the Chicago Film Festival, where it plays to a cheering sellout crowd.

Klady arranges for it to be premiered at Sundance, the festival that jumpstarts edgy films.

But the alcoholic marketing VP of the small company distributing the film says, "Forget Sundance, I know a great shopping mall in Austin. We're too big for some little festival in the mountains."

The film goes unnoticed in the USA, deep in the heart of Texas.

On the Croisette of Cannes, not presenting myself as affiliated with the film, I talk to countless buyers at the festival, mentioning only incidentally that I had seen an incredible movie about assassinating President George Bush, *The November Men*.

My international sales rep, John Rodsett, soon calls, "The office is flooded with buyers, but they all say they need a 'name.'"

I say, "Would Robert Davi do?" He's visible worldwide now for his roles in the new James Bond film and *Predator*.

John says, "Davi is great."

I say, "Tell them Davi is in the film. I'll shoot two scenes with him." I know Jimmy can get Davi to help out.

On the phone from LA, Davi says, "I'll shoot two scenes. In one, I have to be on a horse, and in the other, I'm skeet shooting. And I want you to bring me two boxes of Cuban Romeo and Juliets when you come back."

Foreign sales make back the cost of the film. It is released in many countries as *Double Exposure*.

In one of Robert's scenes, he sits in the saddle smoking a cigar and writes a check to my character, the seditious filmmaker, to finish his movie, and Davi says, "Don't tell anyone I gave you the money. Arnold is my buddy." Schwarzenegger is his buddy and plans to be governor of California.

Susan and I debate going to Charles and Caroline Muir's retreat in Maui to learn about tantric sex. I hope these sexual yogas by the authors of *The Art of Conscious Loving* will make Susan more enthusiastic in this realm. She reluctantly agrees.

At the first meeting of the class of fifteen couples, I see that the other men are all rich business executives, hair impeccably groomed. We sit in a circle on a rug, and I hear during "sharing" that these clearly uncomfortable husbands are here only because their wives demanded they learn how to make real love or they would be sued for divorce.

Instructions are given by Charles and Caroline with two cloth hand puppets—one resembles a penis, the other a vagina—"Lingham" and "Yoni." A long ritual of arousal before intercourse is detailed. The couples leave for their cabins to do the "homework."

In the preliminaries of the homework, Susan—who not incidentally has perfect pitch and is a descendant of Transcendental Ralph Waldo (Class of 1821)—looks deeply into her beloved's eyes—mine. She makes beautiful "expressive sound" but we never get to the intercourse part because she transforms in front of my eyes into a column of shining pinkish-gold light—we both see the entire room in a pink glow. As Emerson, Ralph, said, the light "makes us aware we are nothing, but the light is all."

We have been instructed that the end goal of tantra is not orgasm but enjoying the extended width and elongation of sexual sensations of the body—the bridge to the divine.

At the next group session, Charles extols the benefits of prostate massage in preventing cancer. Caroline explains to the women how to enter the man's anus and stroke the gland with sensitivity. As I look around the sitting circle, I see the face of every husband flushed in deep panic.

When the couples disband and head for homework, I hear all the masters of the universe announce to their wives their various plans to immediately pack bags and leave the island on the next plane.

The following day, when the couples sit cross-legged on the rug in the large circle, I see the husbands all present—smiling like Cheshire cats.

Some months later, I return with a tiny video crew and shoot *The Best Ever*, about a young man with HIV who wants the joys of ecstasy that are possible with tantra—without communicable penetration. When I show this beautiful, intelligent piece of transcendent artistry to distributors, they say, "It's porno!" It is too much, too soon.

1995

I need to make some money. Even my minimal satisfactory survival level is in danger. The only thing I know how to do that will be profitable is to make a movie. Light is the answer.

Agfa has created a new superfast 35mm color film stock that can make rich exposures in dim natural settings without any lights. I can make a low-budget film look beautifully lit, like an expensive production. Light is the key.

Jimmy writes a murder mystery script, *Smoke*, for two stars and two supporting bad guy roles that we will play. Director Wayne Wang and actor Harvey Keitel then announce their new big movie, using our title. Harvey Weinstein pays us a significant fee, and we change our name to *Mirage*.

It is six months before the shoot when I direct Susan, now my platonic friend, to go live in Palm Springs to research light in all the locations. She was a successful regional painter when I met her. She sees light well. Susan's task is to find interior and exterior locations that have interesting natural light either in the morning or in late afternoon.

I look for an actor "name" that we can afford. Sean Young has seen her career plummet because she was fired from Warren Beatty's *Dick Tracy*, she told me, because she wouldn't fuck the director. And then Sean was defamed and sued by actor Jimmy (*Salvador*) Woods after they broke up and she put a disfigured doll on his doorstep. The court ordered Woods to pay $277,000 ($471,000 today) for her legal expenses. She may have won in court, but her career was caput.

I drive eight hours to Sean's house in Sedona, Arizona. The daughter of two journalists, she was a ballet dancer and *Vogue* model before starring in Ridley Scott's *Blade Runner*. Sean is smart, articulate, spiritual, and a classic beauty. In a tipi, she agrees to do the film. I like her.

Sean suggests I meet Edward James Olmos (*Stand and Deliver*) to play the male lead. I drive to San Diego, where he is on location. He loved *The November Men*. An icon of Latino activism, he commits to the role.

Each day of the shoot, I assemble the crew two hours before daybreak. They eat and set up in faint light for the first shot. When the sun first appears over the mountain ridge line, we get many shots rapidly because we do not need any time to set any lights. We are divinely side-lit by God. The sun is angled enough until nine thirty. Then we start planning all the setups for later in the afternoon, eat lunch, and rest and rehearse until the sun is low in the sky again. We have double the number of "magic hours" of other movies, sunset and sunrise.

The rushes look like we have a John Huston–size company and at least a dozen huge arcs and lighting trucks and generators on hand every day.

Universal buys *Mirage* for twice its cost. In the movie I play the role of Donald Gale—a con man with a cash flow problem.

1997

Zoe is twenty-two and wants to use an unknown actress named Gwyneth Paltrow to play the lead in her first film, *Men*, based on Margaret Diehl's novel. Zoe loves Paltrow. Zoe's best friend is an actor whose lowbrow father finances the film just after salivating at rushes of Sean Young doing a pole dance in a scene from *Mirage*. This ex-McKinsey consultant insists that Sean must be the star—he knows her from *Blade Runner* and *No Way Out*, with Kevin Costner. He does not want to put up his money for an unknown kid named Paltrow. It reminds me of my wanting Jon Voight before he did *Midnight Cowboy*, and Ed insisting on Barry Gordon. The past hides, but it is present.

Men wins Best First Film at the Hollywood Film Festival and other prizes at festivals in Spain, Portugal, Greece, and the Philippines. Zoe gets to see some of this world. Paltrow's next film is *Se7en* with Brad Pitt, soon followed by *Shakespeare in Love*, for which she wins the Oscar for Best Actress.

Frank Mancuso at MGM hires Zoe to direct a $12 million film for the studio, *My New Best Friend*.

Zoe hates the people in the feature film business. She drops out and starts to work with autistic children. Then she organizes a documentary, *Autism: The Musical*. She finds the people in the documentary business worse than the feature people. The film wins the Emmy for Outstanding Nonfiction Special, but Zoe now wants only to be a poet and leaves the West Coast to study creative writing at Columbia.

Is my daughter being punished for the sins of her father? Nah.

2000

Osama bin Laden masterminds attacks in Africa—a year ago, al-Qaeda cells blew up the American embassies in Nairobi and Dar es Salaam.

I feel I know what he is up to. He approaches old age as I did—assassinating George H. W. Bush—but he has not yet struck directly at the Devil's home. My instinct is that soon he must attack the USA on its own soil.

At Christmas, Heidi throws a party for her daughter and the young children of her friends. I give each of the rich kiddies a briquette of coal (inside Saran Wrap) with a tag attached: "Darfur." I tell them about the Sudanese genocide and how this gift can make them appreciate their happy lives. Some cry. The mothers don't know what to do.

I also mail an end-of-year 2000 holiday greeting to my friends—an eight-by-ten, black-and-white headshot of bin Laden under a banner headline, "Have a Good Year, America." I do not mention that we're all astronauts on Earth—on a beautiful blue marble traveling at 490,000 miles per hour.

I pick up my cell phone when I hear Robin Hood's trumpet "Sherwood Forest" alert. Dennis Ardi, my old friend and lawyer, is in a hurry.

He says, "Listen, there's this eccentric Catholic billionaire, he founded Domino's Pizza. He owned the Detroit Tigers. He's ultraconservative, and he wants to make a movie about his friend the pope."

I say, "The pope? John Paul the Second?"

He says, "He's meeting guys here tomorrow. I can fit you in around four, and you can take a shot at giving him advice about how to go about it. Maybe get a consulting fee."

I say, "How much?"

He says, "Maybe twenty-five thousand."

I need money.

That night I google Tom Monaghan and John Paul II. After a few hours, I am up-to-date on current issues in the Church and on Karol Wojtyla's biography. I also find out that three-quarters of everything that has been written about sex within the Church since the time of Christ has been written by this pope. His first book, *Love and Responsibility*, teaches that sexual union is a sacred path to union with God. Wojtyla of course insists on the prior sacrament of marriage and, surprise, insists on the prior obligation of the man at intercourse to make sure his beloved is physically and emotionally ready to receive. That's why the Polish students were hanging from the rafters at the University of Cracow when Wojtyla, who had been an actor and playwright before becoming a priest, taught there. His teachings about intercourse are right in line with the Tantric Charles and Caroline Muir.

I discover too that Bain Capital of Boston paid Monaghan $1.4 billion for Domino's.

I walk into Dennis's office in Beverly Hills. Monaghan is there with his lawyer.

For three hours, the slim, bespectacled midwesterner from Ann Arbor and I talk about His Holiness. I focus on the pope's expanded consciousness, his combining mysticism and realpolitik. Tom is engaged—he has found a kindred spirit. My good fortune.

Tom says, "Would you come to dinner with us? I'd like to keep this discussion going."

I say, "Sure."

Dennis says, "Okay. Let me call my wife."

At the Four Seasons, where Tom's sommelier had earlier selected the rare wines now decanted and ready, Tom says he has taken a vow of partial poverty—he only spends money on food, wine, and travel. The rest he gives away through his Ave Maria Foundation (that will fund the movie).

He says, "I don't want to have any money when I die."

I ask him, "Tom, when are you going to die?"

Tom's lawyer looks crossly at me.

Dennis says, "Now, Paul . . ."

I say, "No, no, Tom? You need a reverse amortization schedule if you're going to die near-broke, right?"

He says, "Of course."

I say, "I have the same plan."

He says, "I've given my kids a few million each, and that's enough for them. The rest will be gone."

After another three hours, Dennis walks Tom and his lawyer to their waiting limo.

Tom says to Dennis, "He's the only guy I've met with in Hollywood who didn't say a word about the deal. And the only one who talks about the spirit. I want him to produce the film."

Dennis says, "Produce it? The whole picture?"

Tom says, "Draw up papers."

I fly up to Sun Valley, Idaho, three times. I finally persuade Jack Briley to work with me on the movie only when I abandon my idea for the film—following in parallel the life of the assassin Mehmet Ali Agca and the pope, Karol Wojtyla, until they meet in his prison cell. Jack won the Oscar for his screenplay *Gandhi* and wants to do a similar straight historical biography. And *Gandhi* turns out to be the pope's favorite movie.

I introduce Briley to an old acquaintance, William K. Reilly (a Yalie who headed the EPA under George H. W. Bush and was a student anthropologist in Laurence Wylie's French village, Chanzeaux, with Cliffie Libby Buxton, who starred in my short *Don't Walk* and who is now his wife). Bill Reilly had helped this pope write his encyclical on the environment and helps us contact Robert M. Gates, who had been head of the CIA during the assassination attempt on JP2.

In Texas, Gates tells Jack and me that the pope was "the best political operative I ever knew."

To prevent a bloodbath like Hungary's from happening in Poland, the pope played our CIA and the Soviets' KGB without their knowing: "William Casey, head of the CIA, put on a Groucho Marx big-nose-and-horn-rim-eyeglasses mask and takes an unidentified flight twice a week to Rome. At midnight he secretly meets John Paul II in the Vatican. Casey has in hand US spy satellite photos of Russian troop movements. Once Casey is on his way home, John Paul meets with the Russians at 3:00 a.m."

Gates says, "John Paul always played his cards very close to his vestments."

In Rome, unlike twenty years ago, I find that Italians at every level want to practice their English on me—now the universal language of capitalism.

I meet an American businesswoman and ex-TV–soap opera actress who is friendly with all the cardinals—kind of an exalted enabler. She tells Catholic Jack she will inquire about the pope's hearing Jack's confession. She tells me later at dinner that she has an extra ticket for the next day so the two of us can sit right next to His Holiness.

The following day, Pope John Paul II sits on a throne on a platform in front of Filarete's twenty-three-feet-high, fifteenth-century bronze door of Saint Peter's. I am about ten feet away sitting on a folding chair, understanding none of his Holiness's multilingual slurring. I do remember that this man called American capitalism the most ruthless in the world and deplored the domination of things over people.

I see a clear, bubble-shaped change in the atmosphere that extends out fifteen feet around the pope. This bubble remains all during his address. It is extraordinary—a palpable radiation—of compassion? The vibration of spirit is visible?

"Be not afraid," is Wojtyla's motto and principal teaching. My bravery has sat on top of the fear and shame that have been lifelong silent companions.

He looks intensely into the middle distance, focusing on no one I can see.

Zbigniew Brzezinski (a Polish American, Harvard Ph.D. 1953, who served as Jimmy Carter's national security advisor) later tells me at lunch in Washington, "I've known a lot of popes, but this is the first one I ever met who believed in God."

Tom Monaghan, his lawyer, Dennis, and I sit for two hours with the archbishop of Denver, Charles J. Chaput. He wears two hats: the top-swelling miter and the hat of the Vatican's designated movie expert. He approves Jack's script *And the Walls Came Tumbling Down* . . .

We celebrate at a nearby restaurant. As usual, Tom's sommelier in Ann Arbor has called hours before our lunch. As the third carafe of $2,500 wine is poured, Tom reveals he is a fan of Al Jolson imitators and says, "My favorite song is 'Home on the Range.'"

He sings, "Home, home on the range, / where the deer and the antelope play, / where seldom is heard / a discouraging word, / and the skies are not cloudy all day."

Tipsy, he smiles and looks me in the eye.

From music assembly in Public School 108, I know the second verse.

I sing, "How often at night / when the heavens are bright / by the light of the silvery moon / have I stood there amazed / as I asked as I gazed / does their glory / exceed that of ours."

Tom has tears in his eyes. We are bombed and bonded.

We drink more wine.

I say, "But now and then a man wants a change, and champagne is the most complete and exhilarating change from Bordeaux; it is like the woman of the streets: everybody that can afford it tries it sooner or later, but it has no real attraction—it is always within reach and its price is out of all proportion to its worth."

Tom laughs out loud.

I had memorized the passage decades earlier from my favorite teenage book, Frank Harris's *My Life and Loves*.

2001

My friend Noel and I go out to sea most weekends on his sloop, sometimes out of sight of land—a sweeping connection to the natural world with glimmerings of infinity.

Noel says, "If you know what you're doing, you don't much need a rudder."

I sit at the rudder only used for coming about.

Noel adjusts the sails for the changing wind and currents, sets them again and again for the course—his meditation. I sit still as the open sky is above my head, the horizon circles my throat, and the ocean fills my core—I am happy with my sedentary contemplation.

In bed with Heidi Lloyd at her house in Santa Monica at daybreak on the morning of September 11, we switch on the TV news and all we see are replays of American Airlines Flight 11 crashing into the North Tower of the World Trade Center. We are transfixed.

She says it is an act of terrorism. Heidi is deeply knowledgeable about geopolitics. For a decade, she traveled the globe as a close associate of Maharishi Mahesh Yogi, the founder of Transcendental Meditation—the Beatles' guru.

We watch the attack on the homeland from the big bed.

United Airlines Flight 175 crashes into the South Tower.

I say, "It's bin Laden."

She says, "How can you be so sure?"

I say, "He loves planes. He tried to blow up the pope with altitude bombs in the Philippines."

She says, "You may be in trouble."

I say, "It was just my intuition."

She says, "You sent big pictures of bin Laden to everyone for Christmas."

I say, "If I know it's bin Laden, then plenty of people in the CIA know."

She says, "I wouldn't be so sure."

I say, "Not to worry—this is a time for forgiveness, not vengeance."

She says, "Dream on. You have a file."

I'm certain that I'm in no trouble—when no one paid attention to our assassination film *The November Men,* and everyone made a fuss a year later about *In the Line of Fire,* Jimmy said, "We're just the shit on Clint Eastwood's heel."

The next day, the mystic activist Pope John Paul II, says, "Let us beg the Lord that the spiral of hatred and violence will not prevail. May the Blessed Virgin, Mother of Mercy, fill the hearts of all with wise thoughts and peaceful intentions."

2002

In Aldous Huxley's *After Many a Summer Dies the Swan,* I read that all human activity is driven by ego—even a doctor doing brain surgery. Huxley writes that the only two worthwhile activities of the higher consciousness are the study of methods of ego transcendence and the study of the instinctual behavior of animals.

Susan proposes making a feature movie with no humans, just cats. A cat has absolute emotional honesty. The star will be Marcello, her new kitty. She has had her new video camera on him since he arrived and unknowingly has imprinted the feline with camera-as-mother, analogous to Konrad Lorenz being the first vision of his ducklings.

I have rented a big house in Brentwood, and we live there with separate bedrooms. I mount long lengths of one-inch-by-six-inch boards ramping up and down all around the rooms and walls for Marcello's racing delight.

While I work on preparing the pope movie, she spends three years shooting the film and I then show it to Universal. The VP there says he likes it, but it needs "more story." Three years later, Pinky's scenes with Marcello have been added as an antagonist, and the film is ready for voice-overs.

Zoe's friend Troy Garity—Jane Fonda and Tom Hayden's son—calls and asks me if I can talk down his crazy best friend who just returned from aya-huasca rituals in the Amazon. Raphael Monserrate tells me about seeing his mother and the fiery energy that violently flew through the air, back and forth between them, and his endless vomiting. I talk to Rafael about coming to terms with our parents and redirecting our connections to them from passion to spirit. I read aloud to him from "Throwing up in Mexico," in Andy Weil's *The Marriage of the Sun and the Moon: Dispatches from the Frontiers of Consciousness*, including the "practical clues about the possibilities of coordinating conscious and unconscious mental energies . . . most of us have vomited only in association with illness and do not think of it as something we could feel good about . . . [yogis], and practice it regularly and perform it as a morning ritual (called *jala dhauti*) . . . American Indians who eat hallucinogenic plants that cause nausea often vomit effortlessly and unself-consciously." It takes me a few hours to give Raphael Monserrate the knowledge he needs to understand his experience.

Raphael is all better.

On the way out, he says, "If there's anything I can do for you, just let me know."

I say, "What do you do?"

He says, "I am a voice-over director on big animation films."

I say, "What a coincidence."

He calls in favors and gets us an all-star cast at SAG minimums, including Jeremy Piven (*Entourage*) and Michelle Rodriguez (*Fast & Furious*).

We show the Universal VP the film again, with Marcello and Pinky. It is a remarkable achievement.

Universal does not buy the digital film because those huge-budget animated films with lip-synch talking animals have saturated the kids 'market during our six-year shooting schedule.

We find a small distributor, but the $100,000 ($150,000 today) the film earns in video sales is eaten up by marketing and distribution costs.

The greedy, binge-drinking, deep-pockets sadist who financed *Men* brings a baseless lawsuit to take away the cat film. He says, "You know the Golden Rule? He with the gold, rules."

Her Honor listens carefully to the lawyers on both sides, who have done the minimum of preparation.

One of plaintiff's lawyers says, "This cat is the very basis of the movie . . ."

She says, "Wait, wait. There are two cats. Why do you say one cat?"

The lawyer says, "No, Your Honor, I believe there is one cat, named Marcello."

I stand up in the back of the gallery and take a deep breath to project across the courtroom.

I say, "No, no. You are right, Your Honor. The other cat is named Pinky."

She looks up and finds me.

She says, "Oh!"

I say, "He's an extraordinary pink-nosed Maine Coon."

She says, "My cat is named Pinky too!"

Synchronicity! Laughter in the court.

She says, "Case dismissed. I find for the defendant."

Eventually, Random Media picks up *The Amazing Adventure of Marcello the Cat*, and they are still distributing it on the internet. Returns are a few thousand dollars so far—the remaining $275,000 of production costs are unrecovered. I lose my money, my way, on the path.

The pope and I have paid for a worthwhile spiritual effort.

2003

I am in Warsaw on the final reconnaissance trip to prepare for *And the Walls Came Tumbling Down* . . . about the pope's major role in the fall of communism in Eastern Europe. Tom Monaghan asked me to direct the film, as well as produce.

This preproduction group includes forty Poles and a half dozen English below-the-line department heads—director of photography, production designer, line producer, et al.

We take everyone to dinner. The head waiter gives me the menu. It is all in Polish. I don't speak a word of the language, but I read in a loud voice to all, in my presumptive Polish voice, the menu cover's history of the famous old Fukiera Restaurant.

The assembly sits around one giant table. I have my eyes on the printed nonsense syllables as I orate. But I hear no laughter. I raise my head and look around.

The jaws of the Poles have dropped. They stare at me.

I say, "What's going on? What's going on?"

They say, "You have a perfect Polish accent."

What is this? My shared ancestors' genes? My paternal great-grandparents were immigrants from Frankfurt, Germany, but my maternal grandparents were immigrants from Lomza, Poland.

I have often had dreams of mounted cavalry surprising people around fires in an encampment at night, torching their huts and slaughtering them with flashing sabers while I run away on little feet into the darkness.

"Xenoglossia" is "the putative paranormal phenomenon in which a person is able to speak a language they could not have acquired through natural means." There are biblical and Middle Age references as well as nineteenth-century Spiritualist examples of this ability.

Who am I to blow against the windpipes?

In my rooms at the Four Seasons Hotel in Prague, two weeks later, the phone rings. It is Paul Rooney, head of the Ave Maria Foundation.

He says, "The film is called off. I am canceling it. Close it down right away."

I say, "What are you talking about. I don't work for you, I work for Tom."

He says, "Tom! Tell Paul the movie is canceled."

I hear Tom, voice cracking, distant from the phone, "Yeah. It's over."

I feel like a medicine ball has hit me in the stomach. Out of nowhere.

We were weeks away from principal photography. We were scheduled to finish around Christmas next year.

2004

Under the Golden Gate Bridge, our cell phones hidden in our cars a half mile away, I stand with an officer of the CIA who asks for my blessing to make a formal recruitment offer to my daughter.

I tell him it is solely her decision.

I say, "I'd like to know why hasn't anybody ever tried to recruit me? I travel everywhere, and I have a perfect movie cover."

He says, "Number one: you can't keep a secret."

I remember my compulsive spill-the-beans dinnertime training in Massapequa. I am distracted by the memories and hardly notice when he continues.

"Number two: you're on the wrong side."

Yes, the United States has become the most powerful without becoming commensurately wise.

Later, Zoe says to him, "No way. I'm on the wrong side, too."

2005

On April 2 Pope John Paul II dies. To the surprise of all except Tom Monaghan, the funeral is the biggest in two thousand years of papal history—hundreds of millions of Catholics attend masses worldwide and seventy heads of state join four million mourners in Rome. Our movie would have been just released with a billion-dollar box office.

I remember, Tom founded Domino's Pizza—the pope movie would have been as big.

In May, Liz and I have dinner together at the fortieth reunion of the Class of '65 in what was called Memorial Hall when we were undergraduates. It is now called Annenberg Hall because Walter Annenberg (who went to Penn) donated $25 million to refurbish the kitchen and huge dining room—after which, incidentally, his son was admitted to Harvard. Elizabeth's famous post-Harvard success is her purchase of El Pollo Loco Corporation for $300 million that she sold a few years later after improvements for $600 million.

I remember her father's excuse for her not being able to help me out on *The Secret Life of Plants*.

I ask her, "What do you mean, you don't invest in retail? They sell chicken by the plate!"

She smiles and says, "Paul, it's all about deals now, not about products. You buy and sell deals."

I am just another crazy chicken.

Ed Pressman calls me, to my surprise. He's produced sixty more movies since we terminated Pressman Williams Enterprises. He thinks his son, Sammy, needs urgent help adjusting after a psychedelic experience at Stanford. I meet Sam and like him a lot. He is insightful and funny and in better shape than his parents understand. ("I was just standing on the edge of the roof—I wasn't going to jump.") My important help is reassuring his distraught mother and father.

When Zoe is diagnosed not long after with late-stage Lyme disease, Ed's wife, Annie McEnroe, comes to Zoe's aid with support and medical savvy.

Ed's feelings of betrayal have been largely overcome by his years of success. I have long ago realized that we are all victims, he and I, of his youthful selfish anger. Among other things, in a 2013 interview, Ed did say, "The original relationship I had with Paul was a wonderful experience. In some ways, trying to recreate that kind of partnership is what I've been after ever since. It was never producer against director; it was a collaboration of us against the world, and a real friendship."

Zoe and Sammy are friends.

In December 2005, the CBS miniseries *Pope John Paul II* starring Jon Voight airs across the nation—it had been rushed through production to exploit JP2's immense worldwide popularity that surprised Americans and the movie business after he died.

Jon does look like a younger Karol Wojtyla. I had mulled the difficult thought for a while in 2003 of offering him the role in our movie.

A dozen other productions surface soon in various countries on Earth.

2006

After a year's preparation with my Harvard Law attorney who volunteered to take the case upon speculation, we sit in the federal courthouse in Los Angeles for the four days of a bench trial.

Tom Monaghan owes me $2.3 million that remain under my contract to produce and direct *And the Walls Came Tumbling Down* . . . Tom and Paul Rooney, president of the Ave Maria Foundation, have seven gray-haired lawyers arrayed at the defendant's table.

The film was canceled only weeks before principal photography was to begin because, according to Rooney, the Vatican said it would look like John Paul II was "campaigning" for sainthood to become "Paul the Great."

Kept secret, the Foundation did not want $55 million to be spent on a movie. The Foundation intends to spend $300 million to move their conservative Catholic university from cold Anne Arbor, Michigan, to a new, warm city they would build near Naples, Florida—named Ave Maria, Florida.

Rooney conspired with the head of the Entertainment Group of Comerica Bank before a meeting with Jack Briley and me on the top floor of the Comerica Building in Beverly Hills. The banker lied to Monaghan's face that *Gandhi* had lost money and had not made three times its investment as was the fact. Tom had to no choice but to believe in his corrupt Foundation president.

Tom visits President George W. Bush in the White House just before the trial.

On the last day, the federal judge appointed for life by Bush says, "I award compensation only for quantum meruit."

Another medicine ball wallop into my stomach.

The judge's decision calls only for compensation for the two years' work I had actually done (for which I had been already paid and had used to finance *The Amazing Adventure of Marcello the Cat*).

My award, therefore, is zero.

TIME STOPS again.

I see the road in front of me continues—the boy's spare road of his demon mother now excused as the magical Fool's path of the Buddha. So it shall be. What to do? Head through the eye of a needle? Breathe.

I give up my office in Santa Monica and make a pilgrimage into the pristine valley on the other side of the hill from the old ranch. I leave behind most conveniences of home in search of something more—illegal under zoning laws of Ventura County but a holy stewardship of a tiny part of Mother Earth, off-grid, in a seventeen-foot trailer, with two shipping containers, nearby solar panels, and a well. We call it "Camp Afghanistan" because one of Zoe's young friends visits and says, "This looks like an advance camp outside Kabul."

Will this story turn into an account of collapse and recovery following a devastating midlife crisis? Or will it be a tale of transfiguration? Will I unite with the universe with less distinction between me and the rest of nature? Or will my ignorance only become more focused?

Henry Thoreau spent two and a half years at Walden Pond. This is a new adventure, extreme and simple—with no exit strategy.

2008

Presidential candidate Barack Obama tells a San Francisco donor audience that working-class voters in the Rust Belt "cling to guns or religion" as a way to express their frustrations. The great divide.

But, like Thoreau who visited rich slaveholding friends in Concord to get adequate protein in his diet, I find myself periodically at swanky Trancas Market in Malibu.

2009

Over the years, I have looked into the eyes of Buddha statues, of other people, and of my own eyes longer than usual.

In the beginning of a one-year affair with Melissa, driving on weekends to her apartment in Carlsbad, I often see her left eye turn into a perfectly round dark circle and then expand into the profile of the wrinkled gray head of an elephant.

Eventually, I mention it to her.

She smiles, gets up, disappears into another room. When she reappears, she holds a large box with both hands. In it is her extensive personal library of elephant books which she shows me, one by one.

She says, "Since I was a toddler, my 'secret friend' has been 'Eli' the elephant. My shrink wrote it up as a case for her book, but I knew Eli was for real."

I do not mention the Hindu deity, traditionally worshipped before any major enterprise.

Ed Pressman's mother, Lynn, is ninety-seven years old and close to expiring. In the hospital, she hears that Ed has finally made over half a million dollars for himself in the deal for the sequel to *Wall Street* (directed by Oliver Stone, starring Michael Douglas), *Wall Street: Money Never Sleeps* (Stone and Douglas, again, thirteen years later). Lynn Pressman smiles and dies peacefully after her last, single-word utterance, "Money."

My mother, Mildred, is ninety-two years old. She lies on a hospice bed in her own bedroom.

She stares into the middle distance as John Paul II did in front of Saint Peter's.

She reaches upward with outstretched frail arms.

She smiles toothlessly at something into a dimension I cannot see.

She repeats again and again during these last hours, "Esther, Esther . . . Esther . . ."

It is the first time I have heard my mother mention that name, Esther.

Her tone is satisfied and happy.

Zoe leaves the apartment to go home, uptown to Columbia, where she's now a thirty-two-year-old junior.

Mom passes away. Or, as she would insist when she was alive, "People don't pass away. They die."

My mother dies at 11:20 a.m. on December 27, 2009. A milestone. Orphaned. A child feels his love.

An hour and a half later, I squat in order to shoot up past Mildred's corpse with the Blackberry cell phone camera in order to frame Melissa and

Miss P. and their loving faces as they clean a woman they did not know. I email the cell phone images to my Mac laptop.

Later I call Zoe and say, "Did you ever hear Grandma mention the name 'Esther'? Did she ever have a Scrabble partner named Esther?"

She says, "After she broke both wrists when she fell over the curb on Twenty-Fourth Street—we were in the hospital and they gave her a ton of Vicodin. She told me about her childhood and I took notes."

I say, "And?"

She says, "Grandma's favorite friend in 1921 was from the Amalgamated Housing Development in the Bronx. She had a four-year-old friend. Her favorite playmate—Esther. Smoke. Esther Smoke. Esther Smoke from the Amalgamated."

Zoe arrives at Apartment 10-F at five o'clock. We look at the cell phone photographs now enlarged on my laptop. In the shot from below of Melissa and the soulful Jamaican hospice worker, Miss P., hovering over the corpse, there is a clear, distinct image of a humanlike entity in the lower part of the frame.

It looks like the homunculus I saw during the Alchemical Transformation in the motel room in Pueblo, Colorado.

Zoe says, "But what is it? This is weird, weird shit!"

Professor Hany Farid, head of the Computer Sciences Lab at Dartmouth, partnered with Adobe Corporation and Photoshop to devise a fool-proof forensic analysis system for digital photos. They utilized all of the ten thousand digital cameras extant on Earth. This system is now used by intelligence agencies, courts, and the *New York Times* to verify the authenticity of digital photographs.

The world's foremost authority in photo forensics, Farid, analyzes the image from the Blackberry in his lab and says, "I confirm that the image is authentic."

A year later, I finally meet Dean I. Radin, senior scientist at the Institute of Noetic Sciences in Petaluma, California. Previously, he was in charge of vetting parapsychological matters for the CIA. He wrote the recent *Entangled Minds* and the classic *The Conscious Universe*, now translated into twenty-eight languages.

Radin says, "I have never seen such a photograph before—a 'ghost' image that, one, was not amorphous and cloud-like and, two, was comparable to an actual person in continuous time and space—much less one a few inches away and dead less than two hours. I do not know of anyone taking a picture of a specific loved one, so soon after death."

Emboldened the next morning, I take a walk along Fisherman's Wharf with my Blackberry and text Standish Meacham and William K. Reilly. Standish calls and says he will meet me at the Asian Art Museum at one o'clock to take a look. Reilly is out of town helping the president of China, Hu Jintao, set up a Chinese version of the Environmental Protection Agency.

I approach the coat check just off the marble-columned central atrium of the Asia Museum. I spot Standish, into his seventies now, in good form and cheer. We sit down in the cafeteria with beers and after a bit of catching up, he wants to get to it. I explain quickly the context of the picture taking and show him the photo of Mildred when she died and then the *psi* shot, up at Melissa and Miss P.

"That's it," he says pointing.

"Yes," I say. "You can see it?"

He looks intently. He says, "Yes. I see it."

Standish looks for a minute, and I see tears slowly well up in his eyes. Tears roll down from both my eyes. I wipe them away.

He turns from the image and speaks of his early religious upbringing in Ohio, "an upbringing from which I had turned away, unsurprisingly, even before I entered academia. But seeing this picture is bringing back early memories of those years."

That two agnostics were here, now entertaining spirits, somehow seems timely, perfectly appropriate to him. I point out that now I think of myself more as an ignoramus. Standish says, "This photo certainly communicates to me on some deep level. It moves me."

I fight back tears, listening.

He says, "Thank you, sincerely. I am so glad that you wanted me to see it and, more importantly, that I have seen it. But don't show it to anyone. There's no point."

I say, "You mean this shopping-obsessed, competitive materialism that is Reality to mature capitalism's greedy egomaniacs will only cause my dismissal as a fraud?"

He says, "That's right. Don't show it to anyone."

Mildred skipped four grades in high school and was an immature nineteen-year-old living at home when she met my father in graduate school. She never had time to experience herself as an independent woman before she had two kids in quick succession. She had confidence only in how to be an obedient student and how to be a faithful mother.

Despite my father's dream of going off to see the world after my sister and I were out of the house, she insisted on giving birth again. My father hated my young brother for this reason—which my brother could not fathom. My mother continued to infantilize me—for reasons she could not fathom. I treasured her as my love, beyond the dictates of my autocratic father—an excessive need it took me too long to fathom.

If I were independent, who would she be? Who would I be? So, she never taught me anything useful after childhood.

She was an antireligious fanatic rationalist who said, "Emotions are stupid"—but she freely expressed her excessive emotion, loving kids. She became a children's special needs teacher in hospitals after my father died, working until she was in her late seventies. She served the people, and she served in the way that she knew best.

Now she is dead. Her little boy hid behind a Brownie Hawkeye film camera and now reached for a Blackberry digital camera at her deathbed. Believing is seeing, or vice versa? I start to research *psi* photography.

Is this my unspoken inheritance? Did she show herself from another dimension to say, "I am sorry, I was wrong. You took a wise path. See, here I am."

26

Magic Johnson

2010–2021

2010

I sit in my off-grid reconditioned shipping crate in a remote section of the Malibu coast and glance up at the foot-wide circular clock with relentless black hands and numerals and, right next to it, I see Mildred's foot-wide circular black Japanese wrought-iron relief that I took back with me from Apartment 10-F after her death. I have them both on a high shelf over a window through which I can see the frantic hummingbirds feed. When the birds are gone, it is still. I see only the yellow and green lacy tops of the fennel and the gray sky beyond.

It was under a lone eucalyptus with a great view of the Pacific that I spread her ashes—on top of the indigenous rocks that mark the grave of Pinkus Pidinkus, our Maine Coon cat. Pinky loved just the right amount—when it was needed and never when it was not; unlike my mother, who gave love in such excess that it sometimes elevated and just as often oppressed.

My mother's death brings stillness.

The light of the purple hour at Camp Afghanistan penetrates my trailer window. I open the screen door and stand on the steps. The different cloud forms and colors in the sky now wash over me.

I chant like a shaman of the Chumash Native Americans who lived on these same pristine acres for millennia before me, "Hey-yah, Ho-yah, Ho-yah, Ho-yah / Hey-yah, Hey-yah, Hey-yah, Ho-yah . . ."

The sounds I make vibrate my entire spine, fill me from head to belly.

My eyes flit from cloud to cloud: gray, brown, salmon, gold—each pulls forth a different sound, "Yah-yah, yah-yah, hy-yah, hy-yah, yay-yay, yay-yay . . ."

The sounds enlarge as they merge with my vision.

No neighbors here for half a mile. There is nothing constructed by the City of Man. Fennel and king grass, wrentits and scrub jays, mule deer and bobcats—the City of God.

Fifteen minutes pass and I sit down in front of a laptop. It is silent in the small main cabin of the Prowler module. All is still.

I read from his singular book that parapsychologist Gary E. Schwartz gave me, "What is it like to experience your guides seemingly showing up in your car ... or a bathtub, and having them give you guidance ... Clarissa says it's rarely intrusive and often in response to a silent prayer or request."

In the seventy years of my lifetime, I have never asked spirits anything. I look around: one stove burner under the small Eco-fan heats the room, and a single overhead light provides a chiaroscuro view of the interior.

I say, "Hey, if there are any spirits or guardian angels or spirit guides around here, I could really use some help. I've had a degenerating lower spine for ten years and it hurts. It hurts when I sit here. It hurts when I drive. You know, can you help me out? I'd really appreciate it, guys."

I laugh.

"Can you hear me?"

Ten seconds later, my limbs feel wired into a 110-volt electrical outlet. My body buzzes. After twenty more seconds, I lean my head way back and create pressure in the muscle between my top vertebrae and my skull.

A rectangle of white light perches at the juncture and grows brighter as I bend my head even farther back. But it is in the front of my neck that a deep relaxation starts: one cartilage after another, the muscles let go and my throat lengthens. I cannot remember having ever felt so much neck. I am a Modigliani.

My eyes are closed and I focus on the rectangle of white light, now bright at the juncture of my spine and my cranium—the center of the pain.

The rectangle floats up along the back of my skull and when the light reaches the top, it lifts my head up—and my neck follows.

When my head can rise no more, the rectangle descends back down the rear of my skull into the length of my spine. It illuminates as it drops, relaxes and elongates.

Am I taller?

I feel no pain in my lower back. I swivel the chair and stand up. For the last decade, I'd been at least grunting loudly when I stand up. No grunt now. I sit down.

I get up again and sit down again. No pain. I get up and walk twelve feet to the sink and then turn and walk fifteen back to the crapper. No pain. Only a silly smile.

I say, "Thank you, guys! Thank you. I really do appreciate this!"

Angels?

My oldest friend, Dyanne, who once studied at the Jung Institute in Switzerland, calls about another matter and I immediately debrief her.

She says, "I'm proud of you, Paul. I feel like your mother. You've been living out there in the wilds for so long noodling around, I am so glad to hear about your allies!"

A few days later, I am in my brother's house. He notices that I sit down and get up from his low Eames chair calmly without the grunt.

He says, "You should get an X-ray and see if something really happened. Compare it to the one you got when you slipped down the hill two years ago."

Days later with my old wise friends Wendy and Charlie, I squeeze my six-foot frame easily into the cramped booth of the Reel Inn without the grimace and grunt. They both look surprised. I jump in and out of the booth several times to get tartar sauce and utensils. Then again for coffees.

Charlie says, "That's quite something."

In bed later, I lie on my back and look into the blackness. I am happy and pain free.

I say, "Thank you, spirits. Thank you for your help." And I mean it.

In a few moments, out of the Void descends Pinky, the only animal I ever loved, who died two years ago.

How sensitive was Pinky? On the two days I felt depressed in the wilds, I took refuge "under the covers" (as actors say). Each time, within ten minutes, Pinky came from far afield into the trailer and sat on my chest, his eyes fixed on me, his mind engaged in rapt contemplation. I looked back into his steady eyes and he purred. And each time, my balance was restored within a minute or two. As soon as I felt relieved, Pinky promptly left to continue his vermin hunting or bird search.

When Pinky now appears in this vision, his black-and-white coat is as clean and shiny as I've ever seen it. He has no bump on his forehead from the cancer he died of. His countenance is in high definition. He is in perfect holographic form. He looks at me steadily, and I look at him totally absorbed and I feel goose bumps all over.

And then my fucking ego pipes up into thought, "Incredible, incredible. Pinky! A damn animal. Spirits! Oh, Pinky, Pinky."

When the wordy thought ends, Pinky recedes and is gone.

An X-ray soon reveals that the compressions in my two lower vertebrae are gone.

2011

I say, "I don't want another relationship with another personality. I want it to be just an essence-to-essence connection—one spirit recognizing itself in someone else—winning the battle between being conscious of our breath and being conscious of our brain's chattering thoughts. I don't want to hear about your mother or sister or any of your history now. No personality. Maybe after a month or two we can have normal conversation where our ruthless egos can be 'I'—that one who claims to be you or to be me."

She must think I'm a ridiculous curmudgeon.

She says, "A month?"

I say, "Can we just look at each other when we are together? I mean it's okay to say 'pass the salt' or 'open the door' but otherwise let's be quiet and look."

She says, "Okay. A man who doesn't want to hear himself talk!"

I say, "The Sufis call it 'objective silence.'"

She says, "Sounds interesting."

I say, "I'm sixty-eight. I've got to tell you that I know that I am good for a relationship of one year, three years, at the most."

She says, "I haven't got anything more exciting to be doing right now. It works for me. I'm fifty-six."

We are in my small shipping container bedroom. It has white Styrofoam walls. She undresses in front of the closed entrance doors eight feet from me. I take off my clothes at the foot of the big bed and in the kinetic stillness see beautiful Vivian Johnson fully naked for the first time. Her deep red hair hangs down to the many deep surgical scars that crisscross her abdomen, and one extends to her pelvis.

I look in wonder—she has been through major hurt. How can I best alleviate her pain? I feel "the trembling vital spirit that dwells in the secret chamber of the heart," as Dante Alighieri described it in *Purgatory*.

Before anything else can happen, I see my heart float out of my chest toward Vivian. My buoyant heart is white.

Sufis say the conscience is in the spirit and the spirit in the heart and the heart in the body. Now, no blood vessels extrude from my cleanly detached white heart. It just floats freely into her chest cavity and disappears. She didn't steal it. I didn't give it away. It just went.

This ridiculously literal phenomenological vision is beyond my prior experience. But I have loved her from the first day in the liquor store when we bought cigars and champagne in Malibu Canyon, a month ago. Her loving gaze replied to mine. In the air around her, all was safe, serene, easy—to stay with her was a no-brainer—it is the place to be.

My heart is now hers—lost somewhere in her thorax—as she stands naked in the container we now call the Magic Box.

We gaze silently for hours. She is a great spirit.

One day as I look at her, I see the small head of a snake peek out between her perfect teeth. I gaze at it curiously.

Then, the oval head emerges from her mouth and the yellow snake grows until it is four feet wide—overwhelming—and stares at me in profile with one black eye from three feet away. I immediately notice her round head—she's not a poisonous viper.

TIME STOPS.

A fast strike with an open mouth will swallow me head first.

I look directly in the snake's eye.

I hear, "Wish her all the love you can"—words of instruction from decades before.

She is coy. This snake and I like each other. I do wish her love. After two minutes, the penetrating friendly serpent shrinks and returns into Vivian's mouth and disappears.

I say, "Did you see that?"

She says, "I didn't see anything."

I say, "You didn't see a giant yellow snake?"

She says, "The police came to my house last year and took me to the looney bin for three days of involuntary observation because my daughter called them and said I was trying to set myself on fire. But I was just using a cigarette lighter flame to prod out the evil spirits around my stomach. I did not burn myself. There was an open wound there from days before."

She says, "In the looney bin, I did regression all by myself and started to recover my memories of abuse. Each time I had to break through the post-traumatic stress."

I say, "There is no line between sanity and insanity. People draw the line in different places, depending on their own experience." Shaman? Guru? Transcendent being? Dissociated? Delusional? Schizophrenic? We function though these realms are extraordinary.

Later, I am lying in bed with thought suspended when inch-thick, silver-strand cables descend through the metal roof and hang like a magical forest. When I breathe, silvery foot-long air bubbles escape my mouth as if I were underwater, and rise up through the roof. A vision of Paradise? The final destination of love?

Thrusting into her sex, her exquisite back and long deep red hair in front of me, I get an overwhelming feeling that she doesn't like this sex. I love her. My heart is hers.

My kundalini recedes down my spine. I lose my enthusiasm.

I say, "You don't like this."

She says, "It's okay. You can do whatever you want."

I say, "I don't want to do anything that hurts our love."

She says, "I really don't like it."

I say, "You can be in charge of sex. I only want to have sex when it makes you feel good."

She says, "I love you."

I say, "The most important thing is that I love you. And I do."

Her vulnerability pushes sex into the background and brings me closer to any meaning in this life.

We look into each other's eyes, into a different sphere of reality. She disappears into visions that I see one after another. A dead ringer of the terrified woman in Munch's *The Scream*. A Native American squaw with one feather in her headband. Then, another head with no skull or skin—just brain-like tissue everywhere.

She says she does not get any different visions of me from her point of view.

I see a face with dark eyes the size of cue balls. The first time I look deeply into the left cue ball, I see a thick cock pushing right through it.

When time resumes, I say, "I know it's not literally true, but I just saw a penis fucking your left eye."

Vivian tells me all about her experiences in Brazil of brutal sexual abuse that began in infancy and continued into her teenage years.

She must have detached at a young age in order to separate from the horrendous memories of pain—pain without death, and split off her essential self so completely that it wasn't destroyed—it survives. That abuse has made her capable of including and transcending almost any tragedy that might happen from the highest perspective looking down. I can hear its pure notes accompanied by overtones when she sings.

Vivian says, "When I was sixteen, I went with my mother to hear a lecture by Fazal Inayat-Kahn at a big apartment in Rio de Janeiro. Afterward, he came over to me and asked me to meet with him" (Inayat-Kahn, a psychotherapist and poet, then led the international Sufi movement).

She says, "Two days later, in a private audience with him, he held me by the shoulders and looked straight into my eyes for an hour. Then he sat on a pillow and played his sitar for me during the rest of the afternoon."

Sometimes I see a white aura around her head and shoulders. Sometimes it is a couple of inches thick, sometimes, almost six inches.

I have seen a bright golden halo behind her head, just like a medieval biblical illumination. And once, above her angelic face, floated a female Buddha whose penetrating silver lines of vision traveled from her eyes into my eyes

Vivian's spirit smiles through her heart and her heart smiles through her eyes.

2012

Republican presidential candidate John McCain says forty-seven percent of Americans will vote for Obama because they are dependent on government handouts. "I'll never convince them that they should take personal responsibility and care for their lives."

I load up on caulk, and continually climb on top the trailer after rains, to seal new leaks in the trailer roof.

2013

I visit Karen in the hospice unit of Saint John's hospital in Santa Monica before she dies of cancer.

Her eyes shine as always. We have an intimate chat. She is the one who is reassuring and considerate. Her light is serene.

But then she looks cross.

She says, "You ate my chocolate-chip cookie."

I say, "Oh my, I'm sorry. It was so delicious."

She says, "I love those cookies."

"I'll be right back. Don't worry."

I jump up and run out of the hospice room, through the long hallway and down two flights of steps to the closed hospital kitchen.

I jump over a gate and head toward a refrigerator when a worker intercepts me—I tell him my crime and my urgent need to repair the situation. He unlocks the fridge door, hands me a bag of chocolate-chip cookies. I run back to where I came from.

I smile at Karen, "Got 'em."

She says, "Oh, goody. Thank you."

Karen was constantly present—and by her constant example—taught me.

Her son Hunter is now in his forties. He stands at the bottom of Karen's hospice bedside.

I say, "I don't know if you remember, but I once squeezed your arms so hard that I'm sure you were traumatized. I've often felt sorry about that. So I want to apologize."

He says, "Yes. I do remember. I have a daughter now. I'd do the same thing. It's okay."

I wake up this morning; the sun almost hits the solar panels.

A star mandala of grass shines razor-keen blades in my third eye.

I pulled king grass from the garden yesterday.

It happens when I pull weeds too.

Or trim the sumac tree.

Or in the old days, when I pulled out the mustard after a rain.

Tons of mustard.

And I went to mustard heaven and flew over endless rolling hills and fields of nothing but shining mustard. Perfect, healthy mustard.

Mustard fields, forever.

I pick grass again today—I wonder if each bunch of grass that connects to a main root is just one soul.

So many seasons. So many years. So many souls. Centuries of souls.

Are there hierarchies of souls?

If there are too many human souls accumulated from the beginning of sapiens' existence, do some of the excess enter into grass?

When I drive all night and lie down to sleep, I see the cars in grays and blacks and white beams still coming in my mind's eye—it is just a repeat. But in this grass vision, I see pure color, vibrant rays of light.

Is this the collective consciousness of plants?

Downloaded from the day, at night before sleep, new plant souls—of plants killed by me during the day—present themselves: now in their timeless perfect forms, not their temporary manifestations.

These dead forgive me.

"Download"? It is not just exhuming a dormant memory and elevating it to a wakeful one. When the picture of a moment is accepted here, it sheds the emotion accumulated in a lifetime—those slings and arrows that originally infused, and continue to attach, feeling to the memory. Experience is now a history less distorted by hurt and defense—simply more objective, liberated from victimhood.

Downloaded, I see it purely—its essence.

2015

At our landmark fiftieth reunion, I stand at a lectern in a lecture hall with three hundred members of the Harvard Class of 1965 in front of me to give a "Ten Minute Talk." Among other things, I say, "In one of his arguments, Socrates explains that Plato's Forms are 'eternal and unchanging, and as the soul always brings life, then it must not die, and is, necessarily, "imperishable." As the body is mortal and is subject to physical death, the soul must be its indestructible opposite.'"

I say, "But now, today at Harvard, research is ongoing in a recent field: 'Asymmetrical Physics'—utilizing Einstein's notion of 'Entanglement': Einstein called entanglement 'spooky action at a distance'—the way two objects remain connected through time and space, without communicating in any conventional way, long after their initial interaction has taken place.

"The government right now is funding this research (which is so interesting to mystics). The research was described by the *Harvard Gazette*, thusly:

'. . . to enable the military to shoot down an incoming ICBM, by throwing a screwdriver at a wall.'"

The classmates all laugh.

"But, all I want to show you here, now, is that in fact we have some manifestation after death. I actually just finished a book about my research, *Image of a Spirit.*"

An image of the "*psi*-photo" is projected on a large screen above and behind me.

I say, "Andrew T. Weil, MD, Class of '64, wrote, quote, 'I find the image captured an hour after the death, above the corpse, of the mother of Paul Williams, is a really interesting anomaly. It cries out for an explanation. What does it mean? I don't know but I'd like to know more about it. I've never seen anything like it.' End quote. This image may change your notion of life and death. It certainly changed me, from an agnostic to an ignoramus."

Then images are projected onto the screen—various close-ups of the *psi*-photo.

I say, "I ended up my research with Sandra O'Hara, the renowned medium used by the CIA—Dean Radin got her in for a couple of hours to meet me. O'Hara looked at the picture for two minutes and said, 'Oh, there's your father! And who's that little boy over there?' (She did not know that my mother's brother was run over by a horse when he was six, and died.) O'Hara then said, 'See, there's another head up there,' and she showed me more images within the one of my mother. I could show you more, but I don't want to strain your credulity."

The classmates have their biggest laugh of the morning.

I say, "In the end, we do give up something. I don't know if it's the ghost, but it is a fact. I don't know a fact of what, but it's a fact."

The Class applauds.

Afterward, one old friend says, "It took a lot of guts to make that speech to this audience."

2016

One night, head on the pillow, my eyes closed but not asleep, I float above the left shoulder of a handsome black-eared bobcat that saunters up the dirt road.

The sleek animal begins to canter, and I float with it. He looks over his shoulder at me for a moment. I see his eyes clearly. The bobcat begins to trot, but I float close. He looks up at me again and breaks into a run. He leaves me behind.

The next afternoon, I drive up the dirt road to the rise by my bench where often I sit with coffee and cigar, and contemplate the ocean to the horizon.

A large bobcat sits beside the bench.

He leaps forty feet to the storage container, and in a second leap, almost to the ravine.

I get out of the car and walk down toward the bobcat. He watches me. When I am twenty feet away, I stand stock-still. I look at the bobcat—no thought, total focus. He looks at me. I look at him. Brown and cream with a freckled muzzle and pointed black ears. He turns his head slightly away, then returns to my eyes. I swivel my head away and then slowly look back at him. He still looks at me. I exhale in a chant from my heart. He watches. I slowly turn my head away again, then back, looking directly at him—and slowly finish my long, "Ooommm." And then a longer, lower, guttural, "Huuummm." After another minute, I slowly step back at a 45-degree angle (I remember Robert Redford retreating from lions in *Out of Africa*), and the bobcat unlocks his eyes and turns away, sauntering down into the ravine. I hear the cry of quail as my gaze remains focused on the spot of his disappearance.

Aristotle said "phantasia" is not one of the five senses; that it is a unique avenue of communication between man and animal.

Soon after the bobcat encounter, multimillionaire candidate Hillary Clinton, in a singularly authentic moment, identifies her opponents as a "basket of deplorables" and warns that, "I am all that stands between you and the apocalypse." Have compassion for some of the people all of the time, and be afraid of the others all of the time? The new populism will be split—progressive like FDR and fascist like Mussolini.

When Vivian tells me she is returning to Rio de Janeiro with her mother and sister, I decide to follow her soon to Brazil. Yes. "What happened to Williams?" "Who knows—he took off for South America . . ."

Do I flee the backlash to the forty years of neoliberalism that emerged after Ronald Reagan's ruthless brand of capitalism, and now surfaces in the deranged new American president Trump? Or am I just fleeing the apotheosis of greed and ego endemic in the mighty USA? Or, just an old 1960s hippie, am I hightailing it for the hills?

Don Regan, President Reagan's chief of staff, wrote in his memoir, "Virtually every major move and decision the Reagans made during my time in The White House was cleared in advance with a woman in San Francisco who drew up horoscopes to make certain that the planets were in a favorable alignment for the enterprise." This woman was Joan Quigley, who did one for me, ten years earlier, in 1971. She drew a longitudinal line around the planet that touched land only in one place, Rio de Janeiro. And she said I would be most happy there, for some reason.

I give Vivian my Tempur-Pedic bed and massage table to put in the family duty-free shipping container and listen to her sing, "When my baby smiles at me I go to Rio / De Janeiro / I'm a Salsa fellow / When my baby smiles at me / The sun'll lightens up my li-ife / And I am free at last, what a blast."

2018

Alone, back in Malibu (because an American can only reside in Brazil for six months in any twelve-month period), I am underwater as eight, fleshy, pink, suction-cupped tentacles about four feet long and four inches in diameter slowly float toward me. As they advance in the dark water, the tentacles loosely surround me. Tentacles have distributive brains, I remember. I grow short of breath. I'm afraid I'll be suffocated and sit up, suddenly awake.

In the trailer's four-foot-high sleeping alcove, my eyes open, these tentacles still float around me. When they touch me, there is no physical feeling. But it is sensory and emotional. This floating holographic octopus above my bed has no molecular substance and, clearly, no active life. It is dead.

I get up and take a few steps to exit to the dark outdoors. I am dazzled by sixty powerful searchlights atop commercial fishing vessels in a battle group that closely parallel the coast—now a holocaust for teeming giant squid. Under the high stars of Malibu, it is their season to die.

I wonder how many dead squid souls are there in the sea out there? I must testify to the transcendent nature of reality—I'll bet the quantum physicists and cosmologists will one day prove beyond doubt the infinite reality of our everyday world.

2019

There is one primary religion on Earth, Capitalism, and one universally accepted god, Money. Ruthless economies grind on.

I sell the land in Malibu. Soon, I say goodbye to my best friends Wendy and Charlie, and Dyanne, and my brother, Ted. We head off 6,400 miles to Rio to live our sunset years in the Southern Hemisphere, far from any of the Earth's nuclear powers. I will get a green card, an RNE—Registro Nacional de Estrangeiros, so I can stay without limit in the land of *Black Orpheus*.

2020

Now I get my existential news on BBC–Brasil. It is clear to me that if the US Pledge of Allegiance were exchanged for the BBC World Weather Report, world peace rather than atmospheric degeneration of our home planet would be more likely.

I am amazed in March that an exponential expansion of consciousness is at hand as a result of a black swan event—the coronavirus pandemic—like cholera, tuberculosis, syphilis, bubonic plague, and smallpox that in the long past fanned out across the world's trade routes. I hear, "We're all in this together," morning, noon, and night. Suddenly, we are all one body (though we still have separate but unequal bank accounts—any one of the three richest men in America can afford to vaccinate the whole world many times over for a paltry slice of their billions). The millions of paycheck-to-paycheck frontline brothers around the world nevertheless are motivated without compensation to work their compassionate hearts out in lethal danger. A half century ago, Marshall McLuhan said, "The medium is the message." On TV, the people of Earth can see that their tribe is just the same as the other human tribes around the world—"planetary intercommunalism." Now the global shock of coronavirus is in everyone's community.

And then in June, a second black swan event: God or the Over-mind or Cosmic Coincidence Control plants the same image into the brains of all Earthlings at the same time. The web smartphone nervous system of the planet compels all to see the last eight minutes and forty-two seconds of the life of George Floyd.

The greatest political motion picture ever made is by a seventeen-year-old woman, Darnella Frazier, who implores the racist cops to stop killing a defenseless man. The cries from her heart for compassion are ignored, as she records pure, banal evil. George Floyd repeats, again and again, "I can't breathe." We watch him die. Just like someone infected by the coronavirus.

There is no "suspension of disbelief" required to believe this murder. It is long enough to be emotionally unavoidable and short enough for all the mortally threatened Earthlings to pay complete attention. There is a common heartbeat.

The virus and the murder create a planetary feedback loop of awareness.

Suddenly in July, a third black swan event: the "Pole of Cold" in Siberia registers more than 100 degrees Fahrenheit, and wildfires rage throughout what was the coldest region on Earth. The prediction had been that these temperatures of "Arctic Amplification" would not occur for seventy more years. But CO_2 (carbon dioxide) and CH_4 (methane) now surge from the tundra's permafrost at an unprecedented rate and multiply the toxicity of the warming atmosphere past irreversible tipping points. This quickening approach of the sixth extinction of the animal kingdom wakes up all Earthlings to the reality of the mortality of their race, but it is too little, too late for our near demolition of the biosphere.

Decarbonization of the atmosphere is a delusion of politicians and hopeful young people, a concept embraced by those Earthlings who cannot entertain the cataclysmic fact that this century will not be Chinese or American. It will belong to Thomas Malthus—famine, disease, natural disasters, mass population crises, and clashes of arms, foreign and domestic. The speed and scale of the global demise will take the optimists by surprise. Compassion, too, may be extinguished in the collective trauma.

Civilization lives in the face of being torn apart as a million and a half babies are born every week.

Einstein said, "Let the people know that a new type of thinking is essential if mankind is to survive and move toward higher levels."

I may float in the cosmos, a benefit from childhood abuse and the work on myself, but industrial humankind is mesmerized by its greedy technical triumphalists and remains faithful to its materialist Pollyanna religion of constant-growth capitalism and its monumental income disparities—even though the only sustainable prosperity is shared prosperity.

Instead, they watch depraved billionaires head for short dips into space and they despair they cannot afford a seat on a slow fantasy trip of two years through lethal radiation to Mars. Of course, the Jet Propulsion Laboratory has started their research on modified human genomes resistant to radiation needed by a human body beyond Mother Earth on such a resettlement trip.

Unable to face their fear, hope springs eternal. Humanity has the faith but not the capacity for the all-encompassing reorganization that the world needs to take in concert to evade its self-made gas chamber.

A box of N-95 masks, seven standing turbofans and open windows, 70 percent alcohol in spray bottles—we isolate at home. We have projects and take care of each other in a country of profound inequality where delivery is cheap—groceries, medications, wine, cigars. Vivian's daughter brings a home-cooked curry dish to the porch door and Biera's restaurant sends seafood vinaigrette and *pastel* up our steep cul-de-sac via *mototaxi*. Two thousand miles southeast of the burning Earth lungs of the Amazon and Pantanal, three hundred feet high on the edge of the jungle in a house where inside is close to outside, our porch and windows overlook a vast twenty-six-mile view of Rio's Marambaia Peninsula forest. Toward the horizon, Guaratiba Bay blends into the mountains of the Costa Verde and meets the Atlantic Ocean. As Thoreau said in the Harvard Yard in 1837, "This curious world which we inhabit is more wonderful than it is convenient; more beautiful than it is useful; it is more to be admired and enjoyed than used."

2021

Is a fourth black swan event at hand? The Department of Defense reports on June 21 that it is stymied by 140 "unidentified aerial phenomena," or UAPs, that "were registered by multiple sensors, including simultaneous radar, infrared and electro-optical trackers, weapons seekers, and visual observations."

Gideon Lewis-Kraus writes in the May *New Yorker*, "How the Pentagon Started Taking U.F.O.s Seriously: For decades, flying saucers were a punch line. Then the U.S. government got over the taboo." A couple of weeks later, Barack Obama seconds the need to find out what this new reality is. It is time for a new conversation, but the ephemeral news cycle will only sustain a brief chat.

These objects fly faster—without sonic booms—beyond our understanding of propulsion, flight control, and materials. Furthermore, they disappear and reappear, as if they are intersecting from another dimension. Science fiction exists.

When I was a senior working for John and Faith Hubley at Harvard's Carpenter Center, Eric Martin made an animation film based on Edwin Abbott's novel—*Flatland*. Flatlanders can see only a two-dimensional sliver of any three-dimensional object that passes through their world. Could UFOs operate in 5-D or 6-D worlds? Seem to us to wink on when they enter our 3-D world and then wink off when they leave? That's why there is no sonic boom? They have their own bubble of energy as they just pass through ours?

I like the notion that we are just a zoo of primitives being watched by ETs for entertainment. Leslie Kean, a preeminent UFO researcher and a descendant of John Winthrop, says, "Why should we assume we already understand everything there is to know, in our infancy here on this planet?"

I would enjoy an explanation as simple as Occam's razor—that these ETs, thousands or millions of years ahead of our primitive civilization, know that

All is one big hologram; that consciousness and the material world are part of one continuum—interconnected and capable of seamlessly interacting with each other—unlimited by material, linear time and space. That would be splendid—everything including consciousness itself is part of a single system where separation does not exist. Thought materializes faster than the speed of light and an Ox walks by me in a loft in Manhattan.

Just in the nick of time, this all-encompassing hedgehog's paradigm would give new dignity to the altered realities of my prior pages. I am not dead yet, Horatio. Yes, the ETs are just hovering until the milestone event of human maturation—a paranormal, unified prayer from Earthlings for world peace—after which the extraterrestrials shall land to say to us, as in Vonnegut's *The Sirens of Titan*, "Greetings."

Vivian and I talk about mundane house needs and garden insights, and the pandemic. We read aloud the last chapter, "New Fidelity," of Marquez's *Love in the Time of Cholera*, where Fermina Daza says she wants to "keep going, going, going, and never come back." Via FaceTime from North America, my daughter rails against my political incorrectness when I tell her that I have nicknamed Vivian: Bouquet-Creamy-White Cloud—her fragrance, her skin, her field of energy, within which we snuggle in our bubble. We have both had more than our share of shame in this lifetime and in old age reap the benefit—we are shamans.

Inside, I read and write and watch the daily opera on the world news. Once a month, we argue about accounting, and she berates me for not overcoming my mommy-money trauma earlier in life. I try to learn the language here from audiotapes but their well-enunciated São Paolo Portuguese is nothing like the Carioca accent of Rio de Janeiro spoken around here that makes every word sound like "goulashes." Vivian's eighteen-month-old granddaughter lives nearby, and we speak the same innocent language. I smile when I go to sleep, thankful that I've made it through another day at our home, our planet.

Waking in the morning is also good news. Exercise and stretching too. Finished, I tap a Tibetan singing bowl with a soft mallet and listen until the sound dissipates and I hear just the distant surf—and then look at the face of a small bronze Buddha. She opens her eyes as long as I stay empty. The better shape I'm in, the larger and brighter her eyes. When I become thoughtful, she gently shuts them and remains on the bookcase until tomorrow.

This morning I think about how there is no need to frame out anything from my vision of the sunsets on the porch to see the beauty. And about Venezia, the only city I know where, too, it is not necessary to subtract from all I see. But when I look into the empty white metal *doppio* cup in my hand I must look for a few seconds before I can subtract and only see in a crescent of its bottom, the dancing rhythms of the remaining coffee drops.

I say, "I have been faithful since I met you eight years ago."

Vivian says, "Well, that's excellent, but you were sixty-seven when we met."

I say, "That's my personal best by five years."

She says, "You were a bad boy. Maybe you grew up?"

I say, "Well, I found the gold. I found the gold—I finally found the gold!"

She laughs.

She says, "I would like an ultrasound to see if my blood clot is gone."

I say, "Like lake sounds? To see if my bloody clock is gone?"

She starts laughing.

I say, "The world is happiest for me when you laugh."

She says, "Our gold is not common gold, Mister Goldberg."

I am grown old on Earth in the Milky Way galaxy that contains our solar system and two hundred billion more solar systems and, beyond, two hundred billion more galaxies.

On this side of the jungle mountain, the pitch and moment of the generative years has faded away. The many mistakes of my lifetime are old battles fought. Everyone is forgiven.

In this world of man, I have been far less useful to movies than Oliver Stone and to politics than Huey P. Newton, or to dancing than Helena Kallianiotes. The drama of shrinks, actors, and gurus is over. It is what it is. I too am forgiven. I am refined.

I realize attention is a limited resource, so I pay more attention to what is real—receptive so I can be filled with more.

I say, "I didn't become anything."

She says, "You became everything."

I smile. I am where my eyes can see.

She says, "Now, be quiet."

The sunsets mesmerize me time after time. They don't belong to me. I'm a visitor. I photograph the wonder of the sunrise and the evening spread out against the sky.

Just a glance from the porch makes it impossible to keep the illusion that any human being is greater than nature.

The story written, the life lived. I remember myself.

Memory stored, no past, no future, no time.

Only now.

A privilege of a lifetime.

It is the writer's convention to have a conclusion:

> Nature and I are one—most of the time.
> Until it shall be for all of the time.
> I am now, finally.
> a forest.
> ranger
> .

Epilogue

The 10 Most Important Practical Things I Learned by 10

1. Older kids always feel they are superior to you.
2. When it rains, go outside—use dirt and pebbles to build dams and canals all the way to the sewer.
3. Don't ever pass up a chance to buy the expensive properties in Monopoly.
4. Ask for an allowance.
5. The best thing you can buy for a nickel at Woolworth's 5-and-10-cent store is a small pad with colored pages.
6. People believe all kinds of weird ideas.
7. If someone is going to hit you, run away before they get close enough.
8. Learn the rules of all their games—parents, teachers, kids.
9. Break any rule if you want to, if you can—without getting too hurt.
10. Be loyal to your friends.

The 10 Most Important Practical Things I Learned by 20

1. When turning into a sharp curve, brake as you enter, accelerate midway as you pull out.
2. The best way to start talking to a woman who attracts you—who you do not know—is to ask her about the music she likes.
3. It doesn't hurt as much as you think it will, to get punched.
4. If you don't know the SOURCE of a drug, wait for some others to do it first, and see if they die.
5. If you're a girl, never believe what a boy says about love and sex—only do it if you really feel like doing it.
6. If you're a boy, play music—a guitar is best but a car radio can do it too.

7. Everybody is different and has had different experiences, and every-body's family is fucked-up somehow.
8. If you don't know the proper DOSAGE of a drug, wait for some others to do it first, and see if they die.
9. Get out of the house and put yourself in the way of opportunity—that's how you have good luck.
10. Try everything once. Masturbate whenever you feel like it (not in public).

The 10 Most Important Practical Things I Learned by 30
1. On frequent occasions, caress every imaginable part of your lover's body before the moment of penetration.
2. Boys, after an orgasm, don't look for something else to do. Just wait fif-teen minutes—"recovery time"—and you can go again.
3. Girls, don't be embarrassed to bellow—deep, full, loud, long—as you approach and during orgasm—it makes them bigger, multiple, and longer lasting.
4. Kids need three years to get their basic trust and confidence in the world—don't split up until they are three years old.
5. Realize that democracy is just public theater—the ultrarich are far more mind-bogglingly rich and powerful than anyone knows—including the best journalists, the most radical activists. It's worse than you think.
6. Go into nature once in a while, away from all man-made things—and dance.
7. Wait and see what kids do—only stop them if they are about to hurt themselves or you.
8. Unbeknownst to them, almost everybody's god is money and almost everybody's religion is capitalism—being an atheist is challenging.
9. Take trips to foreign lands.
10. Don't be afraid.

The 10 Most Important Practical Things I Learned by 40
1. Everyone is a child pretending to be grown up—there are no adults.
2. Exercise your core muscles and stretch—stops throwing your back out.
3. If you have a problem in life or art, think about it, and then stop and go do something mindless like gardening or going to sleep—get out of your own way. Then the answers come to you.
4. Buy land in the mountains. Live in another part of the world for a while.

5. The world is filled with barbarians, as well as nice people—don't be surprised.
6. It's time to fall out of love with your personality—work on yourself. Start the never-ending path to serenity.
7. You will die one day, for sure—dance.
8. People are often so damaged by life that they are not trustworthy.
9. Treasure your friends.
10. Be smart about what you eat.

The 10 Most Important Practical Things I Learned by 50

1. When your dad dies, your load may lighten—let it.
2. Get a full panel blood check every six months—any disease will only have a six-month head start.
3. Remember to dance, or meditate and contemplate.
4. To better understand anyone, ask yourself, "Who do they think they appear to be in the eyes of others?"
5. If you want to memorize lyrics, or poems, or dialogue, repeat a line aloud twenty times—not ten—and repeat it with NO expression in your voice. Absolutely flat tone.
6. If someone pulls a gun, run—and not in a straight line. Only go back when you have a gun—really, don't go back.
7. Use the computer and internet but don't let them use you.
8. The overburdened bureaucrat handling you just wants to be able to check the box and get his pile for the day finished—stay inside his box. You'll win—he just wants to keep it simple and keep his job.
9. Everyone is responsible for their own evolution. But be kind, every day.
10. Soaking in a mud bath takes away the deep bone pain from the withdrawal from three or more days of smoking opium.

The 10 Most Important Practical Things I Learned by 60

1. Hughes satellite internet is a miracle—go live in the wild country.
2. Revelations off-grid—sunrise, weather, water, solar panels, soil, animals, birds, sunset.
3. You can find anything or anyone on the internet.
4. A cat is a sphinx—and a vermin eliminator.
5. It's the space—how you get there is not important.
6. Throw out or donate as much of your stuff as you can.

7. A mountain lion's eye shine at night is not as tall as a mule deer's but higher than a coyote's.
8. Mitch Cohen, my MD, keeps current with the medical literature.
9. Be eccentric with adults and silly with toddlers.
10. Everyone is a victim—remember compassion.

The 10 Most Important Practical Things I Learned by 75

1. Wear your suspenders OVER your sweatshirt so you can drop your sweat pants fast.
2. Wear two pairs of Thorlos hiking socks on cold mornings.
3. Drink celery, kale, cucumber, beets—they are juices, like carrot or apple.
4. Isolate and dance—even if it's sit-down salsa.
5. Zoom anyone from nuclear-free South American jungle and watch the world flail on BBC.
6. Mount safety grab bars in the shower.
7. Befriend a toddler.
8. A Cuban Partagas No. 4 cigar is a smoke.
9. Rock in a chair with a panoramic view of nature.
10. Lose your heart in someone—leave it there.

The 10 Most Important Practical Things I Learned after 75

1. How to open a sauerkraut jar—impossible—but not if you use a butter knife on the side of lid to pry it up a tiny bit to let in air and break the vacuum.
2. If you get down on your left knee and place the right leg forward and bend the knee down at a 90-degree angle, and then tuck your pelvis forward for 30 seconds—and then switch to the right knee, and do it again for another 30 seconds—your lower back pain upon getting up in the morning will improve 75 percent immediately and 100 percent by the third day. A revelation.
3. The two most important material possessions are: a massage table so you don't have to get down on the floor to do core exercises and get up afterward AND a good espresso machine and Brazilian coffee.
4. If you consume fewer than 1,600 calories a day, you lose one or two pounds a month.
5. The Australian "Moo Position" makes defecation almost effortless—unbelievable (google it—"Moo to Poo"!). Another revelation.

6. A plastic urinal bottle beside your bed makes it unnecessary to get out of bed to visit the toilet at night.

7. Writing each day an honest memoir of your traumas and defeats will make you happy. Forgive everyone. Go easy on yourself.

8. If you call AppleCare, young people are patient and can usually solve your iPhone or computer problem.

9. Know the difference between opinion and wisdom.

10. If you stare at a small statue of a Buddha head, its eyes will open as soon as you are thoughtless and close when you start to think.

And would it have been worth it, after all,
After the cups, the marmalade, the tea,
Among the porcelain, among some talk of you and me,
Would it have been worth while,
To have bitten off the matter with a smile,
To have squeezed the universe into a ball
To roll it towards some overwhelming question,
To say: "I am Lazarus, come from the dead,
Come back to tell you all, I shall tell you all"—
T. S. Eliot, from "The Love Song of J Alfred Prufrock"

Acknowledgments

To my great friend who five years ago told me that at my advanced age I should "deal with this Goldberg thing," and two years ago, that the manuscript "turned to mush after page one hundred" and needed more work—Charlie Plotkin.

To the historian who championed this last draft through passageways unknown to me to get it published—Paul Cronin.

And to the nurturing writers who generously provided expert editorial insights at various stages of the writing—Dyanne Asimow, Ronda Gómez-Quiñones, Barbara Bottner, Margaret Diehl, and historian Standish Meacham.

Constant friends of more than half a century provided essential encouragement and advice at key moments of the process: Wendy Brandchaft, Sylvain Despretz, Eldon Greenberg, John Young, Barbara Lilly, John Rodsett, Stephen Eckelberry, Susan Emerson, Dennis Ardi, and John Steiner.

The manuscript has materially benefited from the wisdom of John D. Hancock, Elliott Gould, John Briley, Andras Jones, Jeffrey Kennedy, and my brother, Theodore Williams.

Susan A. Murray amazed me with her meticulous proofing of the manuscript.

Finally, thanks to my domestic partner, Vivian d'Affonseca Johnson, and my daughter, Zoe Clarke-Williams, who never flagged in their astute editorial help and wild enthusiasm.

By the Same Author

Books

1965 "The Expressive Meaning of Body Positions in the Male-Female Encounter," senior thesis, Harvard Department of Social Relations

1974 *Messages of the Body* by John Spiegel and Pavel Machotka (Free Press)

2015 *Image of a Spirit* (Waterside Press)

2022 *Psi Photo*

Movies

D–Director, W–Writer, P–Producer, A–Actor, PW–Paul Williams

1965 *Crew* [10 min.] (Carpenter Center for the Visual Arts) D, W, P

1965 *Chanzeaux* [17 min.] (L. Wylie/C. D. Dillon) with Tom Yager D, W, P

1965 *Don't Walk* [17 min.] (Ford Foundation/John Winthrop House) D, W, P

1966 *Girl* [12 min.] (Pressman Williams Enterprises)

1968 *Out of It* (Independent/United Artists) D, W

1970 *The Revolutionary* (United Artists) D, uncredited W

1972 *Dealing: or the Berkeley-to-Boston, Twenty-Brick Lost-Bag Blues* (Warner Bros.) D, W with David Odell

1972 *Sisters* (American International Pictures) P

1973 *Badlands* (Warner Bros.) P

1974 *Phantom of the Paradise* (20th Century Fox) P

1978 *Nunzio* (Universal) D

1981 *Miss Right* (Independent/Sony) D

1982 *Jazzwork* [22 min.] (Independent) D, P, A

1988 *To Heal a Nation* (ABC-TV), A

1993 *The November Men* (aka *Double Exposure*) (Independent/Arrow Ent.) D, P, A

1995 *The Best Ever* (Independent) D, W, P

1996 *Mirage* (Independent/Universal) D, P, A

1997 *Men* (Independent/Unapix Films) P

1998 *Charades* (aka *Felons*) P

2003 *And the Walls Came Tumbling Down . . .* [30-min. documentary] (The Ave Maria Foundation) Susan Emerson D; PW—P, A

2007 *The Amazing Adventure of Marcello the Cat* (Independent/Random Media) Susan Emerson D; PW—P

2009 *Beyond Greed and Ego: Interview* [OnTheRiverEnt.] A

Unproduced Original Screenplays

1966 "The Man Who Killed Men"

1968 "The Genius and the Gunfighter"

By the Same Author

Screen Classics

Screen Classics is a series of critical biographies, film histories, and analytical studies focusing on neglected filmmakers and important screen artists and subjects, from the era of silent cinema through the golden age of Hollywood to the international generation of today. Books in the Screen Classics series are intended for scholars and general readers alike. The contributing authors are established figures in their respective fields. This series also serves the purpose of advancing scholarship on film personalities and themes with ties to Kentucky.

Series Editor
Patrick McGilligan

Books in the Series

My Life in Focus: A Photographer's Journey with Elizabeth Taylor and the Hollywood Jet Set
    Gianni Bozzacchi with Joey Tayler
Hollywood Divided: The 1950 Screen Directors Guild Meeting and the Impact of the Blacklist
    Kevin Brianton
He's Got Rhythm: The Life and Career of Gene Kelly
    Cynthia Brideson and Sara Brideson
Ziegfeld and His Follies: A Biography of Broadway's Greatest Producer
    Cynthia Brideson and Sara Brideson
The Marxist and the Movies: A Biography of Paul Jarrico
    Larry Ceplair
Dalton Trumbo: Blacklisted Hollywood Radical
    Larry Ceplair and Christopher Trumbo
    Warren Oates: A Wild Life
    Susan Compo
Improvising Out Loud: My Life Teaching Hollywood How to Act
    Jeff Corey with Emily Corey
Crane: Sex, Celebrity, and My Father's Unsolved Murder
    Robert Crane and Christopher Fryer
Jack Nicholson: The Early Years
    Robert Crane and Christopher Fryer
Anne Bancroft: A Life
    Douglass K. Daniel
Being Hal Ashby: Life of a Hollywood Rebel
    Nick Dawson
Bruce Dern: A Memoir
    Bruce Dern with Christopher Fryer and Robert Crane
Intrepid Laughter: Preston Sturges and the Movies
    Andrew Dickos
The Woman Who Dared: The Life and Times of Pearl White, Queen of the Serials
    William M. Drew
Miriam Hopkins: Life and Films of a Hollywood Rebel
    Allan R. Ellenberger
Vitagraph: America's First Great Motion Picture Studio
    Andrew A. Erish
Jayne Mansfield: The Girl Couldn't Help It
    Eve Golden
John Gilbert: The Last of the Silent Film Stars
    Eve Golden
Stuntwomen: The Untold Hollywood Story
    Mollie Gregory
Jean Gabin: The Actor Who Was France
    Joseph Harriss
Otto Preminger: The Man Who Would Be King, updated edition
    Foster Hirsch
Saul Bass: Anatomy of Film Design
    Jan-Christopher Horak
Lawrence Tierney: Hollywood's Real-Life Tough Guy
    Burt Kearns
Hitchcock Lost and Found: The Forgotten Films
    Alain Kerzoncuf and Charles Barr
Pola Negri: Hollywood's First Femme Fatale
    Mariusz Kotowski